The Wisdom of Strategic Learning

Titles available in the McGraw-Hill Developing Organizations Series

THE ORGANIZATIONAL LEARNING CYCLE
How We Can Learn Collectively
Nancy Dixon
ISBN 0-07707937-X

THE WISDOM OF STRATEGIC LEARNING
The Self Managed Learning Solution
Ian Cunningham
ISBN 0-07707894-2

DEVELOPING STRATEGIC THINKING
Edited by Bob Garratt
ISBN 0-07707986-8

For further information on these titles and other forthcoming books please contact

The Product Manager, Professional Books, McGraw-Hill Book Company Europe, Shoppenhangers Road, Maidenhead, Berkshire SL6 2QL, United Kingdom
Telephone 0628 23432   Fax + + 0628 770224

The Wisdom of Strategic Learning

The self managed learning solution

IAN CUNNINGHAM

McGraw-Hill Book Company

London · New York · St Louis · San Francisco · Auckland
Bogotá · Caracas · Lisbon · Madrid · Mexico
Milan · Montreal · New Delhi · Panama · Paris · San Juan
São Paulo · Singapore · Sydney · Tokyo · Toronto

Published by
McGRAW-HILL Book Company Europe
Shoppenhangers Road, Maidenhead, Berkshire, SL6 2QL, England
Telephone: 0628 23432
Fax: 0628 770224

British Library Cataloguing in Publication Data

Cunningham, Ian
  Strategic Learning. – (Developing
  Organizations Series)
  I. Title   II. Series
  658.4012

ISBN 0-07-707894-2

Library of Congress Cataloging-in-Publication Data

Cunningham, Ian
  The wisdom of strategic learning / Ian Cunningham.
    p.   cm.
  Includes index.
  ISNB 0-07-707894-2
  1. Organizational change–Management.   2. Learning.
  HD58.8.C857   1994
  658.4'06–dc20

94-2167
CIP

12345 CUP 97654

Typeset by TecSet Ltd, Wallington, Surrey
and printed and bound at the University Press, Cambridge

Contents

Series Preface

The McGraw-Hill *Developing Organizations* series is for people in the business of changing, developing and transforming their organizations. The books in the series bring together ideas and practice in the emerging field of organizational learning and development. Bridging theory and action, they contain new ideas, methods and models of how to get things done.

Organizational learning and development is the child of the organization development (OD) movement of the 1960s and 1970s. Then people like Schein, Beckhard, Bennis, Walton, Blake and Mouton *et al.* defined a *change technology* which was exciting and revolutionary. Now the world has moved on.

The word 'technology' goes with the organization-as-machine metaphor. OD emphasized the *outside-in* application of 'behavioural science' which seems naive in the context of the power-broking, influence and leverage of today's language. Our dominant metaphor of organizations as organisms or collective living beings requires a balancing *inside-out* focus of development and transformation of what is already there.

Learning is the key to our current dilemmas. We are not just talking about change. Learning starts with me and you, with the person—and spreads to others—if we can organize in ways which encourage it.

Learning is at a premium because we are not so much masters of change as beset by it. There is no single formula or image for the excellent company. Even the idea of 'progress' is problematic as companies stick to the knitting and go to the wall. Multiple possible futures, the need for discontinuity almost for the sake of it, means that we must be able to think imaginatively, to be able to develop ourselves and, in generative relationships with others, to continuously organize and reorganize ourselves.

Organizations are unique, with distinctive biographies, strengths, opportunities. Each creates its own future and finds its own development paths. The purpose of these books is not to offer ready-made tools, but to help you create your own tools from the best new ideas and practices around.

The authors in the series have been picked because they have something to say. You will find in all of the books the personal voice of the writer, and this reflects the voice which each of us needs in our own organizations to do the best we can.

I'm very pleased to see this book by Ian Cunningham as one of the standard bearers for the Developing Organizations series. I met Ian some twenty years ago and for me our relationship has always had both qualities of colleagueship and friendly rivalry. Although he's always had a distinctive and important voice, I think this is his first book, and long overdue.

You will find The Wisdom of Strategic Learning *personal, opinionated in places, with all manner of insights popping off the page. It rarely fails to be lively and sustains a powerful belief in the self managed learning approach from start to finish. The writing displays the energy which Ian puts into all his activities, and I'll be suprised if you are not energized in turn.*

I hope you enjoy the reading and find inspiration in your efforts.

Mike Pedler.

Preface

This book presents a number of arguments. I am making a case for a particular focus on organizational life which views learning as central to organizational and individual success. My case also includes the notion that 'success' is necessary but it isn't enough in the life of a person or an organization. Learning to *be* underpins learning to *do*. The book develops the idea that a *strategic* approach to learning is necessary. This is important for individuals *and* organizations. This point leads to the view that people with a strategic interest in themselves or their organizations ought to pay attention to learning issues.

I want to establish the concept of 'strategic learning' as an all-encompassing strategic approach to learning. It includes management development and training, but it is much more extensive. Also, strategic learning *starts* with strategic imperatives — the direction the organization is taking, its purpose, its vision, its mission, its strategic goals (or whatever language and approaches are used by the organization). Training programmes *may* then follow as tactics to use — but they may not (and it's not apparent that training *has* to be used). Also, *most* learning needs are not best met through training. This leads to the view that individuals need to consider their roles in assisting others to learn. The concept of 'assisting' is crucial to making organizations *good* places in which to learn. I shall weave in to the text some ideas about what makes 'goodness': such as, good learning; a good learner; a good organization; a good learning assistant. I shall, as often as possible, draw on evidence from research (my own and others). Each chapter is an overview of certain issues, which, in some cases, are complex. Literary references in the text are idiosyncratic, as this is not a book that reviews other texts in the field. You may have a preference for classics that I don't mention: the choices are mine, and relate to the material being presented; that is, I want to refer you to texts that may add to what I have written rather than throw in references as a way of providing spurious credibility for what I have said. As well as being researched as far as ideas go, the methods and techniques suggested have all been tested in actual situations, so they are not the product of mere armchair theorizing.

The reader

This book is intended for anyone who cares to read it. I recognize that it may appeal most to those interested in learning issues, and that might imply only those with a professional interest in the subject (for example, HR managers, trainers, educators). However, I hope that my argument that *everyone* in an organization needs to be attentive to learning is accepted. Hence the suggestion that it has a wider appeal than merely for the 'professional'. Assisting others to learn is part of what makes us human. Parents, as a natural part of their role, assist their children to learn, so the idea of assisting others at work to learn ought not to be entirely foreign.

A strategic approach to learning

'Strategic' as a word has a hard bite to it, whereas 'learning' is often seen as a soft topic (flabby, psychological stuff removed from business realities). I want to combine hard and soft in this book—and in thinking about problems of making organizations work better.

I know that 'strategy' has a basis in a war metaphor: it belongs to a school of thought that sees organizations as competing aggressively in a hostile, difficult world. And, like so much in this book, it is both true and not true. Yes, organizational life is difficult—we live in turbulent, uncertain and complex times. Survival is high on many agendas for organizational action. Survival is sometimes from the attacks of predators—that is, from takeovers or from competitors determined to drive a company out of business. I accept the warfare side of business, but I also want to balance this with a concern for organizations being *good* places for people to be, where it feels *good* for an individual to spend a high proportion of his or her waking hours. This is the soft side of strategic development and in many respects the soft side is harder to achieve and to maintain.[1]

As well as wanting a hard/soft balance in thinking about strategy I also want a hard/soft balance in an approach to learning. The kind of learning I see as necessary for modern organizations is not some easy-going, sponge-like absorption of new knowledge, but a tough, searching and bone-deep personal change process. It is mostly accomplished through the struggle of adjusting to change or making change happen, rather than by absorbing ideas in a classroom. This does not, however, support the 'no pain, no gain' school of thought. Learning is sometimes pleasurable, and sometimes not. But learning is what has brought us to where we are—collectively and individually. Whatever abilities, skills, thoughts, beliefs and attitudes we possess, they have *all been learned*. We are as we are because it is either in our genes or it has been learned. Our genes provide us with the basis for learning, but we are not born with the knowledge and skills we all individually possess.

All this can seem pretty trite stuff if you accept my basic propositions. I am, nevertheless, amazed by the number of managers who seem to work on different assumptions—for example, when they bring in new systems or technologies and assume that these innovations will be implemented without people *learning* to use them. They seem to assume that by issuing instructions, or by just telling people, implementation comes naturally.

I also see this in the actions of consultants who produce erudite, rigorously argued reports for new structures or systems of working and assume that their implementation is no problem: it will just happen. They seem to have little or no sense of the learning necessary in their client organizations.

An old story concerns a grasshopper.[2] As he got older he found winters more difficult to cope with. His joints and bones ached so much that he went to the wise owl, the consultant of the animal kingdom, for advice. When the owl had heard his tale he recommended that the grasshopper change himself into a cricket. As the owl pointed out, crickets hibernate in winter, so his problems would be solved. The grasshopper was delighted with the proposed solution, but somehow could not implement it, try as he did. He went back to the owl to complain that he couldn't make this transformation. The owl replied 'Look, I come up with the solutions; it's your job to learn how to implement them.'

Writing style

I shall be making a case for what I regard as 'best practice'. Sometimes I am challenged to be more accepting of other practices. My view is that if something is less than best, why accept it when there is something better? Toyota has a motto: 'Compromise is the enemy of achievement.' I agree; but that is only my view. Hence, in this book there are a lot of 'I' statements. That is because I want to own them as *my* views, *my* opinions. They are not truths or absolutes; it is just how I see the world. And if I were to write in a neutral way, it would be less honest and less authentic. I have also written about my reasons for coming to particular conclusions—for example, my personal experiences—because you, as a reader, can then see the basis of my assumptions and make up your own mind about whether to accept them or not. So the book is something to argue with, or to disagree with. And I would rather have you angered by it than bored with it.

Notes

1. The idea of the 'soft being hard' comes from, among others, Tom Lupton (former director of the Manchester Business School).
2. The story of the grasshopper and the owl is modified from one in Bennis, W.G., Benne, K.D. and Chin, R. (1970) *The Planning of Change* (2nd edn), New York: Holt, Rinehart and Winston (page 3). This is a fine book on the 1960s/early 1970s ideas about managing change. A lot of it is now dated and seems naive, but there are some good papers in it (and in later editions of this text).

Ian Cunningham
1993

Acknowledgements

Although I take responsibility for all that the book contains, I want to acknowledge the help, support, advice and assistance of others. In no particular order of importance, these include: hundreds of managers and students with whom I've worked and learned from over the years; current colleagues, including especially Graham Dawes, Andy Smith, Andre Mailer, Janet Adams, Ben Bennett, Eden Charles, Kathy Moore and Jackie Draper; past colleagues, too numerous to mention; the series editor, Mike Pedler; Julia Riddlesdell at McGraw-Hill Europe; those providing secretarial, word-processing and desktop-publishing help, with a special thanks for coping with a difficult task to Frances Watt, Jennie Johnson and Stephanie Carter; Andrew Constable, who thought of the term 'strategic learning' before I did; colleagues at Sheffield Business School with whom we are collaborating in providing an MSc in Managing Change, especially Stuart Smith and Morris Foster; a long-standing network of professional colleagues who have provided ideas and stimulus over many years, including John Burgoyne, John Morris, Alan Mumford, Tom Boydell, Richard Boot, Mike Reynolds, Vivien Hodgson, Sarah Mann, Magda Csath, Bob Garratt, Alistair Mant, Phil Boxer, Roger Harrison and Ron Smart; the Chairman and the Board of Roffey Park Management Institute for providing a senior fellowship during which time I wrote much of the book; David Cunningham and Lucy Cunningham for their own brands of thinking and for being themselves; and Caroline Cunningham for many things, but especially for her help in editing the text.

PART ONE

INTRODUCTION

The book is in five parts. This first part contains just one chapter and provides some opening thoughts. I introduce some themes to be explored later.

Chapter 1 provides clues towards understanding some key ideas I shall use. These include

- strategic learning
- self managed learning

In Part Two I shall define more precisely what I mean by strategy in the context of learning and in Part Three I shall discuss what I mean by 'good learning'. Self managed learning is introduced as an idea in Chapter 1 and elucidated more fully in Part Four. Part Five looks at some issues of practical application.

1   Introduction: some basics

The basic issues   René Fichant, the CEO of Michelin Tyre, once told a story which I shall modify here. Three men were shown a room with two doors. They were told that behind one door was wealth beyond their wildest dreams—gold, silver, priceless jewels. Behind the other door was a hungry man-eating tiger. They were each given the option of entering the room and opening a door. The first man refused the choice and left. The second man—a good strategic planner—hauled out his computer, analysed probability data, performed some risk analyses, plotted graphs, produced charts, created scenarios, etc., and after much deliberation he opened a door and was eaten by a low probability man-eating tiger. The third man (and, of course, the third one is always the winner) spent his time learning to tame tigers.

Learning in organizations makes sense. Indeed, organizations in which there is little learning, or the wrong kind of learning, do not survive in the modern world. Some, such as IBM, can survive a long time because of their size and monopolistic position. But even IBM's poor learning culture eventually caught up with it.[1]

The trouble is that learning is not a very visible process. It is internal to people and often takes time. In a world that values the obvious, the immediate and the concrete, learning gets undervalued. Many organizations seem to have taken to heart the graffiti I once saw which said '500 million lemmings can't be wrong'. And as they hurl themselves off the cliff shouting 'so far, so good' they take with them many innocents—into unemployment or impoverished jobs.

When I harangue top managers about the importance of learning—and the need to take a strategic view of it—I get a sense of how Kirkegaard felt in his dismay at how his words were received. As he said, he felt like a theatre manager who runs on stage to warn the audience of a fire. But they take his appearance to be part of the farce they are enjoying, and the more he shouts the louder they applaud. Of course, it is not applause that is required, but another kind of action.

The situation may be changing, however. My modification of the 'Law of Revolutionary Ideas[2] suggests that a new proposal goes through three stages of reaction:

1. 'It's stupid and irrelevant—don't waste my time.'
2. 'It's interesting, but not worth doing.'
3. 'I said it was important all along.'

I believe many organizations are at stage 2, and a few are at stage 3. Although this comment is valid, it relates mainly to the English-speaking world. Japan is an example of a society that has taken learning extremely seriously for a long time, and has reaped the benefits of its rapid learning. Other parts of the Asia Pacific region are also culturally highly tuned to learning (Hong Kong, Taiwan, Singapore, etc.).

Learning levels   While this book has its main focus on organizational life (and it is part of a series on 'Developing Organizations'), I want to draw attention to wider issues. There are various levels at which we can pay attention to learning. These can be delineated, as shown in Figure 1.1.

While I believe that, strictly speaking, learning is done by individuals, there has been a growth of attention on 'learning organizations'. Usually this latter means creating a 'context for good learning' (and the latter will be explicitly addressed in

Individual
|
Group/Team
|
Organization
|
Community
|
Society/Nation state
|
World

Figure 1.1   Levels for learning

Chapters 4 and 5). However, the other levels (that is, other than individual and organization) are also important. It's clear, for instance, that some work groups or teams seem rich in learning whereas others in the same organization are 'learning impoverished'. Also, particular communities within nation states seem to provide a better learning culture than others. In the UK, Wales and Scotland are significantly more learning oriented than the East End of London. Working-class children in Cardiff and Glasgow are much more likely to gain qualifications and to enter post-school education than equivalent children in London's East End.

I have already mentioned that Japan[3] is more of a 'learning society'[4] than any English-speaking country, and when we reach the global level we have to ask: 'How well is the human race doing?' Are we learning fast enough to deal with global environmental and ecological problems?

Issues of learning are of major significance to us all—in all the roles we play—as individuals; as members of groups, organizations and communities; as citizens of our countries and of the world. If the emphasis on learning in organizations de-emphasizes these other levels, then this is an unbalanced focus. If, on the other hand, learning to make organizations better places within which to learn helps us to focus on other contexts as well, then it must be a good thing. (Wider aspects of 'good learning' are discussed in Chapters 4 and 5.)

Big picture and little picture

A famous 1960s writer, Baba Ram Dass, once said that when you're floating in inter-galactic ecstasy you need to remember your zip code. Somehow we have to hold together the big picture and the little picture. We have to integrate the visions for our organizations with day-to-day practice. Otherwise we have what we so often see in organizations: dead vision/mission statements devised through some detached bureaucratic process. They do not relate to people in their daily lives and hence become the butt of cynical banter from secretaries and shop-floor workers. ('Have you seen the latest nonsense to come from the top floor?')

Examples

I would like to introduce a few cases of learning-based approaches that address these and other problems, and this chapter will show some concrete examples that link the big picture and the little picture. They will provide a basis for what is to come in later chapters, and I shall signpost references for the reader who wants to leap ahead—or at least to know what follows the 'hors d'oeuvre'. This hors d'oeuvre provides small tasters of what follows—but please do not confuse it with the main meal.

At the core of this chapter are the outlines of two cases of strategic learning. The cases throw up a range of issues, a few of which will be addressed in this chapter. The remainder will emerge as the book progresses. I want to start with concrete examples so that the ideas and discussion that follow are grounded in real-life issues.

The two cases are presented fairly baldly. At first sight the aims of the programmes and the claims of their efficacy may seem familiar. After all, everyone in the business of promoting organizational learning claims that what they are doing is good. I hope in later chapters to demonstrate that there is genuinely something different, special and especially excellent, about strategic learning and about the self managed learning method as part of this approach.

The active reader

You will find examples of models, checklists, and other materials used in strategic learning approaches scattered through the text. I would encourage you to test them. Like clothes bought off the rail, they may not fit, but you'll only know this for certain by trying them on. And the process of 'trying them on' may help you to see what else you could use. Also, this kind of process is consonant with the self managed learning mode of operating that I shall emphasize in this book.

Strategic learning in a drinks business[5]

The Hiram Walker group is an international drinks business and part of the Allied-Lyons group. The Hiram Walker group mission statement is reproduced here:

> Our mission is to create value for Allied-Lyons and its shareholders by building our wines and spirits business into the leading international drinks group.
> In attaining this goal, we will be noted for the high quality of our people and products, for our ethical standards and for the care and consideration we give to our customers, our employees, our business partners and the communities around the world in which we operate.

Hiram Walker distribute a wide range of wines and spirits (for example, Courvoisier brandy and Beefeater gin). The Hiram Walker group was formed from a merger of well-established companies, and in its merger saw the need for significant change. Top management wanted to move the culture from the cosy, patriarchal model that had been common in the drinks business towards a faster-moving, more entrepreneurial culture. They also knew that they needed to change strategically to operate in a highly competitive marketplace. With increasingly sophisticated approaches to purchasing, especially from the large retail groups, Hiram Walker needed to develop highly capable managers to operate in these new environments. (Chapters 2 and 3 discuss the wider aspects of the environments and markets in which organizations operate.)

They decided that their entire management team needed extensive and coordinated development if the business was to compete effectively. However, the history of the companies that had merged into the new organization was one of fragmented management development. Also, the whole personnel/human resources (HR) function had had an 'industrial relations' attitude, rather than a developmental one.

When I was asked to talk with their human resources development director they had already decided that they wanted a management development approach that would put *all* their senior managers through a significant learning process over approximately a three-year period. They were also clear that they wanted something that responded to individual needs. I and my colleagues worked with them in designing a self managed learning programme that would take about 60 to 70 managers initially, expanding to cover all their senior people in the three-year time scale.

The first step was getting the buy-in of top management (at chairman and board level) to a process that was going to meet their strategic needs but would not look anything like a traditional management training course.

Hiram Walker wanted to develop a culture that supported learning and change. Within this it realized that managers needed to take responsibility for their own learning, while the company needed to accept its responsibility to support managers in their learning. The self managed learning approach appealed because it met those needs and also allowed managers to work on job-related issues, hence overcoming transfer of learning problems.

The first stage was to put specific proposals to the board of Hiram Walker Agencies (the company, within the group, that handled the spirits business). They were to be the first part of the group to adopt the new approach.

The board recognized that they themselves needed to model this new approach. They had to give overt purposive support to the change, and they needed to learn better how to mentor and coach their senior managers (hence modelling a key aspect of the new culture). Therefore, in parallel with developing the self managed learning programme the board members attended a workshop on mentoring and coaching.

In designing the senior management programme it was clear that the links between it and the strategic direction of the business had to be made explicit. Also, the programme needed to mirror the new culture being established. A more entrepreneurial culture needed more entrepreneurial managers. But managers would not become more entrepreneurial by sitting in classrooms listening to lectures, or by doing case studies. This would produce people who could *talk about* being entrepreneurial, but they would not necessarily *become* entrepreneurial.

The self managed learning approach addresses this issue. For instance, it demands that managers manage their own learning. They set their own objectives, decide how to achieve them, how to measure them and how to integrate their learning with organizational needs. As part of the programme individual managers join 'learning sets' with five or six other managers. These sets meet once a month for a whole day. In the Hiram Walker programme they met over a period of nine months, which constituted the first phase of the work. The sets provide a place to negotiate learning objectives, agree a written 'learning contract' to carry out these objectives and get support to implement the contract. At the end of the nine months the individuals in their sets were required to assess themselves against the objectives they had set. (Chapters 6, 7 and 8 in Part Four explain more about self managed learning and how it works.)

The set is assisted in its working by a set adviser. This person's role is to help the set function. It is not a teaching role, nor is it the same as being a facilitator (as the term has come to be used in training and development circles). (This role is explained more fully in Chapter 9.) In Hiram Walker, we initially chose 11 senior people from different departments of the company (mostly in the number two position in the department, just below board level) to act as set advisers. They attended a three-day workshop to develop their ability to fulfil the role, and they also received ongoing supervision and support from experienced set advisers (from outside the company) throughout the programme. This feature is important as it was part of our role to develop the strategic capability of the organization to continue to support this approach to learning.

The first programme was launched with a two-day residential event. The role of external consultants (such as myself) was to stay as much as possible in the background to support the company people. So, for instance, explanations about the programme were delivered by board members, and the role of the company set advisers was stressed. During the two days the sets were formed, and emphasis was given to the fact that these groupings were not teams with a common goal, but were there to help individuals meet their own defined learning objectives.

The first three months of the programme were spent in developing and agreeing learning contracts, and the following six months were spent in meeting the requirements of these contracts. The contracts were drawn up by answering five questions:

1. Where have I been? (What have been my past experiences?)
2. Where am I now? (What kind of person/manager am I? What abilities do I possess? What are my strengths and weaknesses?)
3. Where do I want to get to? (What kind of person/manager do I want to become? What abilities do I want to develop? What learning goals shall I set?)
4. How shall I get there? (What programme of learning and development do I need to undertake? What resources do I need to do it? How shall I overcome obstacles to my learning?)
5. How shall I know if I've arrived? (How do I measure achievement of goals? Who will provide measures of learning?)

The 'contract' was between the individual, their learning set and the organization (usually represented by the boss).

Learning sets were seen as a critical element in helping people to succeed in meeting their contracts. As evidence of top management commitment, and the strategic importance of the programme, people were not allowed to be taken out of set meetings (e.g. by their boss) unless sanctioned by the managing director. This ensured that short-term crises did not override the strategic imperative of the learning programme. A flavour of the programme is given by the comments of Ruth Harley, planning and inventory manager in the operations department of Hiram Walker's head office. She was among the 66 managers on the first nine-month

Hiram Walker programme and she became involved in a second phase:

> Before I got involved in the programme, I didn't really know what to expect, as I hadn't heard of self managed learning before. I felt pleased that the company was making some provision for our development as managers. My phase one learning objectives were quite general: to improve my Lotus and PC skills in order to produce better management information reports, to build my confidence at doing stand-up presentations, and to broaden my knowledge of accounts and finance and depot operations at Hiram Walker.
>
> I liked the self managed learning process because I was the one that was identifying and taking responsibility for my own learning. You benefit from the knowledge and experience of your fellow set members, especially if you have a good cross-section of different departments with different viewpoints in the same set. It is a safe, supportive and challenging environment in which to learn.
>
> I felt that, as a result of self managed learning, people in the different departments involved started to work more closely together, both inside and outside the set environment. At first it was a very foreign process, and it seemed odd to meet and talk in a group in such an unstructured way. The lack of structure makes you look to the set adviser for direction, but your questions are reflected back to you and the group, and you discover your own answers. It is definitely not the usual teacher/student relationship. I have achieved the learning objectives I set in phase one, and I am sure that the programme will bring further improvements as time goes on.
>
> I am also linking my phase two learning objectives more closely into my work: as you become more experienced at self managed learning, you are able to focus more clearly on what you need. We are also setting some short-term objectives, as achieving short-term goals is very satisfying and spreads the development work more evenly across the year—and makes the end of the year less worrying.

This is only one view out of 66, but it is fairly representative. However, all the learning contracts were different. In essence there were 66 courses running in parallel, as people pursued their own needs. Learning sets, though, had some common patterns, including the technique of giving each person time to talk about personal needs and issues, and get support from others. Sometimes the support came through challenging questions, but the set's focus was always on how to assist good learning. (See Chapters 4 and 5 for a discussion on 'good learning'.)

Most of the learning activity, outside sets, took place in the company. People took the opportunity to learn from other managers in the organization. Participants also had a comprehensive handbook of materials on a wide range of topics. It was almost a mini learning resource centre for each person, providing diagnostic questionnaires, handouts, guidance to accessing other resources, etc. Where needed, participants could get access to outside specialists, and this was supported by the company. (Chapters 6, 7 and 8 in Part Four give more information on these aspects of self managed learning.)

At the end of the programme there was an important phase of assessment. Individuals presented evidence of achievement to their peers in the set. They also met with the director responsible for their own division for a debriefing on the programme. The results of the assessment process were logged on individuals' personnel records, hence acknowledging the place of the programme in a person's career development. Hiram Walker Agencies has evaluated the programme and identified a range of benefits, which include:

- Increased self-motivation, self-awareness and personal initiative
- Reduced departmental barriers and increased cohesion in the company
- Broadened skills and abilities in managers
- Greater understanding of roles (personal and others)
- Greater business awareness and strategic abilities
- Managers more open and receptive to change
- A positive attitude to learning and development

The company has assessed the cost-effectiveness of the programme, and it has proved to be the most cost-effective approach it has undertaken. As one director stated, in presenting the programme to participants, the company was not engaging in this management development for altruistic purposes. The ultimate benefit of the strategic approach to learning is more profit.

Strategic learning in the public sector

The National Health Service in Britain is one of the world's largest employers (with almost one million employees) and it has been going through massive strategic change. My colleagues and I worked in one region (the South West Thames Region) to support these changes through learning-based approaches. As with the previous example, our objective was to help the organization be as self-supporting as possible. For instance, we undertook development workshops for personnel and training staff throughout the region so that they could learn how to use a self managed learning (SML) approach integrated with other strategic initiatives. In some cases this meant new regional level initiatives; in other cases districts within the region started programmes. The case I shall mention here was within one of the first wave of autonomous hospital trusts established.

The St Helier Trust was the largest hospital trust established in the region at the time. Trust status had been applied for to give the hospitals in the proposed trust more autonomy, and the top management involved decided on a process of strategic and cultural change. The chief executive wanted to develop his managers in a way that was congruent with the radical changes occurring in the health service in Britain. He specifically made a commitment to support an organization-wide strategic learning initiative as well as provide means for individuals to meet their own learning objectives.

The change process initially went through three phases. The first phase (July–November 1990) was based around 'focus groups' of managers developing ideas about what would be needed of managers in the new style organization. Phase two consisted of setting up a managers' conference, which was attended by 70 of the 78 senior/top managers in the organization. This one-day conference was led by the chief executive who gave personal backing to the proposal for a self managed learning (SML) programme for *all* the senior/top managers.

Prior to this conference, my colleagues and I had assisted in developing the set advisers who were to handle the SML programme, and in designing the programme. At the conference the SML approach was explained to the managers and 13 sets, with six managers in each, were formed. These sets then, in phase three of the initiative, met about once a month for four or five hours until June 1991 (that is, just over six months). Twelve of the 13 sets were judged by the organization to have been successful.

This SML programme had similarities to the one in Hiram Walker, with the use of learning contracts and internal set advisers. The organization went this route for the following six reasons:

1. The SML approach reflected the change process in the health service.

2. SML mirrors the managerial process (in demanding of managers to set objectives, allocate resources, measure results, etc.).
3. It stresses learning and development rather than purely training.
4. It emphasizes career, personal and organizational development.
5. It breaks down internal professional barriers (a key issue in hospital settings) through the use of cross-disciplinary sets.
6. It is a 'learning umbrella', not an enforced learning style (people could use whatever learning methods suited them).

An independent evaluation of SML programmes at the regional level showed considerable success in the venture. A typical quote from the report was:

> All had found it an unfamiliar process on first acquaintance, using words like 'floundering', 'difficult', 'battled with it'. They described SML as causing them to think more, to be more reflective, to assess and look at themselves, to take responsibility, to take more initiatives, eg in choosing mentors, getting secondments, asking people for information. SML is seen as being both about career development and personal development.

Why 'strategic learning'?

The two examples show a strategic approach to learning. I shall elaborate 12 criteria, or factors, that indicate that this approach is different from others. First, however, I shall give a brief outline of other approaches.

From research we conducted on a range of small, medium and large organizations in the public and private sector[6] we identified four main organizational approaches to management learning, development and training. These, known collectively as the ARBS model, are summarized below:

Apathetic/antagonistic These organizations were especially characterized by top management apathy or outright antagonism to supporting and resourcing training and development. Many small firms fell into this category. The boss was convinced that funding and giving time to such activity was either a waste of time or downright harmful. The latter position was taken by those who felt that supporting training and development would lead people to learn things that would make them more marketable (especially if they obtained qualifications) or raise their sights to look elsewhere for a job. The apathetic (the larger group) tended not to see learning as a priority. They felt that in difficult economic times their business survival was linked to other activities (for example, more aggressive selling) than to their employees learning new skills and abilities through organized development activity.

Organizations in this category not only didn't sponsor people for courses, they also didn't foster a learning environment. There was minimal coaching and mentoring, induction of new employees was haphazard and there were no rewards for learning.

Reactive

These organizations did provide support for learning, but purely (or mainly) on a reactive basis. If employees pushed their bosses they might get funding for an external course. If individuals took initiatives they might find someone to coach them or, at the very least, to share knowledge and expertise. At one extreme, reactive organizations are close to apathetic. At the other extreme, they could be quite supportive of individual learning (see Figure 1.2). However, there was no strategic imperative guiding learning, and little or no evidence of attempts to evaluate courses or other developmental activity. Learning was hit-and-miss with no systematic planning (though there might be a designated training budget in the better examples of this type).

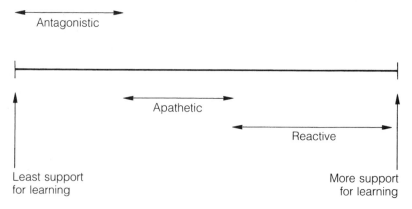

Figure 1.2   Spectrum of antagonistic/apathetic/reactive organizations

Bureaucratic

These organizations (typically relatively large) did have training budgets and either ran internal training courses or sent people on external courses (or both). Internal courses were highly standardized and often linked to particular grades or levels in the organization. In many organizations people had to go through a particular course when they reached (or were about to reach) a particular level in the hierarchy. The main overt commitment to learning in these organizations was through training. People were sent on courses if learning needs were identified (for example, in an appraisal interview). There was usually little emphasis on job-based learning (projects, secondments, mentoring, etc.), though this would often occur informally. In large organizations with regional offices, we found considerable resentment towards head-office-driven training. The training department would carry out a mechanistic questionnaire-based training needs analysis and would design courses for the whole company based on an average of the identified needs. Managers outside head offices usually felt that the standardized offerings that resulted were unresponsive to their needs, and provided little value added to the business (and were certainly not cost-effective). However, the bureaucracy required that they conform to head office systems.

Strategic

These were the minority. They encompassed small, medium and large companies and were characterized by board level commitment to learning and development. In the medium and large companies there was an active personnel/HR/management development function which had access to the CEO. The people in HR/development were typically energetic, able, committed people who cared deeply about the business and its success. They were respected by senior managers and their expertise was regularly called upon. They sometimes directly supported line managers in coaching and counselling their staff. They were good networkers, well connected inside the organization and outside. They could readily access external sources of expertise as needed and were knowledgeable about current thinking on management, organizations and learning.

In taking a strategic approach to learning, these organizations would look for direct linkage between business needs and learning activity. They would pragmatically support learning methods that met specific needs. They were flexible and responsive to the differing needs of different parts of the organization.

In order to exemplify further this strategic approach, I shall again refer to the two examples outlined above, and suggest 12 reasons why the specific initiatives were consonant with strategic learning.

1. Organization wide commitment

Both examples were high profile, centrally resourced, across-the-board developments. They were in no sense marginal or peripheral 'extras'. All managers knew of the programmes, and all were to be involved (in the Hiram Walker case, in stages). The programmes were seen as a collective responsibility, and there was widespread commitment to their success.

2. Top management giving demonstrable support

This support was demonstrated by top level involvement in learning. In the St Helier case, the CEO had just completed an executive MBA by action learning, and he made certain that all his top team entered fully into the SML approach.

3. Linked to strategic direction and cultural change

The learning approach was directly integrated into the change process at all levels. As both organizations wanted to be more customer oriented, more outgoing and more entrepreneurial, the *process* of learning had to match this. Standardized training courses teaching how to be responsive to customers are a nonsense. People on a course are 'internal customers'; if their requirements are ignored in the course design, that is the message transmitted even if the content of the course says otherwise.

A classic example of process/content mismatch was when I attended a lecture by an eminent psychologist. Near the end of one and a half hours of non-stop lecturing he mentioned some research evidence which showed that people's ability to concentrate in a lecture diminished rapidly after 45 minutes. He saw no incongruence between the process (a long lecture) and the content (long lectures are bad).

4. Large-scale development

In both examples *all* relevant managers were going to experience the programme. It was not a case of selecting managers to go on a course, but rather an integrated, strategic initiative.

Figure 1.3 shows how, over time, the focus of learning has changed. The model is crude as there have been many exceptions, but as a generalization for the English-speaking world it holds up.

Up to the 1960s and 1970s the emphasis of management development (and most other training/learning activities in organizations) was on the course as the unit of analysis. Managers attended courses either on a reactive or a bureaucratic basis. During the 1970s and 1980s two challenges to this emerged. On the one hand organizations saw that small numbers of people going through expensive courses was of limited value. These organizations opted for a 'mass' approach, and began to use some of the methods indicated in Figure 1.3.

1960s/1970s

Group based
– course as unit
(lectures, syndicates, etc.)

C
O
N
T
I
N
U
I
N
G

1970s/1980s

Mass (examples)
- Distance learning
- Open learning
- Compulsory mass training
- Computer-based training
- Learning resource centres

Individual (examples)
- Self-development
- Action learning
- Self managed learning
- Individualized learning
- Independent study

Figure 1.3　Focus of learning

One example was distance learning, which is an update of the old correspondence course method. It promised cheap, mass training to large numbers of managers with no necessity for them to leave the workplace. Where this was attached to a degree, such as an MBA, it proved attractive to managers who wanted the qualification. The problem with this approach, as with other 'mass' methods, was that it was usually detached from work issues and had a rigidity and lack of responsiveness to individual needs that was worse than the standard taught course. At least on courses there was interaction with tutors which allowed questions to be asked by learners in order to pursue some of their own interests. In pure distance learning the learner receives material through the post (print based as well as possibly audio and/or video tapes) and is restricted to responding to this. Some tutor contact has been added to many programmes to alleviate the problem, but it is usually limited. There are also wider issues about the kind of learning that can occur on such courses. (This is discussed more fully in Chapters 4 and 5 in Part Three.)

There was another kind of reaction against the taught course in other organizations, who saw the need to respond to individual differences, and to promote a more holistic approach to learning. Hence self-development (see Figure 1.3) became popular.

Learners on self-development programmes have usually welcomed the freedom and responsiveness of such pro- grammes. However, concern has grown that they may become detached from the organizational mainstream and that the small numbers of people going through programmes had limited impact on organizational development.

In the late 1980s and early 1990s there has been an effort to develop ideas, evolved in self-development and cultural change work, into a more sophisticated learning organiza- tion/learning company model (to be discussed in Chapter 3). Hence, we are now seeing the need to deal with large numbers across whole organizations together with responsiveness to individual differences and a desire to promote a particular kind of learning. The mass and the individual approaches are merging in best practice. Interestingly, action learning, in the hands of most practitioners, became (in the 1980s) very individual or small group focused, but when Revans evolved the ideas of action learning from the late 1940s to the 1970s he was already clear that there was an organizational and a societal level focus. His work in Belgium, for instance, was not just linked into organizational change but, for him, was designed to impact on the Belgium economy. (It is doubtful if it did, but the orientation is interesting, nonetheless.)

Self managed learning started off in the late 1970s as a heavily individually focused approach. While my colleagues and I were always clear that we wanted both a basis for learning in organizational issues and a pay-off for the organization, at that time we had not developed a way of engaging with large numbers across an entire organization. This only came in the mid to late 1980s. (SML programme designs are discussed in Part Four.)

5. Not a one-off project

In some cases, the initial activity is called 'a project', but I am always looking to see the long-term developments. I am, by and large, unhappy with the idea of programmes being 'experimental' or 'pilots'. I appreciate that some practitioners see a strategic choice:

(a) a pilot or experimental scheme leading later to a full-blown organization-wide programme
(b) big bang—going for a full-scale programme immediately.

My experience is that while (a) looks like a sensible option, it usually is not. Experiments tend to stay experiments. If they succeed it is still seen as 'in the lab', but not necessarily suitable for others (for example, if a learning programme is for an élite high-flying group, it may be assumed that it is not right for ordinary mortals).

While organizations also might talk of 'initiatives' or 'programmes' (which is the usual language of an organization) I always want to stress that these terms do not imply one-off action. SML programmes may last for, say, six to nine months (as in the two case examples) but they are a prelude to continued lifelong learning for the people on the programme, and activities initiated on the programme often continue beyond its end date (for example, particular projects or ongoing work with a mentor).

6. Development of organizational capability

Developing set advisers and mentors is often a start point for widespread development of organizational capability to support and foster learning. (I shall discuss other factors in

Chapter 3 and in Part Five.) Also, when managers have been in a set for nine months they know how it works, and they have learned how to assist their peers in their learning. With the growth of flatter organizations (and the concomitant reduction in time that bosses can spend with people who report to them) peer group support for learning is starting to loom larger as a priority in strategic learning.

In the Hiram Walker case there was, from the beginning, an explicit plan to use managers from the first programme as set advisers for the next level down in the organization. Their experience in sets can accelerate their learning to become effective set advisers.

7. Multi-functional development

Both case examples showed the value of bringing together people from different functions in the organization to address learning issues. In a learning set people get to know each other in depth and learn how to support learning across different departments and disciplines. This encourages an integrated approach to learning across the organization through networking. This is not just a spin-off from a programme (as is often the case on training courses). Self managed learning encourages the open exploration of live issues, and this is infinitely superior to telling 'war stories' in the bar between sessions on a training course as a way of getting to know people in other departments.

A strategic approach to learning has to encompass the development of a learning culture across the whole organization. It may seem paradoxical to focus on the personal learning needs of individuals, but when people in a learning set start to see the similarities of some of their problems, this enhances the in-depth development of a learning culture. People feel less isolated and more able to be open with colleagues.

8. Long term, not quick fix

Firstly, self managed learning programmes usually need to last at least four or five months to show real, significant benefits. But as most of this time involves the normal work, this is not an insuperable intrusion into people's jobs. However, by continually looping between live action, and then reflection and analysis in sets, people's learning is greatly enhanced. This is different from the 'quick-fix', where you go to a two-day seminar and learn all you need to know about X (which can be TQM, performance management, or any technique you care to mention). Someone on an SML programme may attend such a two-day seminar, but they will do it as part of an agreed learning contract with agreed learning objectives, and a report back to their learning set on what they have learned.

Another element of long termism is the overall commitment to the continued use of SML. The organizations in the case examples did not see SML stopping at the end of the first programme. As we so often hear in evaluations of SML: 'It becomes a way of life.'

9. Cascading down the organization

Strategic learning means involving everyone in appropriate learning. SML approaches need to cascade down the organization, involving other staff. In other cases I shall mention in later chapters we have used SML with secretaries, technicians and clerical staff. Strategic learning does not stop with managers, but as it usually needs to start there, much of my discussion will focus on managers.

10. Part of the organization's competitive advantage

Strategic learning is becoming a key part of an organization's competitive advantage. Top managers are realizing that unless their organization is learning better and faster than ever before, they will be at a disadvantage. Organizations are starting to make this more explicit.

11. Visibility

Strategic learning is being made visible outside as well as inside the organization. It is recognized as part of the strategic direction of an organization, and is something organizations feel proud of.

12. Integrating strategy and tactics

Strategic visions and missions are unhelpful without a link to tactical action. The long and short terms need to be synchronized. Motivation to stick with long-term goals can come from short-term pay-off (which is seen as part of a bigger picture). (This is discussed further in Chapters 2 and 3 in Part Two, as are other aspects of the points covered above.)

Summary

In this chapter I have made a case for learning in organizations, discussed two case examples and indicated how this use of self managed learning (SML) is part of a strategic learning approach. Issues alluded to here will be covered in more depth in subsequent chapters.

Notes

1. Pascale, R.T. (1993) 'The benefit of a clash of opinions', *Personnel Management* (October), 38–41, specifically criticizes IBM, e.g. for its lack of self-questioning (comparing it unfavourably with Honda and Nordstrom).
2. See Clarke's Law of Revolutionary Ideas on p. 20 of Peers, J. and Bennett, C. (1981) *1,001 Logical Laws*, London: Hamlyn.
3. My reference here is *only* to Japan's general ability to learn. I am not implying that Japan is a Utopia—far from it. In areas where Japan is weak (for example, the political arena) people have not learned as well.
4. The first reference I have seen to this idea is Hutchins, R.M. (1968) *The Learning Society*, New York: Praeger. He defines it as:
   —valuing learning and fulfilment of people
   —*all* institutions were directed to fulfilment of people
   —Athenian model
   —fullest development of highest powers
   —education not segregated from society.
5. Material here is based on Hurley, B. and Cunningham, I. (1993) 'Imbibing a new way of learning', *Personnel Management* (March), 42–45.
6. Cunningham, C. (1991) Report on Management and Development and Training in Central Sussex, Sussex TEC.

PART TWO   BIG PICTURE

This part of the book develops the idea of strategic learning (Chapter 2) and concepts of a learning business (Chapter 3). It attends especially to 'big picture' issues. Later parts move into specifics.

As with other parts of the book, I make an idealized case for a learning business. Few organizations approach the ideal, though many show significant aspects of the ideal and many more clearly want to move in this direction.

The style of treatment of issues here is discursive and exploratory. I am not trying to make neat tight definitions, but rather to sketch out a territory that will be defined in more detail later. As it is probably impossible to prescribe universal models to fit all organizations, my objective is to make a case for a way of thinking that can be shaped to the needs of an individual or an organization.

2   Strategic learning

Introduction

In this chapter I want to elaborate the case for strategic learning; that is, learning that is strategic for individuals, groups, organizations, communities and whole societies. In Chapter 1 I gave some examples of what I see as strategic learning: here I want to present a backcloth to later chapters which will delve more into methods and approaches. I want to say something about the environment in which organizations are operating which justifies a strategic approach to learning. I shall then look at what is going on inside organizations which impacts on learning issues, and mention the needs of managers within modern organizations. The focus of the chapter is thus mainly on organizations and managers. I shall also present a model for balanced development in organizations and indicate the kind of strategic questions that need to be addressed in developing learning in organizations. All this will be a prelude to Chapter 3, which discusses the idea of a 'learning business'.

A little history

In 1987 a colleague and I wrote a list of things we saw going wrong in organizations. The list is as follows:

- Concern that training and development activity is not cost-effective
- Lack of linkage between individual development and organizational needs
- Managers who are intelligent and potentially able, but do not make things happen
- Too much work pressure to allow managers to take extended time off-the-job for training and development
- Lack of internal training and development resources to meet needs
- Managers who have learning needs that cannot be met on standard courses

- Lack of responsiveness to change by middle managers
- Managerial stress due to changed work requirements
- Younger managers who need more experience—and quickly
- Too much emphasis on the latest fad or gimmick—little long-term evaluation of development activity.

You could write the same list today. And it could have been written ten years before it was. There is perhaps now more rhetoric about *training* than there used to be, but serious concern about *learning* is still patchy. I was, however, gratified to see that one organization was appointing a 'Director of Learning' at a senior level, with the specific remit to develop a learning culture in the organization. I hope this might be the start of a changed climate.

The environment of organizations

People in organizations are needing to *learn* to work effectively in the world as it is, as opposed to how they would like it to be. Most strategic planning, forecasting, futurology and predicting is an attempt to introduce a façade of certainty into an uncertain world. We know that economic forecasts do not work. If you track back projections made by Government forecasters, by academics, by independent researchers and by company economists you find that the rare person or group who makes an accurate projection—for example, of GDP growth, unemployment, balance of payments deficits/surpluses (or whatever)—does so by chance, because they do not tend to repeat their 'successes' in subsequent years. And many of their colleagues get it wrong all the time.

World political events in the late 1980s and early 1990s have proved to be equally unpredictable. One week before the Berlin Wall was knocked down you could get odds of 15 to 1 from a bookmaker against the Wall coming down *this century*. I know of *no* political commentator of the mid-1980s who was remotely accurate about what has happened in central and eastern Europe, including the unification of Germany and the break-up of Yugoslavia and the USSR.

White water

Vaill[1] has suggested the metaphor of permanent white water to describe modern organizational life. The metaphor can be described as follows. In the past we have assumed that the way organizations changed has been comparable to the flow of a river. The river has calm periods when it flows smoothly and clearly. Then there may be a period of turbulence—rapids or waterfalls—which produce white water conditions. The river then resumes its normal sedate progress. This metaphor is matched by the common prescription in change literature that in order to manage change you first unfreeze the organization, then change it, then refreeze it in a new state. Both metaphors assume that change occurs in between two steady states. Vaill and others argue that even if this was a sensible metaphor in the past (which is dubious) it certainly is not today. He suggests that we have conditions of permanent, unremitting turbulence: permanent white water. When I first went white water rafting down the Arkansas river in Colorado it was comparable to the way Vaill sees things. In the morning we went down a stretch of river which was mainly calm, with periods of white water intervening (and not too turbulent, either). During the morning our guide taught us how to survive in the conditions we would meet in the afternoon. Firstly you had to learn to survive if you came out of the inflatable raft. Basically, you float on your back, going down the river feet first. If you go on your front you can catch your foot in a rock and drown, or beat your face on the rocks. If you're on your back the most that can happen, usually, is a bruised bottom.

The second thing you learned was how to support and help each other. If someone goes into the water you must learn how to get that person back into the raft as quickly as possible—without capsizing or overturning what is a flat-bottomed vessel. The basic technique is to grab the person by the shoulders of their life jacket and haul them in, the person doing the hauling being held by someone else to ensure that the 'hauler' doesn't go into the water also.

In the afternoon of our trip we put on our helmets and went down a stretch of very turbulent water, which called on what we had learned in the morning as one person *did* fall in when we hit a rock at the bottom of a short waterfall. The link to organizational life seemed quite real. We have to learn how to operate on our own *and* with others in conditions of unpredictable turbulence. Personal (selfish) survival is not enough—because we do need others to make an organization work. Personal survival skills are necessary but not sufficient.

What you also learn in white water rafting is the general value of being prepared. Preparation is about learning relevant skills, about learning to think in the right way, about developing emotional resilience (there is no benefit from panicking in situations of real danger), about learning to value your colleagues, and so on. This *'Preparational Planning'*[2] seems to me infinitely superior to other planning modes currently used by organizations. Crudely, I can identify three main competing modes:

1. *Extrapolation.* This mode assumes that the world of the future will be an extrapolation from the past. There might be odd 'blips' on the graph, but broadly the organization will grow at X per cent per annum for the next Y years in a relatively smooth curve. (And if it is not too smooth, a little creative accounting will soon adjust matters.)
2. *Discontinuous change.* Here planners may assume quantum leaps in performance (never quantum drops) due to some discontinuity. Often such plans come from fantasized futurological scenarios. While Schwartz[3] and others argue that scenarios (as used in Shell) are for learning purposes, often managers come to believe in them as 'real' predictions of the future (and scenario builders also may slip into this).
3. *Short termism.* This mode says that the quarterly figures are as far ahead as we look. We don't concern ourselves with strategic planning; we just get on with earning money. We shall respond to the market and hope for the best.

Preparation planning is a challenge to all three modes. It is essentially a *learning-based* approach. It is at the heart of a strategic learning stance. It responds to the challenges made by Stacey[4] and others from evidence from Chaos Theory. Chaos Theory shows that the future is logically and scientifically unpredictable in the kind of modes in which organizations operate. But Stacey shows that a learning-based approach can lead to a redefinition of traditional approaches to strategic planning.

However, we need to think differently about the nature of change in order to determine our learning needs. Much of the change literature seems to imply that change is all one thing. Changing the paper clips we use is assumed to be the same process as changing strategic direction. Clearly this assumption is unhelpful. A superior assumption is prompted by the work of Bateson[5] and others. In this way of thinking we separate first-order change from second-order change. First-order change is change within defined and accepted parameters: it is about incremental change, which is often doing more of (or better than) what we have done in the past. First-order change might mean producing more widgets than last year—or to a modified design. But they are still widgets.

Second-order change occurs when we move outside existing parameters and frameworks. It can mean changing the way we change. For example, in an airline with which I was consulting, they shifted their thinking from the idea that they were flying aircraft to the idea that they were flying people. So a technical/financial orientation switched to a marketing/customer care focus. In the process the airline became a different kind of organization with a different strategic direction. And the kind of *learning* needed to make this shift was totally different from anything they had experienced previously. It is not simple incremental learning. As the saying goes, 'you can't leap a chasm in two jumps'.

Unfortunately some organizations seem to have an in-built first-order-only change mode, whereas others seem able to operate more broadly. One difference is between

- *the palm tree organization*
  and
- *the redwood organization*

Palm tree organizations grow by first-order change only. Like the palm tree they add to their height, but make no other changes. Eventually there is fatal collapse, as the trunk cannot support itself.

Redwoods are different: they not only grow upwards but also add girth and bulk. They can then last for thousands of years and grow to great heights.

Luck

Many managers come to reject strategic planning approaches (reasonably, given their failures) and to rely on what they term 'luck'. The assumption is that if forecasting and linear old-fashioned planning do not work, we simply have to be fatalistic. If we obtain a large order for a product, it is luck. If a competitor gets the order, we were unlucky. These assumptions support prevailing cultures which undervalue learning and change.

I see this every time I go into a park on a Sunday morning to watch soccer. Someone takes a shot at goal and the ball slices wide. Immediately colleagues shout 'Unlucky'. Now, as far as I can see, luck played no part in this. The person shot at goal and failed. I don't want to berate someone for failure, but unless people realize that they've *failed* in what they were trying to do, will they ever *learn* to improve?

The greatest football player I have ever seen, George Best, *learned* to be great by using direct feedback from his play. For instance, when practising as a youngster, he took out a football to improve his shooting. However, he became bored with kicking the ball into the goal and having to retrieve it, so he practised hitting the ball against the crossbar so that it rebounded to him. If he failed, he had the tedious task of retrieving the ball. George Best, like every great sportsperson, *learned* to be great. He was not born that way, despite misguided journalists talking about people being born as great players. All great sportspeople and athletes practise, and *learn* from practice. When they do great things, it's not from luck. I'm told that after he had won a golf tournament, Gary Player was once confronted by a so-called fan. 'It seems as though you're a lucky golfer,' said the fan. 'Yes,' said Player 'and isn't it interesting that the more I practise the luckier I seem to get.'

My former chairman, when I was a CEO, once chided me for saying that we had been lucky in getting a new contract. 'Luck is preparation meeting opportunity,' he said. And I could not disagree with him. We had *prepared* well and when the opportunity came, we could take it. If we had not done the preparational planning we would not have won the contract.

Pace of change

Will Rogers is reputed to have said that 'even if you're on the right track, if you sit still you'll get run over'. One of the issues in a white water world is living with the pace of change and, indeed, welcoming it. There is an African story about the lion and the antelope. The issue in life for the lion is that it needs to be faster than the slowest antelope otherwise it does not eat. The issue for the antelope is to be faster than the quickest lion otherwise it does not survive. But it doesn't matter if you're a lion or an antelope, when you wake up in the morning you wake up running.

This world of 'hot action'[6] is even more complex. Any study of managerial work shows that managers have to make multiple decisions in real time with inadequate information and to imposed deadlines. This 'hot action' world is totally different in pace, style of thought and activity from the 'cool action' world of the academic, the researcher and many trainers and developers. These latter often have the luxury of working sequentially on problems and recommending others to take action (i.e. take the risks) based on their cool, detached analyses. Training programmes are structured on this basis. Subjects are taught sequentially: case studies are analysed separate from 'real world' action, and participants in case analyses do not have to take the risks of implementing their recommendations (and hence really learning what works and what does not).

Discomfort in learning

British managers sometimes seem to me to be quite prone to blame ill luck (and therefore be unprepared to learn). The Australians have a joke: 'How do you know if an aircraft is full of Poms? Because when the engines are switched off the whining continues.' German top managers have a similarly dismissive view. The general manager of the Commerzbank once made a brilliant summary of the ills of the British economy and then questioned whether British managers and the British Government would do anything about it. His view was that Britain would prefer an elegant funeral to the pain of changing in order to go on living.

Facing up to the need to change (and therefore to learn) is often painful, and this first stage—opening up to new learning—is usually more difficult than the new learning itself. The problem is, therefore, complacency and 'hedgehog management'—that is, faced with an oncoming juggernaut, roll into a ball and pretend you can cope.

A survey of middle managers conducted in 1991 by the then British Institute of Management (now the Institute of Management) showed the extent of managerial delusions.[7] Three-quarters of the managers surveyed expected to remain in a similar role in their present organizations for their *entire* careers, with more than half confident that their next moves will be promotions. Not one admitted to fearing demotion or job loss. These assumptions are manifestly crazy. We *know* that organizations continue to flatten the hierarchy (hence reducing promotion opportunities) and remove layers of management. Roger Young, the Institute's director general, was quoted[8] as saying that 'Middle managers are ignoring all the evidence. [They] persist in the belief that their own job is immune to change.' No wonder, therefore, there is a lack of awareness of the need for rapid, high-quality new learning. But the biggest learning is changing assumptions. Acquiring new knowledge, skills and competences will be irrelevant if managers do not change fundamentally their mind sets, their mental frameworks.

You might like to try an exercise I have often used with groups of managers. Please fold your arms. Now fold them the other way—for example, if you have your left hand with fingers up and your right hand tucked in, reverse it (that is right hand fingers up, left hand tucked in). Some people find this almost impossible to do; others can do it, but feel uncomfortable or strange. This is an example of new learning. If you did it you have quite possibly never done it before in your life, so you have learned something new. In itself, of course, it is quite useless learning. My object in suggesting the exercise was to draw your attention to your own habits (this being one of them), and that changing habits or patterns of working can be uncomfortable.

You may also notice in this exercise that you have not learned something that could sensibly be labelled 'knowledge' or 'skill' or 'competence'. I prefer to call it 'pattern change'— that is, you previously had a pattern of folding your arms one way and I've asked you to change that pattern (or habit).

Much of strategic learning is about pattern change. It is about people in organizations reshaping what they already have. A term to describe a certain kind of pattern change is 'reframing'.[5] The metaphor here is that we look at the world through a frame—through the lenses of spectacles or through a camera's viewfinder. We 'see' what we frame, and we can not frame the whole world. A classic story of reframing is of the two shoe salesmen who, many years ago, went to an African country. The first one wired back that no-one was wearing shoes in this country, there was no market for the product and he was returning home immediately. The second salesman wired back: 'No one is wearing shoes here. An immense market for our product. Ship every shoe you can find.'

Each shoe salesman faced 'reality', but each framed it differently. The key learning for the first salesman was not selling skills, product knowledge or whatever, it was how to look at the world around him in the most appropriate way. How to change his mental patterns.

The kind of change indicated here is within the realm of the second-order change already discussed. Hence pattern change can be seen as part of a second-order learning—it moves up out of an approach which adds on knowledge and skills (first-order learning). It can be characterized as 'metalearning' because typically when this kind of learning occurs, people learn about how to learn for themselves. Experience of pattern change can shift a person's mental frameworks and awareness of this can provide the basis for continued 'self managed learning'.[9]

Let me take another marketing/selling example. In 1961 when I first went to live in London I used to enjoy wandering around the Soho district. In a small, unprepossessing side street a man called John Stephen opened a small men's fashion shop. There were no other shops around as this street was tucked in behind the main shopping areas. However, the shop thrived and was part of a revolution in men's fashion business in the 1960s. The street became famous, and Carnaby Street (for this was its name) became a tourist attraction.

Why was this so? One key element was that John Stephen did what no one else in the trade did: he *looked* at his customers, he *learned* from them and he *responded* to what he had learned. He noticed that the young men coming into his shop were pulling down on the ends of the shirt collars to make them longer, so he ordered shirts with longer collars, and this became a major fashion item in the 1960s. He also noticed that his customers were pushing their trousers further down on their hips. So he made the hipster trousers that also became popular at the time. This was real strategic learning, which required a combination, among other things, of

- *Visual acuity* (really seeing what was going on)
- *Recognition* of the value of this data
- *Linking* this data to a strategic vision
- *Integrating* that with practical action
- *Continual monitoring* of the results.

Visual acuity is an important point as it is linked to the concept of 'feedback': a term that has been horribly misused in management. Leaving aside the distortion of this term from cybernetics (a separate problem), feedback has become associated with someone expressing a view about something to another person—as in the opening gambit 'Let me give you some feedback' (meaning the person is about to jump on you from a great height). This kind of feedback is what I call 'secondary feedback'. It may be based on data, but it is not primary data. It is someone's view/perspective/opinion on something. It often occurs in appraisal interviews where a boss might 'pass on' feedback to a subordinate. For example: 'Feedback from your staff suggests you're not good at ...' or 'Feedback from other departments says they like X about you'.

There are prescriptions for cleaning up feedback—for example:

- Make it timely
- Do not allow it to be highly generalized—make it specific
- Keep it non-evaluative.

The last point is not possible in absolute terms. Any decision to pick something out of the stream of events and activities in an organization and draw someone's attention to it is an evaluation of that activity (positively or negatively).

'Primary feedback' is sensory-based data—it is something you see, hear or feel. John Stephen worked off primary feedback (what he saw) not the views or opinions of his customers (secondary feedback). Good salespeople and presenters work off primary feedback. If, as a presenter, I tell a joke and people laugh, I can *see* it (facial changes, body movement, etc.) and *hear* it. I don't need someone to say 'that was a good joke'. A tennis player or. a golfer can see and feel when the ball has been well hit. They know without being told when they have done well.[10]

No fixed knowledge

Strategic learning is ideally based on primary feedback. One factor that supports this is the shaky nature of generalizations, theories and ideas about management. As soon as someone promulgates a generalization or proposition about good management, counter evidence readily emerges. For example, 'sticking to the knitting' was popular due to Peters and Waterman.[11] However, companies that did this often performed badly (IBM and DEC in the computer business) and companies that did not often performed well (Hanson Trust). Creative, innovative companies are supposed to be unbureaucratic and flexible with flattened pyramids. So how has Sony (which defies these generalizations) been one of the world's most innovative companies?

In running self managed learning programmes we have suggested that introducing learners to theories, generalizations and ideas is useful, but that they cannot be taught as truths. We tend to talk of a mapping process. Maps help you find your way around, but they are not true (in the sense we normally use the term—that is direct correspondence to reality). Maps may help you plan a journey, but they won't tell you what the traffic will be like, or if there will be road works, or if the weather will affect your journey, etc. They are limited in what they can represent and they are static. They do not respond to a changing world. But we shouldn't throw them away. In our use of maps we just need to recognize their limitations. So with all 'secondary data': any generalizations about management and organization are just that—generalizations that could prove untrustworthy.

In discussing this case about the nature of knowledge in a seminar on SML one eminent (but sceptical) professor turned to another (whose subject was accounting and finance) and said: 'Well isn't there some certainty in the knowledge in your field? You deal with numbers and money. Isn't that real?' The other professor said: 'If you note at the bottom of a set of accounts it says that this is 'a true and fair view of the state of the company's affairs'. The operative word here is 'a'. This is 'a' view—there are many views.' And we know from the literature on creative accounting what can be done with figures (see, for instance, Griffiths[12]).

More on managing change

In this book I shall offer models and generalizations. I offer them only as maps, not as rigid truths. However, I have been particularly interested in developing 'process maps' rather than 'content maps'. The former are, as much as possible, content free—that is, they can help you shape up data and ideas, but they do not offer 'content generalizations'. Let me demonstrate two examples, the first of which is from Revans.[13]

Revans has developed ideas on change from his work on action learning. He suggests that a 'coalition of power' that can implement change would be made up of the people in the organization

1. who know about the problem/issue;
2. who care about it;
3. who can do something about it.

This is a process model. The content can be added in the precise circumstances of a particular planned change. We could take a specific change we want to see happen and write the names of people against each of 1. 2. and 3.

I believe that learning to use process models like this is another important aspect of strategic learning. Note that the learning I am suggesting is how to think in a particular way, how to use data, how to sort it and so on. I am suggesting that the *content* issues are less important (from a learning point of view). Knowing how to solve problems (process) is more important than knowing the solution to one particular problem (content).

My own basic process model on managing change is built up, like Revans', from a series of questions. My thesis is that in managing change we need to balance aspects of organizational processes, and that strategic learning is in part learning to do this 'balancing'. I suggest that we need to attend to four basic questions:

1. *WHY?* Why do we want to do it and in what way do we want to do it? This question throws up issues about our values and beliefs, and addresses matters around the fundamental purposes of the organization.
2. *WHAT?* What do we want to do? This raises issues of strategy, tactics, operations, tasks, etc.
3. *HOW?* How do we want to do it? This indicates matters of organizational culture, structure, processes, procedures, etc.
4. *WHO?* Who do we want to do it? The answer to this question is about the people in the organization. Who are they? How should they be recruited, selected, promoted, developed, etc.?

Figure 2.1 shows diagrammatically the linkage of these four basic questions. The 'Why?' question feeds into the other three: values and beliefs underpin decisions about What, How and Who.

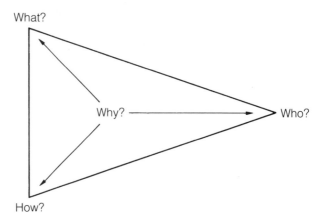

Figure 2.1   Managing change

This, then, is a clear process model. Learning to use it gives managers a series of key questions with which to fill in content. The model is crucial in strategic learning because it postulates that, for instance, individual learning (in the 'Who?' box) has to be linked to

*   strategy, tactics, tasks (answers to the 'What?' question);
*   culture, structure, processes, procedures (answers to the 'How?' question);
*   values and beliefs (answers to the 'Why?' question).

Let me take an idealized case to show the linkages of the four fundamental questions.

Example—an ideal organization

- *Why?* The organization values learning. People are assumed to be able to learn and to change. People are assumed to be trustworthy and be able to make sensible decisions about their own learning.
- *How?* The culture supports learning. People are given freedom to apply new learning. People are challenged to perform better and given support to learn new ways of working. Organizational rules are at a minimum and any structures are designed to assist people in their development. Failures are seen as learning opportunities.
- *What?* The strategic direction of the organization is clear. People know what they are to achieve and they feel committed to it. Strategic goals are linked into day-to-day action. There is congruence and coherence between strategy and tactics. Tasks that people carry out are stretching—causing them continually to learn. But tasks are not so demanding as to cause undue stress.
- *Who?* The organization selects good learners and helps each individuals to learn to their maximum potential. Individuals learn things that are of value to them and to the organization (there is no mismatch).

Real life

In real organizations there is usually a lack of coherence between these four areas. You may like to address these questions to your own organization. Would the answers be different from those in the idealized case above? There would probably be a difference. This can be a starting point for considering action needed to bring strategic coherence to learning activity.

Leadership

An important aspect of developing strategic coherence is strategic leadership. By 'strategic leadership' I mean leadership that is based on integrating the four dimensions I've mentioned and is involved with the broad sweep of strategic change. This is different from 'team' or 'supervisory' leadership, which may be more focused on implementing, on task performance and on maintaining interpersonal relationships. Shop-floor supervisors will have an important implementation role and may also put in ideas at the strategic level, but in a normal hierarchical organization their role will be more oriented to *supporting* strategic leadership than being strategic leaders themselves. The dimensions of strategic leadership, are shown in Figure 2.2.

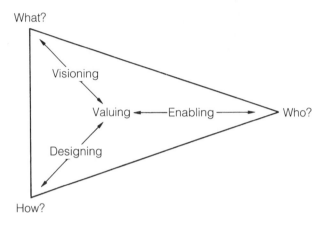

Figure 2.2   Leadership

The four processes of strategic leadership—namely, valuing, visioning, designing and enabling—are linked to answering the four questions Why? What? How? and Who? The ideal strategic leader:

values   (WHY?)
learning and believes in its importance;

visions   (WHAT?)
strategies, tasks and activities which need
learning—and which are learnable;

designs   (HOW?)
processes, structures, cultures which support
learning;

enables   (WHO?)
individuals to learn.

In real organizations all of this will not happen perfectly and easily. Part of the art of leadership can be struggling with and/or coping with mismatches. Such leadership is usually not the responsibility of one individual; leading a strategic learning approach mostly requires the collaboration of a number of key people in power positions. Revans' model (Who knows?, Who can?, Who cares?) can help to identify these crucial people.

Making learning stick

Strategic leaders are important not just in initiating effective learning, but also in making it stick. Often a new CEO will initiate changes which require new learning, but when the CEO goes and a new person takes over, much of this change may be reversed. The concept of hysteresis is helpful here; it is used in physics precisely to indicate the propensity for reversibility. If a piece of metal is magnetized and remains magnetized when the magnetizing field is withdrawn, the metal has high hysteresis. If the magnetism is rapidly lost, it has low hysteresis. Organizations can exhibit analogous properties. What seemed like a fundamental change can prove readily reversible. A new leadership can develop a trusting, supportive, healthy culture; but if the leadership goes, the market turns sour and destructive organizational politics become rife, then the culture can rapidly cease to be trusting and supportive.

Ideal strategic learning would provide a basis for second-order change with high hysteresis (low reversibility). Unfortunately this seems not to be the norm. In the next chapter, on the 'learning business', I shall try to indicate approaches that could improve the chances of high hysteresis.

Strategic excellence

Much of what I have discussed is part of strategic excellence. Note that I am interested in excellence, not competence. I do not support the idea that strategic advantage comes from developing core/strategic competences in an organization. Competence is about being averagely good: at worst it means mediocrity; at best keeping up with the pack. Excellence is about moving beyond the pack. It is a holistic concept—you cannot speak about 'excellences' in the same way as you can about 'competences'. Competence is a reductionist notion. It is assumed that if we learn all the parts well, this will add up to something good. But organizational and business life is not like that. Organizations exist in order to *integrate* individual activity—and integrative learning has to be a facet of strategic learning. The random accumulation of lots of 'competences' will not necessarily produce excellence. (See Chapter 4 for an elaboration of this issue.)

Excellence also has an aesthetic quality. It is about providing products and services which have a particular quality. I remember the managing director of Psion, which makes personal organizers and produces computer software, saying that he wanted his products to be compared to fine Italian glass. Each personal organizer was from a template that he wanted to compare with the template of beautiful Italian glass. He was not saying that his products had the *same* beauty: the aesthetic quality was different. But there had to be an aesthetic dimension to let him feel satisfied about what he was doing.

In sport you find similar notions. The finest sportspeople seem not only to want to win, but to do it in style. They comment on how, in moments of supreme performance, their abilities fuse in a transcendent quality that is well beyond the norm.

Issues for managers

This can seem heady, even unreal, stuff for managers. Yet given the demanding climate of modern management, individual managers do have to face issues of personal excellence. The average (competent) performers with no special talents are the most vulnerable in turbulent times. Vulnerable to losing their jobs and, worse, vulnerable to not finding new jobs.

In Chapter 1 I related examples of self managed learning. In these programmes we have heard managers saying that this is the first time in their lives that they have thought strategically about their own careers. Really strategically. They may have made naive assumptions in the past about a smooth progression up the organizational hierarchy, but through the rigour and challenge of SML they have had to examine seriously how well prepared they really were for different eventualities. They often had, at an individual level, mirrored the fallacies of organizational planning—for example, simplistic extrapolations from the past to the future, or highly short-term target setting.

Strategic learning, then, needs to accommodate individual and collective action. In Chapters 4 and 5 I shall say more about the kind of learning required of individual managers, and about ways of connecting individual and organizational learning.

Conclusion: strategic questions about learning

In making some of the ideas expressed here more concrete, it can be helpful to answer a series of questions specifically about learning activity. This can provide the basis for a link between strategic thinking and operational activity. (A link which will be developed further in Chapter 3.) The questions, with some issues they raise, are:

- *Who?* Who is to learn? Is it everyone in the organization? Will top management give the same commitment to their own continued learning as junior staff? Will age count against people—that is, will it be assumed that, say, those over 50 are not worth further investment? Will women get the same opportunities as men?
- *How?* How will learning occur? Is it to be organized or just expected to happen? Will there be a focus on team/group-based learning as well as individual learning? How will learning be measured? How will learning methods be chosen?
- *Where?* Where will learning take place? On-the-job? Off-the-job and in the organization? Off-the-job and outside the organization? Also how will the different modes be integrated?
- *When?* When in a person's career will there be particular emphases on learning (for example, new entrants, those being promoted, etc.)?
- *How much?* How much will be spent on learning? What resources will be allocated to organized learning activity?
- *What?* What is to be learned? What constitutes 'good learning'? What learning needs will be identified? What will constitute 'quality' in learning? What strategic changes are needed in learning activity?

Table 2.1 suggests a contrast between a typical bureaucratic training-oriented organization and a strategic learning-oriented organization.

Summary

This chapter has made a case for strategic learning, and has considered some ways of developing a strategic approach to learning.

Table 2.1 Bureaucratic vs strategic

Strategic questions	Bureaucratic training oriented	Strategic learning
Who?	Most resources go on younger white able-bodied males. Top management may ask to be briefed on what training is being given to others, but it would not dream of going through such training itself.	Everybody learns. There is a strong commitment to maximizing everyone's potential. And it is assumed that *everyone* has potential to improve.
How?	It is assumed that day-to-day tasks are learned on the job. Training courses are the main *organized* learning activities. Courses are trainer-led with imposed curricula.	A wide range of learning approaches is made available—secondments, projects, study visits, packaged learning resources, etc. All managers act as mentors/coaches to their staff, and take the role seriously. Courses, when used, respond to the needs of those attending—they are not trainer-controlled. (This issue is more fully discussed in Chapter 5.)
Where?	Off-job and on-job learning unintegrated. 'Transfer of training' problems.	Integrated approach. Off-job learning planned to integrate with job needs. No transfer problem.
When?	Main emphasis on training for qualifications for younger staff plus remedial short courses for middle managers.	Throughout a person's career.
How much?	Designated training budget—assumed to cover all costs.	Learning is resourced through a variety of sources.

Notes

1. Vaill, P. (1990) *Managing as a Performing Art*, San Francisco: Jossey-Bass.
2. For a fuller discussion of planning modes, see Cunningham, I. (1984) 'Planning to develop managers', *Management Education and Development*, 15, 2 (Summer), 83–104.
3. Schwartz, P. (1991) *The Art of the Long View*, New York: Doubleday.
4. Stacey, R.D. (1992) *Managing Chaos*, London: Kogan Page.
5. Bateson, G. (1973) *Steps to an Ecology of Mind*, London: Paladin.
6. The distinction between hot and cool action was made by Michael Eraut, a colleague at Sussex University.

7. The survey, by Malcom Wheatley, was entitled 'The Future of Middle Management' and published by BIM (now Institute of Management) in 1991.
8. Roger Young was quoted in a piece by Roger Trapp on p.21 of *The Independent on Sunday* (London, UK), 26 January 1992.
9. For further discussion on 'pattern change' and 'second-order learning' see Cunningham, I. (1988) 'Patterns of managing for the future', *Industrial Management and Data Systems* (Jan./Feb.) 18–22; also Cunningham, I. (1988) 'Learning to learn', in Hodgson, V., Mann, S. and Snell, R. (eds) *Beyond Distance Teaching: Towards Open Learning*, Milton Keynes: OU Press.
10. Tim Gallwey in his writings on 'The Inner Game' is helpful in showing how to work off primary data. The field of neurolinguistic programming is good at showing the needs for sensory-based data, and Richard Bandler and John Grinder's writings are particularly stimulating in this respect (better usually than the more mechanistic writings of their followers). Specific references regarding the above include: Gallwey, W.T. (1974) *The Inner Game of Tennis*, New York: Random House; Bandler, R. and Grinder, J. (1982) *Reframing*, Moab, Utah: Real People Press; Bandler, R. and Grinder, J. (1979) *Frogs into Princes*, Moab, Utah: Real People Press.
11. Peters, T.J. and Waterman, R.H. (1982) *In Search of Excellence*, New York: Harper & Row
12. Griffiths, I. (1986) *Creative Accounting*, London: Firethorn Press.
13. Reg Revans' books and articles on action learning are not always an easy read, but they are stimulating and highly relevant. Some possible texts to check out include: Revans, R.W. (1966) *The Theory of Practice in Management*, London: MacDonald; Revans, R.W. (1971) *Developing Effective Managers*, London: Longman; Revans, R.W. (1980) *Action Learning: New Techniques for Management*, London: Blond & Briggs.

3   A learning business

Introduction

In the early 1970s Peter Drucker wrote some marvellous insightful stuff on Japan and its then growing success.[1] He made specific reference to the Japanese emphasis on learning, including:

- the idea of 'continuous learning'
- *every* employee (including top managers) attended regular training sessions
- learning was seen as part of regular, scheduled work
- training sessions were not, as a rule, run by trainers but by the employees
- experts (e.g. industrial engineers) would *assist* in learning sessions but not take the lead or dominate
- learning did not focus on just one skill at a time—people learned about all the work in a unit: they did not focus on one person or one job but on the *whole* unit or the *whole* plant
- training sessions were oriented to developing new, creative ways of doing things.

This approach made the entire workforce in a company receptive to change and innovation.

Drucker's writing on this topic covered diverse issues, including many of the problems in the Japanese approach. It still stands today as an excellent analysis. Why, then, has he been largely ignored given that:

1. Drucker is probably the world's most respected management writer;
2. his analyses were based on solid data;
3. his analyses were extremely valid;
4. his analyses were clearly and unambiguously expressed?

Only recently has there been any significant interest in these methods of working, and this has largely been because Japanese companies have moved into North America and Europe and shown that the indigenous workforce can learn in similar ways to Japanese employees.

Part of the problem is described by Drucker himself. He argued that the Japanese tradition had a Zen basis which saw learning as a perpetual process of self-improvement. Japanese people understood the concept of a learning curve to mean unending learning—ever-growing visions and abilities. The Western view of a learning curve is an upwards movement followed by a plateau, while the Japanese model allows for plateaux, but assumes that they are only temporary resting places before the next learning phase (see Figure 3.1). In

Western model

Japanese model

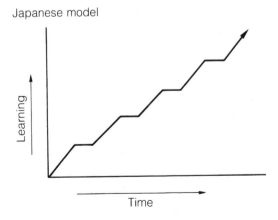

Figure 3.1 The learning process

Western management, there is often reference to a new employee or a newly promoted person 'being on a learning curve'. It is assumed that this learning is a temporary nuisance soon to be cured by the person 'plateauing' into competent performance (and, by implication, ceasing significant learning until the next promotion, unless for remedial reasons).

As Drucker points out, we need to learn about learning in a different way. This is analogous to the difference between first-order and second-order change discussed earlier. Bateson[2] shows that we need to realize that first-order and second-order learning are different. In the Western model, first-order learning is via the 'learning curve' model. In order to release ourselves from that way of thinking we have to learn about learning itself, to understand that there are different models and (I would argue) change to something akin to the Japanese model. But learning to reject an established view of learning is not the same as first-order learning; it requires a mental pattern shift of dramatic proportions—second-order learning. (These issues are more fully discussed in Chapters 4 and 5.)

Getting organizations to become places within which good learning can take place is, therefore, a tricky task. We are faced with the potential paradox that if an organization is not a good place within which to learn, how can it learn to be better (given that it does not learn well)? There are some ways out of this apparent dilemma. A classic one is to bring in new people at the top to make these changes. A more open approach is to rethink the value of the 'it' that I refer to as needing to learn. Most of the literature on 'learning organizations', 'learning companies' and 'organizational learning' assumes that there is an 'it' called an organization that can itself learn. I doubt that this use of language makes sense. Learning for me is most easily attached to a process that individuals undertake. I shall use the concept of a 'learning business' in this chapter, and say something initially about what I mean by that. I shall continue by sketching a definition of a learning business, before launching into more specific points about how a learning business can operate.

Fundamentally a learning business makes strategic learning work. So the ideas discussed in Chapter 2 can be made visible and practical in such a business. A learning business is one in which the internal and external pressures can be addressed in a learning mode.

Some of the issues that organizations face today include:

- a tougher world
- lean organizations—flat pyramid, more fluidity, more pressure

- tensions between centre and periphery: centralize vs decentralize
- faster change
- more demands on managers
- global/international environment
- quality demands
- innovation/speed to market
- customer service demands
- impact of IT
- need for strategic leadership.

All these issues need to be addressed within a learning 'frame'. If organizations are to deal with them effectively, learning has to take place. There is no option.

A learning business

The idea of a 'learning business' is about integrating 'soft' (learning) with 'hard' (business). I fear that today much of what is supposed to constitute a 'learning organization' is a rehash of 1960/70s 'organization development' (OD). The excellent OD practitioners have always seen the need for integration. They have worked with 'touchy/feely' ideas (truth and love) and methods (T groups). They have also paid attention to profits, new technology, quality production, etc. However, often OD practitioners have been trapped (or trapped themselves) in marginalized, semi-subversive roles.[3] They have undermined existing power and authority relationships with paradoxical insensitivity. They have adopted 'holier than thou' postures with barely concealed disdain for engineers, accountants and others who they see as crass, narrow minded and hard nosed.

Again paradoxically, they have paid little attention to learning issues. They have assumed that if people relate to each other more effectively, the organization will automatically improve. Often, though, team-building (to take one method as an example) can create inwardly focused teams that then compete with other teams in the organization (because that is the *raison d'être* of a team in sport—to compete: if there is no competition there is no need for a team and, conversely, if a team is to exist it needs other teams to compete against). Teams can then become places with poor learning cultures where ideas that challenge the status quo are rejected.[4]

All this need not happen, of course. Teams do not have to end up as closed, set cultures. But I believe that unless a more sophisticated approach is taken towards developing the organization, this is a real danger.

The closed approach to developing organizations is one reason why I prefer the concept of a learning business. The term 'business' can be applied to activity on a larger scale than the organization; for instance, we talk of 'the oil business' or 'the airline business' and we mean by this the entire sector. It seems demonstrably sensible to look at learning issues across an entire sector. At the time of writing, the airline business is in turmoil; many companies are losing money and there are major issues about state support for airlines and deregulation (in Europe especially), dirty tricks activity in taking passengers from competitors, safety issues, terrorist activity, etc. Learning to deal with these issues is a global problem affecting the whole airline business. And it also affects passengers: their safety is threatened if airlines and manufacturers do not learn from accidents; and their comfort is affected if airlines do not learn best practice in customer care. In interviewing the cabin crew manager at British Airways in 1986 it was clear to me that his ability to learn from the experience of other airlines was a major contributory factor to British Airways' improved standing with passengers at that time.

Porter[5] has argued (very convincingly) that whole industries in particular countries have benefited from a kind of internal competition and collaboration. Japan is most often quoted in relation to its car industry, consumer electronics industry, etc. Japan has large companies competing against each other in home markets and in export markets, and this has a positive effect on their success. Hence, again, the business sector becomes an important unit of analysis at the country level. This, then, also points to treating countries as 'businesses', as has happened with Japan. Learning at the level of a whole society clearly benefits that society/nation, and it benefits organizations.

In the UK, employers have come together in regional/local groupings (as Training and Enterprise Councils) in order to foster better learning in their locality. At one meeting involved in the setting up of one of these bodies I heard a representative of a public sector body ask why industrial and commercial companies would want to work together on these issues when they might be in competition. There was an immediate response from company representatives that everyone benefited from a more capable, trained workforce. Those involved in purchasing saw the importance of their suppliers *learning* to be better (because they would get better quality goods). Some competitors argued that, as people moved across businesses, it was in everyone's interest to have able people moving through this fluid labour market. These and other benefits point to the need for 'learning societies' and 'learning communities' (in the latter I mean in this context communities such as whole villages and towns or districts of cities).[6]

It is also conceivable to talk of a learning business at the global level. We are aware that the world has to learn together to deal with environmental issues. Richer countries have to learn to use less energy, and poorer countries that cut down tropical forests to make money need to learn new ways of wealth creation. But we all need to support each other in this learning process.

One area in which the term 'business' might not appear to be suitable concerns public organizations and other non-profit-making bodies. Here, however, the need to be more business-like is becoming accepted. Tax-payers in many countries are unhappy with the service they get from public organizations and are demanding to be treated with greater respect. Also, the term 'business' has only recently become associated with commerce (its etymological root is from 'busy') and my Concise Oxford Dictionary defines business-like as 'systematic, practical, prompt, well-ordered' which, while not covering all the facets of business that I want to discuss, is a fair starting point.

Handy makes and excellent case for renaming 'voluntary' or 'non-profit' organizations as 'social businesses'. As he says, 'they are businesses in most senses of the word. They are concerned to turn inputs into outputs as efficiently as possible for the benefit of their clients—not a bad definition for any business'.[7] Sir Duncan Nichol, CEO of the National Health Service in Britain, has commented:

> We run a business which has a vision, some strategic objectives, plans and priorities which feed into these and are discharged down an exective structure which is clear. We may not have a profit motive but we are concerned with the productivity, quality and motivation of the people who work for us. So there are similarities between us and other businesses.[8]

In the industrial sector the Rover car company has created the 'Rover Learning Business' as part of its organization. They say that it works for the 'Extended Enterprise' that is including suppliers and dealers as their 'business partners'. The Rover Group insists that a key part of the successful turnaround of the company has been due to its emphasis on creating a better learning environment. And Paul Kirk, the MD of Rover Power Train, uses all the right language when he argues for a learning focus in the following terms. 'Training is something you have done to you. Learning is something you have to do for yourself'.[9] Rover has clearly made great progress in its work in this field, and the emphasis on a 'learning business' is apt. However, in the context of this book the term is used to cover a whole organization rather than an organization within an organization (which is the Rover model).

Summary of issues

I do not want to use the term 'learning organization' in this book. I accept that some of what I shall cover is also linked by others to the idea of a learning organization. Much, however, is not. I want to· leave aside the idea of focusing on organizations to the detriment of wider concerns.

I have also signalled that I am unhappy with aspects of 'organization development' as the term has been used. Much of the literature in this field uses the metaphor of a human body for an organization as if it were not a metaphor—as if organizations really were living organisms and needed to be treated as such. However, I am comfortable with the body metaphor, as long as it is used in a limited sense. Like most metaphors, it has its strengths and weaknesses. On the down side, ideas of 'organizational health' are overplayed, and can justify 'slimming down/shedding fat' as a nice euphemism for sacking people. Organizations that claim to have become 'leaner and fitter' may not be. Also, organizations that, from a societal point of view, may have outlived their usefulness, are made to survive (because killing off an organization is equivalent to murder, if you take the body/organism metaphor too seriously).

Having made these points I shall be discussing most issues in this book at the organizational level (given the nature of the series within which it is created), but I want to locate all that I say within the wider framework that I have postulated.

Who wants a learning business?

I shall make a generalized and perhaps crude distinction between people who set up and/or run businesses. Firstly, I want to distinguish between *seekers* and *makers*.

Seekers in business are usually of two kinds:

- power seekers
- status seekers.

(There are many other 'seeker' modes, e.g. knowledge-seekers, but they are less relevant in business.) Both kinds of seeker want something from a business, but are less interested in the business itself. Power seekers want to be in positions of power for the ego pay-off that power brings. Politicians are usually strong on power seeking. Status seekers enjoy being in the news, being recognized, gaining titles, and so on. Power and status seekers use the business arena to get what they want. They learn because they must if they are to get what they want. They are, however, less interested in the learning of others around them, and are not too interested in developing learning businesses.

Makers in business are also usually of two kinds:

* money makers
* business makers.

They both want to *make* something in relation to their businesses and so are different from seekers. However, money makers are interested in businesses only as a means to an end: to make money. They are often in the financial sector, but also may be at the top of conglomerates and even manufacturing companies. They tend to be short-term oriented, looking for rapid cash acquisition. They usually have a narrow view of their work and take little interest in wider social issues. As might be expected, they also have little interest in developing learning businesses.

Business makers are in it for the long term. They care about what they make or provide. Many family businesses have this trait and each generation is brought up to identify with the business. Clarks, as a shoe company operating for a number of generations, was noted for its directors putting the word 'shoemaker' on their passport. In Europe, the German family businesses, often not large companies, are strong on business making, as are most Japanese companies.

Business makers may, of course, use power to achieve what they want, but they don't *seek* power for its own sake. Also status may come as a by-product of their business success. They may enjoy such status as they attain, but they do not see status seeking as a basic goal.

Business makers are the prime groups interested in creating learning businesses, though it does not guarantee that they will make a sucess of it. Also, many top managers are a complex mix of aspects of each type; hence, it is not actually a simple matter to put a person or a business into one slot. That being said, the distinctions do seem to help in, for instance, seeing whether it is worth trying to make a business more of a learning business. My experience is that if top management is dominated by the other three types, then it may be pointless to spend time and effort trying to effect a change (unless you can persuade them to alter their basic orientation).

The learning business culture

In writings on learning organizations culture is usually seen as a core determinant of the 'goodness' of the organization. Criteria for a good culture for learning are often commonly agreed in the literature—trust, openness, support, teamworking, etc. While not disagreeing with these criteria, I want to start in a different place. I want to look at three factors (from Sathe[10]) which impact on the strength of a culture and the relevance of these for a learning business.

1. *Thickness*. Thick cultures have many shared values, beliefs and ways of working (thin cultures have few). Hence thicker cultures exert a stronger influence on employees.
2. *Extent of sharing*. If values and ways of working are widely shared, this makes the culture stronger.
3. *Clarity of ordering*. If there is clarity about the relative importance of particular values, this makes the culture stronger.

If the culture is strong on learning it would

- have a shared value for learning and a shared belief in its efficiency (*thickness*);
- these values and beliefs would be widely shared (*extent*);
- these values and beliefs would be rated as important (compared with others) (*clarity*).

Strong cultures have become highly valued as a factor in business success. However, my experience of consulting and researching in strong cultures shows that there can be a downside to this strength. Strong cultures often become arrogant and closed. Competitive advantage may be seen to come from the organization's uniqueness and its strong culture. This can lead to isolationism. This is not to imply that the organization is cut off from its markets, but it can come to deal with its customers in a 'take it or leave it' mode.

Computer companies, such as IBM and Digital, suffered from this syndrome, and this was a factor in the problems they experienced as they entered the 1990s. They did pay attention to learning, but it was largely first-order learning; that is, they worked hard at improving what they were doing, but they did not learn to make the big changes that were necessary (second-order learning). Digital's strong engineering culture was a great strength in its early days, but it needed to learn to deal with its markets and customers in a different way—and did not. There were those in Digital in the late 1980s who felt that they were working hard to fix their problems. But that was the problem (second-order)—attempting to fix problems (first-order). Thus the solution became the problem. The organization was in need of major surgery and was bleeding to death, and top management continued to try to put band-aids on severed arteries, all the time believing it was doing a good job.

In all this Digital's strong culture was a major negative factor. The arrogant belief in its own ways of working caused it to reject the solid, incontrovertible evidence that it needed major change. Strong cultures can find it difficult to deal with mistakes and with major market changes, unless they have in-built second-order change/learning capability. (This issue will be a feature of some of the solutions analysed in this and later chapters.)

Order and disorder

One aspect of fostering second-order change is the need for organizations to accept and even encourage disorder *en route* to creating new kinds of order (to respond to changes in the environment[11] of the organization). Let me quickly summarize an idealized simplified sequence of events.

1. The world/environment is changing—but initially the signs/signals are weak.
2. The signals need amplifying—comparable to the way an amplifier works in a radio or hi-fi system. The organization needs to foster this.
3. The organization needs to allow a variety of messy amplified signals to enter into the business such that they disorient current thinking—like loud-speakers booming out different sounds.
4. This disorienting produces disequilibrium—it knocks the organization off balance.
5. The disorder produced needs to be tolerated. The organization needs to be prepared for it and resilient enough to live with it.
6. Out of the disorder come new shapes, new kinds of order which are better suited to the organization's environment.[12]

I shall give a simplified example of this process at work showing second-order learning. In the English 'new towns' created after the Second World War there was a heavy emphasis on town planning, usually of a rather rigid, centralized, authoritarian nature. One thing planners did was to include open spaces in the new towns and also paths to cross them. Often they would get clever and make the paths run in different shapes, for example curves rather than straight lines. These looked fine and elegant on plans, but in practice people would take short cuts, subverting the planners' aim to keep people to the paths. Hence the grass would get worn in places, or they had to errect fences to stop people doing these unauthorized anarchic things. Practice was less elegant than the plans.

One enlightened new town did it differently. Instead of first-order change (putting paths in different places) they did a creative piece of second-order change: they didn't put paths in at all (at first). They grassed over the open spaces and let people walk where they liked. Gradually the grass wore down in places, and in wet weather parts of these spaces would get quite muddy. This was the disorder phase.

In order to create appropriate order the authorities only had to observe the location of the muddy parts and put paths in those places. So order was created around how people actually behaved, and there was no need for unsightly and wasteful fencing. This sequence follows (approximately) the sequence of amplify signals—create disorder—create order (at a higher level) that I outlined above. It is usually the ideal way for learning businesses to introduce structures and procedures. That is, get on with doing things in a poorly structured, unsystematic way and then, where the messy bits occur, put in procedures and structures—but only in those places. This avoids bureaucracy, which tends to be focused on structuring and proceduralizing for the sake of the structurers and proceduralizers (not customers and suppliers).

I would urge you not, though, to over-focus on the 'disorder to order' sequence. This does not work if the original amplification process is inadequate. The organization needs to be

- prepared to amplify weak signals;
- open to data from the environment;
- non-defensive in its response to amplified data (e.g. welcoming bad news—the best learning businesses *encourage* complaints);
- resourceful—that is, full of resources that are able to respond to amplified signals;
- one which allows considerable freedom in sub-units—these latter, e.g. sales teams, must be free to gather

unwelcome data and spray it around the organization at will;

- reflective—able to ponder on, wallow in, and struggle with new information;
- open to changing beliefs—about itself, its products and services and its markets.

Note: here a distinction is being made between 'beliefs' (what we hold to be true, what we assume the world is like, etc.) and 'values' (what we care about, what we feel is worth while or desirable). Values may be fixed and rooted, while beliefs change. Indeed, a key value may be that we value change at the beliefs level: we accept that beliefs we have held in the past may be unhelpful and need changing. A Taoist metaphor suggests that we need to be like a young sapling. The sapling's strength and resilience comes from its being

- well rooted in the earth—solid and fixed
- flexible, so that it can bend in the wind.

The Taoists contrast this with the old dead tree that stands firm, but when a strong wind blows it snaps and breaks. The message is that organizational resilience comes from a firm solid base in values and ideals, with an ability to bend and move above ground in our contacts with the world.

Diversity

One of the ways to encourage continued fluidity and flexibility in the organization is to value internal diversity. This links to the resourcefulness criterion mentioned above. Diversity provides a variety in the eyes and ears of people in the organization. For instance, people from different cultural or class backgrounds pay attention to different things in their environment.

Organizations lose a great deal by trying to be comfortably homogeneous (usually by hiring young, white, able-bodied, middle-class, heterosexual males for managerial positions). It makes superficial communication easier, but the reduction in the organization's learning capability through this strategy is enormous. Women have shown how they bring a different perspective to organizational life and other discriminated against groups have become more vocal about equal opportunity issues. And, of course, the often illegal, discriminatory practices of organizations are wrong and need to be stopped. However my case here is to put the positive benefits for organizations to welcome difference and diversity. In my first significant managerial post (at the age of 25) I had a manager reporting to me who was a 65-year-old Anglo-Burmese man. I benefited enormously from his wisdom and experience, and the differences between us meant that we complemented each other in ways that benefited the organization.

(In Chapter 10, I shall discuss more fully ways of using diversity positively.)

Organizational types

Another way to approach the issue of recognizing a learning business is to consider organizational types. Like typologies I have already used, the one following is a crude generalization which I offer as a useful map, not as a truth.

Static organizations are classic lumbering bureaucracies. Organizational dinosaurs. But dinosaurs existed for a long time before they expired, and so have the rigid old-fashioned, staid organizations. However, they are recognizably poor learning businesses.

Pendulum organizations move from one side to the other in an illusion of change. Pendulums are, in reality, fixed and allow only a limited movement over a defined territory. Classic pendulum swinging occurs when organizations oscillate across some of the following variables:

Centralized	—	Decentralized
Corporate/strategic long term planning	—	No planning; short termism
Tough management	—	Tender management
Diversify	—	Stick to the knitting

Pendulum organizations lurch from side-to-side across these variables with seemingly no way out of the continual wasteful movement.

Organic organizations use the body/organism metaphor, as earlier described—and, as I indicated earlier, there are limitations to this metaphor. For example, people moving in and out of organizations would be analogous to swapping limbs or organs with other bodies (organizations). Hence, 'organic' organizations can be very conservative ('we don't want to lose or add a limb'). They are what an ex-boss of mine described as 'cosy wrap' organizations—1960s style pseudo-communes imagining that peace and love can prosper within their boundaries while keeping the world out. They are, therefore, rare in a pure form, but the ideal still permeates much of organization development consultancy.

Chaotic organizations are becoming more recognized, though references to organizations as 'organized anarchies' are quite old[13]. Static and pendulum organizations have their own kind of chaos, but the chaotic type is particularly seen as a response to a chaotic, crazy world. The most popular proponent of chaos (in the sense the term is used here) is Tom Peters[14]. He and others encourage the notion that specific kinds of chaos are of value in producing innovative organizations with high levels of responsiveness to markets. Chaos Theory has given a specialized theoretical justification to chaotic organizations, but Chaos Theory has a specific technical way of using the term 'chaos'. In its more common-sense use, unremitting chaos can lead to organizational collapse. Let me side-track to some ideas of Robert Pirsig to help us make sense of this issue.[15]

Pirsig makes a distinction between two concepts: Dynamic and static (he deliberately uses a capital 'D' for Dynamic and a small 's' for static). The distinction is elegantly simple and highly usable, but I do not like 'static' as a term, as it implies a fixedness which is not part of Pirsig's argument, so I shall use the term 'Systematic' (with a capital 'S') in my analysis.

Broadly, the idea of the 'Dynamic' is linked to second-order change and disorderly leaps—often into the unknown. In artistic movements it is the creative leap into a new mode—often initially rejected by 'Systematic' society, as in the outrages over the first exhibitions of the Impressionists, Surrealists and others. Dynamic processes amplify deviations from the norm and provide what in cybernetics is technically called 'positive feedback'. This can enhance deviation to the extent of producing destructive, chaotic situations. As we have seen in such creative individuals as Van Gogh or Nietzsche, this 'chaotic' condition can lead to madness—an inability to live in the world of others. This is where the Systematic forces can apply. They dampen deviations (provide 'negative feedback' in the technical terms of cybernetics) and create homoeostasis (as in the well known example of the thermostat preventing a house from over-heating).

However, if there is only the Systematic dimension, this, in organizations, produces a static organization and eventual bureaucratic death. We need Dynamic leaps to increase choice and versatility while adding the Systematic elements to provide stability and control over hostile forces. Dynamic change produces the creative new ideas, but innovations that work in the marketplace need Systematic procedures to make them work. As Pirsig points out, Dynamic quality is necessary for growth, Systematic quality is necessary for survival. Therefore, in the world of Total Quality Management (TQM), we find organizations that overemphasize—putting in systems and procedures (BS 5750, ISO 9000, etc.) and produce stasis. Other organizations over-emphasize creativity and new ideas (for example, in the computer industry) without the right systems to launch in the market and make profits.

Figure 3.2 shows the problem of the Dynamic leap without 'locking on' devices, and compares this with balanced Dynamic/Systematic progress. Note that this latter has similarities to the Japanese/Zen learning curve discussed earlier in this chapter.

(a)   Dynamic only

(b)   Dynamic and Systematic

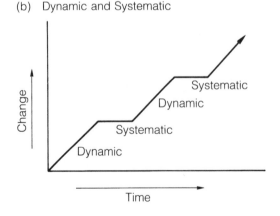

Figure 3.2   Change processes

Pirsig likens the lock-on effect to a ratchet mechanism. There is Dynamic movement upwards which, if it looks right, is prevented from falling back by Systematic procedures. Then there is another Dynamic advance followed by another Systematic patch.

The issue that Pirsig raises is how we disentangle, from all the Dynamic changes, those that are worth having. The person, or group, promoting a seemingly crazy new idea could actually be crazy, or criminal, or both. Cults that seem to promise Dynamic spiritual change usually end in violent disasters, producing the horrors of Jonestown, the Rajneesh organization in Oregon and Waco. In Chapters 4 and 5 I want to address the issues of 'good learning' that can allow us to make good choices, but here I want to signal the importance of these choice issues for organizations. In hiring a new CEO as a saviour with dynamic (Dynamic) new ideas, we have to ask if the person is a con-man in disguise? Learning businesses need to address this.

If, for a moment, we return to the 'chaotic organization' we can say that, as this correlates with high Dynamic, low Systematic, it can be an unproductive option. My preferred option is for a learning business, which is a mix of organic and chaotic. It provides for the Dynamic disjunctures and Systematic procedures, but it does not allow procedures and rules to block Dynamic change. The procedures and rules evolve organically to respond to need as in the example of the paths across open spaces that I discussed earlier.

Creating a balance

If we return to the triangle model used in Chapter 1, we can see how the kind of balance I'm suggesting can work (see Figure 3.3).

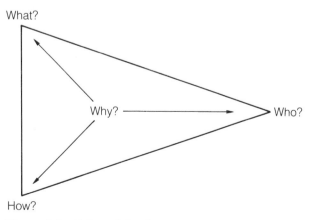

Figure 3.3   Balanced development

If we take the 'How?' corner as an example, the Systematic dimension of this constitutes

- organization structures/organization charts;
- rules for how to do things (e.g. fill in expense claims, do budgets, etc.).

The Dynamic dimension is about culture and cultural change. Culture cannot be pinned down neatly like charts and structures. Indeed, someone once suggested that 'culture', used as a variable in explaining organizational performance, is a word given to what is left when all other explanations have been used. So you could find two organizations with the same technology, same kind of employees, same structure working in the same market providing the same product. If one is better than the other you might have to fall back on saying that one culture is better than the other.

The separation of Dynamic and Systematic is important when we consider learning and change. Dynamic change, such as cultural change, is nothing like Systematic change. It cannot be achieved using the same technology. This is the first thing that must be learned *before* any learning can take place as to how to change Dynamic and Systematic dimensions.

Here is an example. The BBC personnel function over time had gradually been seen as providing interpretations of rules for line managers on such issues as how to discipline someone, when it was possible to dismiss someone, etc. They had volumes of rule books sitting on shelves, and the personnel manager's main job was to react to line management requests for help in interpreting and implementing the rules. Systematic change was the order of the day: changes occurred mainly in terms of modifying rules.

Then there was a decision from the top to change. Personnel would become more proactive in working in a consultancy mode with line managers on cultural/business change. The rule book would be de-emphasized, and decision making would be the responsibility of line managers as often as possible. This was a Dynamic (second-order) change. It required a changed mind-set in everyone, and personnel managers had to engage in Dynamic (second-order) learning to make this work. In Part Four I shall outline the programme the BBC chose—a self managed learning programme for new personnel managers.

Who

Returning to the triangle model in Figure 3.3, I would now like to comment on the 'Who?' corner. A learning business needs to develop people policies and strategies that will help to lock on the changes needed. It will assist organizational hysteresis (the ability to hinder reversing 'good' change).

I shall present a modification of the Birkbeck model[16] as a way of showing an approach. In this model you can distinguish between tactics and methods for

- aligning people with roles, and
- aligning roles with people.

Aligning people with roles

Under *'aligning people with roles'* the main approaches are:

- recruitment and selection
- career guidance
- training and development.

Activity under these headings helps to get the right people in the right positions. These approaches start with an assumption of a role or roles that are defined, and then work on the people dimension to meet needs.

A learning business is one which addresses each of these in the following ways:

Recruitment/selection

The business looks to recruit people who can learn. Learnability is a key criterion at selection. Indeed, often people with lesser abilities/experience are selected over better qualified applicants because the former show higher evidence of learning capability.

Career guidance

People are assisted in choosing career paths from a learning point of view; that is, they are helped to choose options that will enhance their learning and development.

Training and development

This is oriented towards a learning, not a teaching frame as discussed in Chapters 1 and 2.

Aligning roles with people

These tactics and methods reverse the assumptions of the previous category. Roles, tasks and methods of working are adjusted to fit people: people are taken as the defined element (e.g. the capabilities of those already in the organization or available from the labour market). Some of the specific activities available include:

- organization design
- role/job design
- methods design
- design of rewards systems
- equipment design
- environment design.

I shall discuss these activities in turn.

Organization design

The key issue is designing the organization for learnability. This is the area of overlap with the How? question as it affects culture and structure issues. It is clear that a learning business will pay attention to learning factors when engaging in organization design and specifically consider how real people can use the organization for learning purposes. It may be, for instance, that a matrix structure with floating project teams promotes more learning of the right kind than a classic pyramid structure with fixed jobs.

Role/job design

This follows from the above. If jobs are tightly defined, e.g. by rigid job descriptions, this inhibits learning. My preference is for no job descriptions, but rather to have loose role specifications. By the latter I mean simple specifications which delineate different roles in the organization. So it may be useful to specify roles such as 'marketing manager' or 'personnel manager' and provide enough information about the person's role in order to inform other role holders. Also, by avoiding detailed descriptions of duties and responsibilities (as in job descriptions) you avoid constraining people's freedom of movement. It is clear from the available research that if the activities of people are restricted, they do not learn as well and they find more problems in applying new learning.[17]

This whole area is an example of bringing the Dynamic and the Systematic together. The Dynamic forces need freedom, but if people's roles overlap extensively, the level of chaos induced can cause organizational breakdown. Hence, some Systematic role specification is necessary, but always with an in-built capacity for change.

Methods design

This is a subset of the above. Methods of working can be constraining and anti-learning as in the archetypal paper-shuffling methods of bureaucracies, or they can be liberating and open as in an ideal learning business. This is one of the attractions of self-managing teams where individual employees have freedom to develop methods of working to suit themselves (provided, from the Systematic standpoint, that the organization is properly served by the team).

Design of reward systems

This is a crucial area in an organization. From a learning business point of view, the key question is: Is learning rewarded properly? Rewards are, of course, not just monetary. There are perks and there are psychological rewards, for instance. However, I shall refer to money specifically, as it is the base line for rewards strategies.

My starting point is that people should be rewarded for new learning that is significant and of value to the business. This should be the main (or only) criterion for getting pay increments, given that there may be elements in pay increases to cover inflation/market forces. Having given the latter—i.e. if inflation is x per cent, giving x per cent pay rise—then any other increment on pay (for someone in the same role) should be because of what they have learned. (Obviously, if someone is promoted, this is another matter; here I am discussing a situation of no promotion and the decisions to be taken in an annual pay review.) I believe that increases in performance which have come from hard work but not from new learning should be rewarded with bonuses (either individual or collective, or both). A person or group may work less hard next year and therefore warrant less of a bonus. Learning is evidenced by the person

• showing new capabilities and ways of working which provide irreversible changes in performance
• taking on a wider role due to new learning.

These both enhance hysteresis (i.e. irreversibility) and provide a more resourceful person for the business.

The point about a wider role provides a link back to organization/role design issues. It is crucial that individuals, and groups, have a chance to enlarge their roles, so that learning can be enhanced and people rewarded for it.

Equipment design

The equipment people use may inhibit or enhance learning. A good example is IT/computer systems. Some systems liberate people's energies and encourage learning. Others constrain and limit people. In developing IT systems, learning criteria need to play more of a role than they usually do. IT managers are often blinkered in the way they think about the potential for people using the systems they design and the hardware they buy.

Environment design

Some working environments encourage useful interaction between people and enhance learning. This does not necessarily mean open plan offices (and often, if poorly designed, open plan offices fail to fulfil their potential). It can mean areas where people can chat over a coffee, or outdoor space (patios and courtyards) where, in good weather, people can meet and talk. Some organizations have creatively located different departments on the same office floor in order to encourage new interactions.

Integrating alignments

In the above analysis, the danger is that managers focus on one or two areas for change. However, usually all the above choices for action are available, and they overlap and interact enormously. Let me quote one example I experienced in the early 1970s. An English local authority received complaints about the quality of road sweeping and about accidents caused by their drivers. They also discovered that repair bills were high due to these accidents, and that poor driving contributed to increased maintenance costs. Further, government legislation now demanded that drivers of road sweeping and other local authority vehicles gain a Public Service Vehicle (PSV) licence, which is at a significantly higher level than the standard driving test. (Most of the authority's drivers did not have a PSV licence.) The local authority recognized a range of learning needs here, and, at considerable expense, hired an experienced trainer and set up a training programme (with training vehicles and a training area off the roads). In considering the factors in 'aligning roles with people' and 'aligning people with roles', the following occurred.

Selection

Drivers had been selected who were not good learners: most of them struggled in the training programme and the failure rate was high.

Job/method design

The jobs the drivers did and the methods they used were inherently likely to produce accidents. They had to drive around all day at a standard, slow speed in areas with many parked cars.

Equipment design

The vehicles they drove were user unfriendly. For instance, the noise levels were above the permissible values hence causing hearing problems.

Rewards design

Drivers were not rewarded for learning new skills success-fully. Hence the good ones (who got their PSV licences) left to work in the private sector where wages were higher.

A good learning business would have recognized the interaction of these factors and acted accordingly. They would have taken a strategic approach to the issues, and looked at the overall picture rather than just one facet of it.

Appraisal schemes

Appraisal schemes are one aspect of the 'Who?' category (the people dimension) that is perhaps worth mentioning as a specific method which is claimed to help people learn. So often, however, appraisal schemes are poorly used and do not seem to be cost-effective. One reason for this is the negative/ punitive dimension in appraisals. I want here to indicate, in simplified form, what traditional appraisal schemes are like, and what a development approach, as part of a learning business, looks like. The two modes are summarized in Figures 3.4 and 3.5.

Figure 3.4   Appraisal model

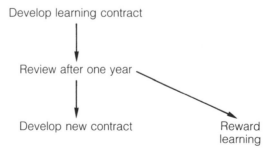

Figure 3.5   Developmental model

The traditional model (Figure 3.4) starts with an appraisal which identifies learning needs. This is a negative, deficiency-based approach. People so often leave an appraisal with the identified weaknesses uppermost in their minds. Learning in this model is associated with something negative: a way of remediating weaknesses.

The developmental model (Figure 3.5) starts differently. People are encouraged to look at themselves, using the Five Questions approach outlined in Chapter 1. They then draw up learning contracts which provide a basis for learning and development activity. This is agreed with the person who will do their annual reviews (one year later). When the reviews take place they are on the basis of documents written by the individuals to which they are committed. As the individuals will have been working on the issues in the documents, the object of the review will be to assess how they have done. A good reviewer will acknowledge first the achievements (and these may feed into rewards decisions) and then help each learner to identify any new learning that is needed in the following year.

The developmental method is significantly fairer than the traditional model. To appraise people *before* they have had a chance to learn is unfair. They have not been given an opportunity to change and are therefore being judged or advised from the wrong base. This is another factor in the failure of traditional appraisal schemes.

In a learning business there would also be greater attention on developing people as good learners than on developing appraisers to check on this. I am not arguing against providing development for those doing performance reviews (apprai-sals), but if an organization is to use appraisals the appraisees need an opportunity to learn how to make the process work for the advantage of themselves and the organization.

The benefit of this is that it encourages more self-responsibility and meets the needs for individuals to manage their own learning and development. In one organization they conducted research on why their annual appraisal scheme was not working. They found that with the pace of change in the company, either the appraiser or the appraisee was likely to have moved in the interval between appraisals. In less than 50 per cent of cases were individuals appraised by the person with whom they had set objectives and written a development plan one year earlier. The only sensible way to deal with this situation is to help the learner (appraisee) manage the process, and de-emphasize the power of the appraiser.

Focused development   One way of describing a learning business is that it focuses a range of issues such that learning is developed in a coherent way. This metaphor is shown diagrammatically in Figure 3.6. The learning business is here compared to a convex lens: various strands that can run in parallel (and therefore may never meet up) are brought to a single point focus, so that learning integrates all these dimensions.

In Figure 3.6 only some of the parallel strands are indicated. The objective of using this diagram is only to show the idea of 'focusing', not to be all encompassing.

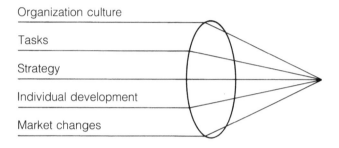

Organization culture

Tasks

Strategy

Individual development

Market changes

Figure 3.6   Focused development

Summary

In this chapter I have moved around the field of learning businesses and I have used a variety of models (maps) to say something of the territory. I have also tried to present a case for the importance of learning businesses as the organizational implementation of the strategic learning discussed in Chapter 2.[18] In Chapter 4 I shall consider these issues in describing 'good learning'.

Notes

1. The most accessible summary of Drucker's views is 'Drucker on Japan' in *Management Today*, June 1974, pp. 89–92 and 138–148.
2. Bateson, G. (1973) *Steps to an Ecology of Mind*, London: Paladin. (See references to Deutero Learning in this collection of readings—not an easy, fun read. Indeed, Bateson can be heavy going if you are not used to his style.)
3. McLean, A.J., Sims, D.B.P., Mangham, I.L. and Tuffield, D. (1982) *Organization Development in Transition*, Chichester: Wiley, is an excellent research-based text showing some of the problems with OD.
4. Janis, I.L. (1971) 'Group think', *Psychology Today* (November) is a neat summary of some key issues on poor team learning.
5. Porter, M. (1990) *The Competitive Advantage of Nations*, London: Macmillan.

6. The Motorola University in Asia is an example of a company seeing its role as developing suppliers. In Singapore I met a trainer whose *sole* job for Motorola was to go into suppliers, mainly in Malaysia, and develop their staff.

7. Handy, C. (1993) 'Make your business a monastery', *The Director* (October), 25.

8. Profile: Sir Duncan Nichol (1993) *Management Today* (October), 66.

9. Quotes here come from the *Rover Learning Business*, Business report 1992 (published by the Rover Group) and from Vallely, I. (1992) 'How Rover drives its learning message home', *Works Management* (August).

10. Sathe, V. (1985) *Culture and Related Corporate Realities*, Homewood, Ill.: Irwin.

11. I am using 'environment' to mean the world around an organization—its markets, suppliers, customers, etc.—rather than 'environment' as ecologists and green activists use it.

12. Ideas expressed here can be pursued with more rigour in the works of Prigogine on dissipative structures, and Bateson on the importance of 'news of difference'. The reference to Bateson is in note 2 above. Prigogine's ideas are most accessibly presented (for the organizational world) in Wheatley, M.J. (1992) *Leadership and the New Science*, San Francisco: Bennett.

13. See March, J.G. and Olsen, J. (1976) *Ambiguity and Choice in Organizations*, Bergen: Universitetsforlaget.

14. Peters, T. (1989) *Thriving on Chaos*, London: Pan.

15. Pirsig, R.M. (1991) *Lila: An Inquiry into Morals*, London: Bantam.

16. The Birkbeck model was developed by Alec Rodger and colleagues at Birkbeck College, London University, mainly in the 1960s. My use of it modifies considerably Alec Rodger's terminology, but the ideas are similar.

17. Current research by my colleagues Ben Bennett, Caroline Cunningham and Graham Dawes on this subject is yet to be published. An already published article which does address this issue is: Kelleher, D., Finestone, P. and Lowy, A. (1986) 'Managerial learning: first notes from an unstudied frontier', *Group and Organization Studies*, 11, 3 (September), 169–201.

18. A good summary of 'learning organization' ideas is in Beard, D. (1993) 'Learning to change organisations', *Personnel Management* (January) p 32–35. He discusses some popular writers, including Peter Senge, Ed Schein, John Burgoyne and Bob Garratt.

PART THREE

GOOD LEARNING

This part follows from the last and acts as a bridge into Part Four. I shall continue the link between a learning business and personal learning and, at the end of Chapter 5, indicate a rationale for self managed learning as the optimal process for achieving 'good learning'. These two chapters will then focus on *what* is to be learned before switching in Part Four to *how* it is to be learned.

I have emphasized the organizational context in Chapter 3. This can be taken also to the level of specific relationships in organizations as a factor in learning. A classic is the boss–subordinate relationship which will be dealt with more fully in Chapter 10. Here I want to take up a concern expressed by Bateson[1] when criticizing 'man's habit of changing his environment rather than changing himself'. While it is important to create good learning environments, it is not of much benefit without good learners.

Indeed, there is evidence to suggest that good learners can learn from and within almost any context. Some Jewish concentration camp survivors (such as Bruno Bettelheim) reported that they treated their situation as a research project—something to be learned from—and this was a major factor in their psychological as well as their physical survival. Yet a concentration camp could be viewed as the worst possible environment that any human being could inhabit.

In psychotherapy there is evidence to suggest that good patients/clients (i.e. good learners) will benefit from almost any brand of psychotherapy (given a not totally incompetent therapist). This line of enquiry may be more fruitful in improving the benefits of psychotherapy (that is, identifying why some individuals benefit more than others) than in a search for the 'best' psychotherapy.

Creating 'good learners' becomes, then, a more important factor than the subject-matter of learning or the improvement of teaching/training. This also seems to be justified by research in universities, which suggests that students who learn how to play the academic game do better (in terms of marks/grades) than those who do not (irrespective of intelligence or other measures of ability). One behaviour to enhance results is 'cue seeking'.[2] This is where students look out for evidence of what their professors/lecturers regard as important, and respond to it. 'Cue deaf' students do not seem to spot the cues provided, sometimes subtly and sometimes blatantly, about how to get good grades.

It is clear that in organizations some people pick up quite quickly what they need to learn in order to progress, and others do not. Traditional IQ and other related measures do not accurately predict these differences, and I shall explore some of these factors using a variety of concepts. In some cases I shall continue ideas already outlined—for instance, the difference between first-order and second-order learning. I shall return to the 'good learner' theme in Chapter 10.

NOTES

1. Bateson, G. (1973) *Steps to an Ecology of Mind*, London: Paladin, p. 420.
2. Miller, C.M.L. and Parlett, M.R. (1974) *Up to the Mark : a Study of the Examination Game*, London: SRHE.

4 Capability and wisdom

Introduction

George Bernard Shaw once said that 'success comes from taking the path of maximum advantage instead of the path of least resistance'. The following section will mention some of the 'maximum advantage' paths that seem apparent in good learning businesses; but, as Shaw implies, they're not easy. In later sections I shall indicate some reasons why only a minority of people and organizations demonstrate these qualities, and some clues as to the kind of orientation needed to get 'good learning' in organizations.

In the following section I shall indicate some examples showing evidence of a learning orientation (or lack of it). The examples are just that: not comprehensive but rather examples of issues.

Learning from all possible sources

Clients, customers, colleagues and competitors are among examples of sources of learning. The problem is that many organizations waste the information they gather. Companies do attitude surveys or benchmarking comparisons with other organizations but often do not know what to do with the data. I have been present at boards that have looked at attitude survey data. They may say 'Oh, that's interesting. We're 2 per cent up on this category this year and 3 per cent down on that. I wonder why?' Others may also wonder, then move to the next item on the agenda. These data-gathering exercises become empty rituals without a learning focus as a starting point. Also, companies tend to invest too much in complex data gathering instead of having a strategic focus on learning needs which can lead to quick, focused data gathering of a much less sophisticated (and more cost-effective) nature.

Let us take some positive examples. Sir Ian MacLaurin was one of those responsible for turning round retailers Tesco from a decaying business into a highly successful one. He demonstrated a clear learning focus. The sequence seems to have been:

1. Identified problems (diminishing market share, reduced profits)
2. Learned why—including the company's commitment to downmarket practices (such as Green Shield Stamps)
3. Studied alternatives (he visited three companies in the USA that had issued stamps, but stopped)
4. Took the best ideas and translated them into his own company's situation.

This was an example of learning from good practice. Richard Branson, who founded Virgin Atlantic Airways at the age of 33, learned from others' mistakes. He studied the reasons why small independent airlines failed (the majority had, up to that time). He realized that competing on price alone would not work (Laker and People Express were notable failures on this score). He learned that service, customer care, uniqueness and specialness would be key criteria for success, and, as a result, the airline, against all the odds, now has a series of 'best airline' awards, and is successful.

Branson's success is all the more remarkable given that he had no experience of the airline industry and was entering an industry where even the large experienced companies were in trouble. He could only do it because he is an excellent learner. But his learning was not a lot of random facts and figures about the airline business. He had a focused attention on what was needed. He connected between his needs and what was to be learned, and after the airline was launched he continued to learn and to apply his learning by making changes in the airline's operations.

Learning and change

Figure 4.1 shows the traditional model for getting change to occur. This is the standard process used by traditional management consultancies: and, generally, it is a poor model. It is fine if you want interesting reports to read, but action/implementation is often limited.

Figure 4.2 shows a learning-based model. Instead of a linear sequential, one-dimensional process of 'study to recommendations to action', this model suggests that 'learnability' is part of the starting point for planning change. There are *two* beginnings, not one. The process has to work as a pincer movement where the problem to be addressed is analysed alongside the analysis for learning and change. An example of

Study problem/situation

Recommendations
(in report usually)

Action
(possibly)

Figure 4.1   Traditional model

Figure 4.2   New model

studying change from the beginning is to use Revans' model
of 'Who knows?, Who can?, Who cares?'.[1]

   The difficulty is that most managers are educated—in
school, business school, etc.—according to the first model.
Case studies in a classic MBA suggest that analysis and
recommendations are all that are required. Because students
on an MBA do not have to implement the recommendations
they make on a case study, they begin to believe that this
linear process will work. They have learned how to learn in a

limited and limiting way, and tend to blame others if their linear thinking does not work. (Argyris[2] is an excellent critic of this problem.) Consultants who work in this way tend to blame resistant or inept clients rather than their own limited methodology.

IT specialists constitute another problem. A paper company decided to computerize its warehouse. Paper was to be stored in fixed points and logged on the computer. Retrieval of paper to send to purchasers could then be done automatically. They had studied the problem, recommended a solution and then acted. The problem was that no one had considered the learning needs of the warehouse staff. They carried on in their old ways, dumping paper from fork-lift trucks in any convenient place. As the computer was unaware of this, errors in shipping were enormous. At one level you can say that this is just common sense. If the IT people had had some common sense they would not have done what they did. However, putting a label on the problem does not solve it, and exhortations to IT staff 'to have more common sense next time' will not necessarily work. They have to *learn* a different way of addressing problems.

Who learns?

There is a danger that more senior people think that others (more junior) are the main focus of learning. However, you may not be able to control someone else's learning, but you can control your own. It is probable that, faced with a change issue, the first person you ought to think of is yourself. Given that you want something different, how can you change?

Let me give the example of a secretary with whom I worked many years ago. She did not like to have more than one or two tasks at any one time. She could not sequence tasks. She panicked, became stressed, felt overloaded if I gave her more than two things at once—even though I would emphasize that they needed to be done in sequence. Task one, then task two, then task three. She somehow wanted to hold all three tasks in her head at once and, given that she could only work on one, the other two swirled around in her head worrying her because they were not being done.

Solutions

(a) *No learning solutions.* These could include dismissing the person. Or leaving the situation as a mess.
(b) *Her learning.* I could have decided that she needed to change. I have no idea how this would have been achieved, but it was a feasible option.

(c) *My learning*. I took the view that I had to learn. I had to change my behaviour and not give her multiple tasks. I had to create a sequencing for myself and feed work to her from that sequence.

Many bosses choose (a) or (b). They only see those two options. They are, of course, genuine options, and I would not argue against them. I am only positing the view that there are at least three, not two, options.

Collaboration and sharing

In a learning business, people share ideas and information. If someone sees something in a newspaper or magazine that might interest someone else, they cut it out for them. If someone goes to a conference, that person is keen to share with others any ideas learned.

This, again, requires a particular mind set; it does not just happen automatically. In some cases, people's experience at school has been not to share learning. In schools that are highly competitive, and where students are ranked in order of performance, it is not in a person's interest to help others. Indeed, collaborating in learning, e.g. over an essay, is called cheating and is punished. This contrasts dramatically with the Japanese school where students see it as their duty to help those who are struggling. I have spoken to a number of British and American teachers who have taught in Japanese schools and they comment on how much easier it was there than in their own countries. Because children are in a culture where they are expected to care for their colleagues, the teacher's job is helped enormously.

Ohmae[3] shows how the 'group harmony' in Japan's educational system contributes to educating Japanese managers in a collaborative style of working. Walzer[4] suggests that the 'democratic' style of learning in Japanese schools develops 'camaraderie and mutuality' and that, unlike some stereotypes, Japanese people become used to a flexible, autonomous way of working. This helps employees in companies to become capable of independent judgements and sophisticated decision making in collaboration with others.

This specific example, from one culture, provides a general challenge to a popular dichotomy. The distinction between individualism and collectivism is used by politicians (especially where individualism is seen as a corollary of right-wing capitalism, and collectivism a correlate of left-wing socialism). Also cross-cultural researchers such as Hofstede[5] have popularized a spectrum of national cultures on an individualism/collectivism dimension.

I believe that Eastern cultures in general (not just Japan) challenge this dichotomy. Merton,[6] in his commentary on Chuang Tzu's writings, suggests that 'personalism' is an apt term for Taoist ideals. As he said:

> Personalism and individualism must not be confused. Personalism gives priority to the *person* and not the individual self. To give priority to the person means respecting the unique and inalienable value of the *other* person, as well as one's own. (p. 7)

He suggests that ego-driven selfish individualism ends up as a self-defeating anti-personalistic position.

There is an important distinction between 'individuality' and 'individualism'. It can be argued that *individuality* is sacrificed in highly *individualistic* modes of acting. If, for instance, a manager is to pursue his[7] own individual, selfish career needs to progress up the organization, it may be that the need to conform and play the game causes him to lose his *individuality*. Here I'm using 'individuality' in the three ways that Squires[8] describes, namely:

- individuality as *uniqueness*—the antithesis of mass standardization
- individuality as *holism*—the antithesis of a partial, usually narrowly cognitive, view of the person
- individuality as *autonomy*—the antithesis of over-dependence on others and excessive conformity to others' views.

The highly individualistic manager may have to disavow uniqueness, pretend that he does not have feelings and values and conform to organizational norms in order to progress selfishly. In this sense, then, I am with Freire[9] in his view that individuality (or, as he put it, 'full humanity') cannot be achieved through individualism but 'only in fellowship' (p. 58).

Personalism also challenges bureaucratic, centralist socialism (for example, as practised until recently in Central and Eastern Europe). It has been suggested that these seemingly collectivist cultures actually promoted selfish individualism[10]. Under communism natural communities broke down and people had to take more responsibility for themselves. Also, where there was covert secret police surveillance of individuals, people could not trust colleagues (for example, at work) and, hence, individuals were thrust into a more closed self-centred mode of being. Also, many individuals joined the Communist Party, not out of ideological belief, but for the sake of their careers and their material well-being.

Individualism and collectivism seem, then, to fold into one another and in their extremes create dehumanized life styles and dehumanized organizations. Neither position is 'personalistic'.

Key concepts

'Personalism' is a key concept. It says something about the person (of their desire to learn with and from others, their desire to support others' learning as well as their own) and about the learning business. The latter needs to be a place that supports a personalistic approach.

In the remainder of this part of the book I want to elaborate some other key concepts and suggest that they go together in saying something about good (desirable) learning. The three main concepts are:

1. Capability
2. Wisdom
3. Holism

This chapter covers capability and wisdom as they balance each other. Chapter 5 covers holism and some relevant subcategories of holism.

I shall also revisit some concepts already introduced including:

- first and second-order learning
- pattern change
- Dynamic and Systematic.

Before discussing these concepts, I would like to indicate another method of elaborating good learning, namely via metaphor.

Metaphor

Metaphor was once considered an interesting poetic speech form of no relevance to practical matters such as business. Lakoff and Johnson[11] were the most influential analysts who changed that view, and Morgan[12] has been a popularizer of the use of metaphor in making sense of organizational life.

We now see that much of our thinking, as well as communicating, is through metaphor. Metaphor provides a way of understanding or interpreting relatively abstract ideas through linkage to familiar concrete objects or modes of behaving. I want here to indicate some metaphors that are used to explicate ideas about learning and, alongside these, to show how the metaphors are applied practically in learning activity. Many of the metaphors used seem to me to restrict and constrain our thinking about learning—and even the good metaphors have their limitations.

Building

Classically much of education has been conceived of as *building* up the person, and 'units of learning' have been seen as building blocks. This has been translated into competency approaches which tend to talk of each competence as a building block towards making a competent manager. This is a reductionist view which assumes that each brick in the building can be neatly mortared to those beneath and produce a nice static building (person) at the end of the process. The concomitant of this is that if all the bricks are not in place, the person is not of much value, since a building without all its walls (and roof) is incomplete and uninhabitable. This metaphor then contributes to 'gap' models of learning, i.e. that learning is to add bricks or fill in holes, and is remedial. Thus we find that competency approaches are almost never applied to top managers (who obviously cannot be incomplete persons!).

Bucket

The bucket metaphor is common. It assumes that the learner is an empty bucket and is filled up with knowledge and skills. Once again it is a deficiency model, though more fluid than the building metaphor. Also, as buckets tend to be leaky, there have to be top-up courses to keep the bucket filled to the brim. The bucket metaphor justifies much of traditional educational activity, especially in schools.

Engineering

The concept of 'human resources' in its strong (economic) sense (people as resources interchangeable with other resources such as machines) is linked to an engineering metaphor. Thus, we have reports on 'making managers'[13] and managers having 'tool kits' of skills. This links to mechanistic human resource development systems and to training courses which assume, at worst, that the person is only a walking tool kit. Resources and tools tend to get worn out and used up, so this metaphor can justify throwing used up resources (people) 'onto the scrap heap'.

Agricultural

People can be seen as organizational seed corn, or as tender shoots needing fertilizing and care. In the Young Professionals Programme at British Airways the symbol for the programme was an acorn—based on the idea that 'mighty oaks grow from little acorns'. This metaphor has many appealing features, but it can also justify 'removing dead wood', 'weeding people out', 'pruning' (sacking) to justify organizational survival or growth. And this may or may not be valid.

Human body

The analogy here is with the physical growth of a human. We know that growing maturity and ability are linked to physical growth (up to adulthood). So developing 'intellectual muscle' and such like has to be a good thing. Also, the idea of people being 'fit' and 'in shape' is appealing. The 'personal growth movement' took on board much of this thinking, and personal growth approaches to training have been popular in some organizations. Like the agricultural metaphor, the challenge here is explicitly to bucket/engineering type metaphors. The assumption is that people have the capability within them— and do not need to be stuffed with facts and theories. Rather they need to be nurtured and supported.

Zoology

This is, at one level, a relative of the above metaphor. However, ideas of 'breeding good staff' link more to the way we see animals than humans. Also, the idea that people are categorizable (for example, in biblical terms, as sheep and goats) can justify stratification which denies learning. This is especially so in ideas that managers are 'born, not made'—and that, encouraging learning is a waste of time.

Craft

The idea of a manager as a craftsperson (and managing as a craft) is common, though usually implicitly. However, young managers are often seen as 'apprentices' learning their craft through watching their 'elders and betters'. The idea of a craft, in its best sense, also encompasses learning the values and ethos of the craft. The true craftsperson finishes the underside of the chair as well as the visible parts, because that is the proper thing to do and they care about the 'total quality' of their work (hence, also, the link to Total Quality Management).

Artist

Vaill[14] talks of 'managing as a performing art'. The notion of 'manager as artist' adds an aesthetic and a creative dimension to managerial activity. It also balances the idea of 'manager as scientist'—and the need for some business schools to want to justify management as a legitimate academic subject through the excessive teaching and study of quantitative and statistical methods.

Medicine

'Diagnostic' activity is justified by a medical metaphor. Diagnosis of ills, weaknesses, etc., justifies action to solve them, and is often at the back of 'training needs analysis'. Also the unpleasantness of some training activities can be alleviated by managers feeling that they have to 'take their medicine' (and an unpleasant taste often correlates with 'good medicine').

War/military

Strategies, tactics and missions came from a military metaphor. They can support aggressive competitive 'fights' with the competition, or with other departments in the organization. The action learning notion of 'comrades in adversity' learning best when their 'backs are against the wall', can have excessively macho overtones for some, which is a pity as action learning has so many good features (see Chapter 6).

The military metaphor can support macho leadership development (especially where military leaders are used as role models, and 'beating the enemy' is used as the *raison d'être* for learning). It can also support the aggressive 'strategic advantage' school of development. Of course, if you are under attack as an organization (for example, in a takeover bid) learning to fight off the enemy can be extremely valid. But continual focus on enemies (real or imaginary) can lead to a. paranoid distortion of the organization's activities, and fundamental learning can be missed.

Another example of different perspectives comes from Eastern writings on warfare. Especially interesting to me are ideas of strategic approaches which avoid battles and bloodshed—that is that war does not have to involve fighting. Also, most martial art forms from the East have evolved as defensive methods and there is much we can learn in the West from the ways of thinking that underpin Aikido, Tai Ji Chuan, Karate and Judo.

Naval/ships

Some aspects of naval metaphors link to war, but others come from the merchant navy. Being 'welcomed aboard' and then 'keeping an even keel' while they get their work 'under way' is common advice to new managers. Of course, they have to make certain they 'don't make waves' or 'go overboard' and then everything will be 'smooth sailing'. They will have to look out for 'fair weather friends', those who 'sail too close to the wind' and those who 'swing the lead'. Learning in this context can be about culture (the organization as a ship, as indicated above) and methods for 'keeping the ship afloat' and not letting projects 'run aground'.

The exploration side of this metaphor can lead to notions of a learning programme as a 'voyage of discovery'. The voyage/journey metaphor has many positive aspects, and is one that is heavily used in self managed learning. (I shall return to this metaphor in Chapter 6.)

Games/sport

Game metaphors are sometimes close to warfare—as games can be ritualized war. There is also a heavy use of the 'team' metaphor in management with overt reference often to sport. This underpins ideas of 'team-building'. Here we have two metaphors that overlap—and in the process cause confusion. 'Building' has a static base in the building metaphor. The notion is of a team as a static entity which is 'built' and then needs regular 'maintenance' (e.g. the annual off-site meeting). This loses the sense of a team as a fluid group where people come and go and where ways of working need to evolve to suit a changing world. I personally prefer notions of 'team development' as these seem more learning oriented.

Game/team/sport metaphors are used in the idea of 'coaching' in organizations, and there is frequently an overt translation of sports coaching methods into organizations. Gallwey's Inner Game[15] approach to coaching is one that I particularly like.

Family

When working in social services organizations I found that the family metaphor was the one most used in relation to work groups. People wanted to be in happy, supportive family groups. In other organizations, ideas of family are more hidden, but in some cases the concept of mentoring is linked to a paternalistic or avuncular model of the older, wiser, family member helping the young learner.

Other metaphors

The list of metaphors could be much longer. My purpose here is to make the point that metaphorical thinking about learning and about organizational life is crucial to understanding different perspectives on 'good learning'. 'Goodness' comes to be defined by the metaphor. So, for instance, competency approaches can be judged, as to goodness, if the building bricks are 'fit for purpose' and can be stacked up over time to make a good manager. In the next section I shall raise some other points about this approach.

As an aside, you might like to consider the metaphors *you* use to think about learning. Have you written anything that you could study to see if your metaphors support the kind of learning you want?

Capability

It is difficult to argue against the case that managing is a *process* that needs, as an outcome, action on live issues. There is, however, no need to postulate a subject or a thing called 'management', and indeed outside the English-speaking world it is difficult to find cultures with a noun that exactly correlates with how 'management' is used in English. Solely analytical learning of a supposed subject called 'management' must, then, be questionable, especially if learning to make things happen is neglected.

Weyrich[16] suggests that MBA programmes typically focus 70–90 per cent on analysis and 10–30 per cent on making things happen. The manager's job is 10–30 per cent analysis and 70–90 per cent making things happen. Research studies on MBAs suggest that indeed there is a major problem here. Even when academics study their own programmes and with a methodology that is potentially biased in favour of finding positive results, problems show up. For instance, Boyatzis and Renio's research[17] suggests that on their MBA, students 'do learn a range of skills' such as planning, quantitative data analysis, etc. However, the MBA had *no* impact 'on abilities that involve interaction with people', including leadership skills, relational skills, helping/delegating skills, setting/ managing to goals skills, learning skills.

The concept of 'capability' can encompass these abilities and is, therefore, of considerable value in considering what kind of learning is needed in a learning business. The Royal Society for the Encouragement of Arts, Manufactures and Commerce (RSA) has, for some years, promoted this concept through its 'Education for Capability' initiative. They suggest that 'Capability is an all-round human quality, an integration of skills, knowledge and personal qualities used appropriately and effectively in a variety of familiar and unfamiliar situations'.[18]

The 'Education for Capability' proponents have suggested that, while capability is a 'whole person' concept, it can be recognized in action and in people through the following:

- openness to learning
- self-awareness
- problem solving
- self-starting
- sense of purpose and will
- courage
- creativity

and so on.

Given the RSA's mission statement of 1754, which included the aims 'to embolden enterprise', these qualities are perhaps unsurprising. They do not reject the detached analysis and scholarships of the traditional educational world but subsume them in this wider framework.

The challenge is how to learn this, given criticisms of traditional education and training activity. That will be covered in Part Four. Here, however, we need to side-step to consider the subject of competence, competences, competency and competencies. This field has become complex and confusing, including the problem of which of the four labels to use. However, most people seem to talk of 'competences' and produce lists of these. The RSA response has been to say that capability is a broader and more holistic concept that would include (or transcend) competence lists.

I shall briefly review some issues about competences, and suggest that the concept can be unhelpful and unnecessary. 'Capability' has its disadvantages as a concept, but is generally more usable and more useful for learning businesses.

Competences

The claims are made that ideal (competent) managerial performance can be identified, codified and taught. Also it is claimed that competences so identified are of universal validity (for the level of management identified). The problem for these claims is that they do not stack up.[19] There is no solid research evidence to support the contention that developing managerial competences of itself improves organizational performance.

Options for use of competences

There seem to be three areas of choice available, each with two options:

1. Level of detail

(a)   Detailed lists of tightly defined competences using lengthy performance criteria lists. (This is favoured at the national level in the UK.)
(b)   General lists usually of around five to ten competences fairly loosely defined without performance criteria. (This is favoured by many organizations.)

2. *Generic or specific*

(a) Generic list of core competences that apply to all managers at a particular level in the organization.
(b) Specific lists linked to precise professional areas. (This latter option seems rare. The attraction for many organizations seems to be the standardized generic list.)

3. *Task/role or person*

(a) Task/role-based lists come from a functional analysis of the supposed needs of a particular job. (This is the favoured mode in the UK at the national level.)
(b) Person-based lists define competences for *managers* (not managerial roles). (This is the dominant mode in the USA and in many organizations in the UK.)

Problems with competences

I shall take the 'generic by level' mode as an exemplar. The claim here would be that first-level managers, middle managers and senior managers would have, at each level, defined competence needs. The dominant metaphor is the building block.

A summary of specific concerns is outlined below with some reference to the preferred option of using 'capability' instead.

1. *Past oriented*

Competence lists are *always* about what has been done in the past. Much of this *may* be valid in the future, but there is usually no basis to decide what. Even in the short time of some organizations using competence lists, they have found the approach undermined by TQM changes in work practices, empowerment policies devolving decision making and de-layering of organizations radically changing managerial roles. The UK Management Charter Initiative (MCI) national 'Guidelines' stated (in 1989) that 'first-level management' (for *all* managers *irrespective* of size of organization, location, organization culture, technology, etc.) was about 'the direction and control of the activities of other people'. Self-managing work teams wiped that out in some organizations. Others had long since moved away from a 'direction and control' view of management.

Capability is about response to changing circumstances. It cannot be defined in terms of the precise tasks of a manager. The capable person needs to be capable of responsiveness to changing needs.

2. Narrowly ethnocentric

Competence lists are usually developed in one country, and are generally inapplicable elsewhere. The idea that a list of competences for middle managers in the UK would have relevance in France or Germany, let alone Nigeria, Japan or Argentina, is untenable. Hofstede, Trompenaars[20] and others have shown quite conclusively that we transfer managerial practices directly from one culture to another at our peril.

Capability, on the other hand, needs to be concerned with capability to work anywhere; not to be perfect, but to be able to learn and to respond to needs in varying cultures.

3. Reductionist/fragmentary

The assumption of competence lists is that people can learn each competence in isolation without reference to other competences, and then unproblematically integrate them. The metaphor here is the notion that one could take an old-fashioned clock apart, take out its wheels and springs, throw the pieces into a box, and assume that it will still work.

Capability is an inherently holistic concept. The facets of capability overlap each other, and cannot be separately identified.

4. Complex, bureaucratic lists

In an effort to develop precision and specificity such that competences are relatively unambiguously defined, lists become long, complex and unusable by managers.

Capability can be kept as a relatively simple, unified concept.

5. Spirit and form

Gil Evans, the great jazz arranger, once said 'Every form, even though it becomes traditional and finally becomes academic, originally came from someone's spirit who created the form. Then it was picked up and taught in schools. But all forms originated from spirit'.[21]

Competences focus on form: capability on spirit and form.

6. Organization culture

Competence lists assume a particular kind of culture, generally that associated with traditional bureaucracies where levels and jobs are tightly defined. The MCI Guidelines for first level managers say 'Such a management task is performed within a fairly tight group of constraints and the individual has limited freedom of action'.[22] So much for empowerment and devolved responsibility!

7. Individualistic

The focus in competence lists is on the isolated individual. It ignores the context within which the person works. Even more fundamentally, it assumes that competences exist in a detached, abstract state. As Wittgenstein[23] said: 'A smiling mouth smiles only in a human face.' The idea that managers can learn, say, 'communication skills' separated from the context in which they communicate is out of keeping with ideas about developing learning businesses.

Day,[24] an advocate of generic competence lists, chose to exemplify the approach by reference to 'oral communication'. His first example of an 'element of competence' was 'communicating clearly to others (groups)'. The assumption here is that we can test a person in this competence and that the test will demonstrate a universal competence applicable to groups of managers or shop-floor workers (or anyone) in *any* organization *anywhere* in the world. He quotes three 'performance criteria' for this element, one of which is 'Delivers the communications continuously, with no major hesitation'. The first problem with this is that many successful CEOs that I have studied would fail this test. They can be brilliant one-to-one or in writing, but tend to ramble or lack coherence in groups. They certainly make 'hesitations'. Yet they are great communicators in the context in which they operate. They use elegant symbolism and rich metaphors in focusing on the strategic needs of their businesses. Two examples would be Ken Olsen, founder of Digital, and Sir Colin Marshall, chairman of British Airways.

One suggestion about great leaders is that (a) they emerge in relation to the needs of the time (like a Winston Churchill who was a failure in peacetime but a success in war) and (b) they play their strengths to the full while being incompetent at a whole range of managerial activities (Eisner at Walt Disney fits this characteristic, as do many other CEOs). Often leaders work in pairs (for example, Hanson and White of the Hanson Trust), each balancing the other (Hanson's solid organizational ability balancing White's creativity). The people I have mentioned above are/were all *capable*, but in many respects incompetent.

8. Not owned

Lists produced by national bodies or by headquarters' HR people are usually not owned by managers down the line/out in the field. The more complex the lists, the less likely are managers to understand them or to accept them.

At one conference a speaker asked the audience how many people had rented or hired a car. Most hands went up. Then he asked how many had washed such a car. One hand went up (out of an audience of hundreds). As he said: 'What's the reason for the difference? Ownership. If you don't own it, why take care of it?' I will focus, in Chapter 6, on ways of helping managers to *own* their learning.

9. Professional/functional differences

Generic, standardized lists of competences do not recognize differences that many managers feel are important. While it is easy to agree that breaking down departmental and functional barriers is important, enforced generalized competence lists are usually not the best way to do it. In a learning business you start where the learner is: you recognize professional values and skills in the engineer and the accountant and help them to broaden these skills to develop the capability to work in the wider interests of the organization. This encourages ownership of learning, and develops learning agendas in the language of the people involved. Imposed centralized lists are usually in the language of bureaucracy and do not generate enthusiasm in professionals.

10. Diversity

Organizations are becoming more diverse. In some cases equal opportunity legislation is forcing businesses to allow women and black people into the ranks of management. In other cases enlightened top managements are seeing the need to broaden recruitment and promotion strategies. It is clearly inappropriate to assume that these new managers have to fit the requirements to be like white, able-bodied, heterosexual, middle-class males. But competence lists tend, implicitly or explicitly, to reflect the assumptions and norms of this previously privileged group both in style (white, male, bureaucratic language) and content.

Capability is about people being themselves and being 'capable' in terms of their roots as black people, disabled people, etc. A learning business needs to welcome this diversity as providing increased opportunities for people to learn from each other—white from black and black from white; men from women and women from men.

11. Systems thinking/Chaos Theory

Senge, from a systemic perspective, and Stacey, from a Chaos Theory perspective, show that addressing individual competences is unhelpful.[25] A systemic view shows that organizational performance is best understood by recognizing a mass of interacting factors, none of which can be viewed on its own as an isolatable reason why an organization is as it is. Therefore, to suggest that the development of more competent managers will *automatically* improve business performance is a fallacious assertion. A capability focus needs to be located in context. A person's development needs to respond to systemic features.

12. Epitaph

My local newspaper has features every week on famous people. They are asked a series of questions and the answers are published. The last question they are asked is what they would want as an epitaph. I have seen no one suggest that 'He or she was competent' would be desirable. And when I have tested this epitaph idea at conferences or in groups, I have found no one who wants to be labelled 'competent' as a farewell image. When asked why they would not want it they say:

- it smacks of mediocrity
- it sounds as though you're barely acceptable
- it's boring.

Capability on its own also does not turn people on: so in the remainder of this part of the book I shall indicate some concepts that do get people's attention, starting with 'Wisdom'.

Wisdom

I was once consulting with a public sector organization and I happened to hear of an incident that had just occurred. The director of one of the departments in which I was consulting received a complaint from an old lady living on her own. The previous Friday, a group of workmen from this organization had been working nearby and had become a bit frisky at the end of the week. The old lady had an apple tree at the front of her house, and the men had decided to climb it and steal some of her apples. She wrote to complain not just about the apples, but as a lonely old lady she had felt disturbed at these boisterous men invading her property. It had upset her.

The director called the men into his office and showed them the letter. They realized that what they had done was not sensible and expected disciplinary action. The director suggested instead that if they tried to put matters right he would not formally discipline them. They agreed. He suggested that they buy the old lady a box of chocolates, take it to her and apologize—which they did. The following week the director received a glowing letter from the old lady saying how kind the men had been, and that she now realized that their high spirits had got out of hand. The men also thanked the director, saying that they had now formed a friendship with the old lady and would call on her when they were in her neighbourhood.

Clearly the director had done a good job. But it goes beyond 'capability'. He had to be *capable* of understanding the problem and communicating with the men. But that alone would not necessarily lead to the *wise* course of action he chose. Capability provides a basis for action—it is 'doing' oriented. Wisdom is more 'being' oriented and is associated with knowing what to do via a reflective/introspective process. Capability without wisdom can lead to unwise action: wisdom without capability can lead to inaction. However, it is not quite as neat as that, as the two concepts overlap, but when put together they can enrich understanding of what constitutes good learning.

One way of conceiving of learning is that capability may come before the wise use of capability. Keeney[26] quotes the example of the Samurai swordsman who spends an enormous amount of time and energy learning skills and techniques. 'After much rigorous training, the pupil is instructed to go meditate on the mountains. When he forgets all that he has learned, he can return and *be* the sword.' Now I do not actually think that 'forgets' should be interpreted in a Western mode. We might more usually say that the skills are internalized so that the person acts unconsciously. This is a point that Bateson[27] makes. As he says, the problem in understanding exceptional artists is that the more brilliant (capable plus wise) the artists become the *less* conscious they are about how they produce great art. So also in management. The exceptional CEOs who seem to be able to cope with overloads of information and activity and yet make wise strategic decisions cannot usually say how they do it. Of course, if asked by a researcher they will say something about what they do and how they do it, but it is probable that these answers would not tell a novice manager how to do it.

This is why a scientific attitude is necessary. Not science purely as measurement, calculation and laboratory experiments but science as understanding and codifying. A scientific approach to management requires the wise balancing of theory and practice: the understanding of managerial practice in depth so that we can develop good theories. (In Chapter 6 I shall suggest that the process of learning wisdom needs this scientific attitude.)

If we just assume that wisdom is inborn or learned through esoteric Zen-like practices we will not progress. We have to map out the territory to assist other explorers.

Beyond knowledge

Not to know is bad: not to wish to know is worse. (African proverb)

The slenderest knowledge that may be obtained of the highest things is more desirable than the most certain knowledge obtained of lesser things. (St. Thomas Aquinas)

Books are there to keep the knowledge in while we use our heads for something better. (Szent-Györgi)[28]

These three quotes permit us to put 'knowledge' in context. They disabuse us of the notion that the wise person is the one who knows the most. We need to backtrack on what constitutes knowledge and wisdom.

Cleveland's[29] hierarchy of

Data → Information → Knowledge → Wisdom

is helpful. Data are unconnected facts—for example, financial data in a book-keeper's records. Data can be analysed to produce information—for example, the accountant's financial analysis of the book-keeper's records. However, if this information is just stored somewhere and not used it remains as information, not knowledge. Knowledge is information in use—often through the grouping of pieces of information into models. So the board that integrates financial information with marketing information, HR information, etc., will eventually *know* better what is going on in the business. However, wisdom is related to the way we use this knowledge. Does the board make wise decisions based on this knowledge? These wise decisions must include value judgements, beliefs about the available knowledge and assumptions about aspects of the organization and/or of the world of which they have little or no knowledge. Often this activity is called 'strategic thinking' but because of this label it is assumed to be a purely cognitive, mental activity. However, wisdom includes beliefs, values and feelings as well as thoughts. Deciding what to do also demands moral choices. If we know that closing a factory in an area of high unemployment is going to create a great deal of human misery, but if we do not do it the whole organization may be put at risk (and hence create even greater misery), we have to grapple with this not just as a rational problem but as a non-rational, moral problem. We must also have the *wisdom* to recognize that the judgements we make have these dimensions.

Schumacher[30] suggests that there are four useful knowledge-gaining activities:

(a) Finding out about ourselves
(b) Finding out about others (people, animals, things, etc.)
(c) Finding out about others' views of us
(d) Finding out about our views of others.

Activity (b) tends to be the only one in our society given the label 'knowledge'. However, the wise manager needs to develop all four. In the self managed learning work to be discussed in the Part Four, we have always taken the development of all four areas seriously. However, we have found academics claiming that only (b) has any status. And, worse, they have assumed that if we pay attention to self-knowledge (category (a)) then we must, by definition, be paying little attention to (b). This either/or thinking has always made little sense to me—and I shall return to this issue in Chapter 5.

Wisdom and age

T.S. Eliot, in the *Four Quartets*, criticizes the 'wisdom of age' as a wisdom of 'dead secrets'.[31] In its place he praises the 'wisdom of humility'. Margaret Mead would have agreed. In some of her last writings she argued that in past time the young would learn from the old as the culture and its technology hardly changed from generation to generation. In the modern world this is not so. The world in which young people are growing up is vastly different from that of previous generations. It is not just that new technology makes life more complex: it requires a whole new way of thinking. Mead argued that in this kind of world adults have to learn from their children. This requires a 'wisdom of humility'—a recognition that the young IT specialist will have something to teach the middle-aged manager—and not just about hardware but about different ways of thinking. As Mead said:

> Until recently, the elders could say: 'You know, I have been young and *you* have never been old.' But today's young people can reply: 'You never have been young in the world I am young in and you never can be.'[32]

This has a whole range of implications for learning, but it especially challenges educational assumptions about passing on knowledge to the next generation. The status of this knowledge is called into question.

Summary

This chapter has emphasized the personalistic approach to learning, and discussed the concepts of capability and wisdom. The next chapter considers aspects of integration.

Notes

1. See Chapter 2.
2. Chris Argyris has produced much penetrating stuff on this issue. His book with Donald Schön is a major text: Argyris, C. and Schön, D. (1974) *Theory in Practice*, San Francisco: Jossey-

Bass. His 1991 paper 'Teaching smart people to learn', *Harvard Business Review*. (May/June), 99–109 is also useful.

3. Ohmae, K. (1982) *The Mind of the Strategist*, London: Penguin.
4. Walzer, M. (1983) *Spheres of Justice*, Oxford: Blackwell.
5. Hofstede, G. (1980) *Cultures Consequences*, London: Sage.
6. Merton, T. (1965) *The Way of Chuang Tzu*, Boston, Mass.: Shambhala.
7. I deliberately use the masculine gender here: it is possible that individualism is more a male trap.
8. Squires, G. (1980) 'Individuality in Higher Education', *Studies in Higher Education*, 5 (2), 217–226.
9. Freire, P. (1972) *The Pedagogy of the Oppressed*, London: Penguin.
10. Hankiss, E. (1990) *East European Alternatives*, Oxford: Clarendon Press.
11. Lakoff, G. and Johnson, M. (1980) *Metaphors We Live By*, Chicago: University Press.
12. Morgan, G.M. (1980) 'Paradigms, metaphors and puzzle-solving in organization theory', in *Administrative Science Quarterly*, 25, 605–622.
13. Handy, C. (1987) *The Making of Managers*, London: NEDC/BIM/MSC.
14. Vaill, P.B. (1990) *Managing as a Performing Art*, San Francisco: Jossey-Bass.
15. Gallwey, W.T. (1974) *The Inner Game of Tennis*, New York: Random House.
16. Weyrich, K.D. (1993) 'Key issues for business schools and executive development centres: a business viewpoint', Oslo: Paper to EFMD Deans and Directors Meeting. Consider also the following quote from *The Independent on Sunday*, 6 June 1993, p.14, in an article by Roger Trapp:
    'There is plenty of scepticism among senior business people and MBA graduates over the value of what an MBA course teaches. "I have always found that thinking about a problem is the easy bit. Implementing the strategy is the hard part," said Alan Bowkett, head of Berisford International. "But it was the implementation that my MBA did not teach."
    A conspicuous success (he was a millionaire before he was 40), Mr Bowkett took his business degree from the LBS in the mid-1970s but remains sceptical of the benefits. "It gives you a terrific bag of analytical tools; it stretches you and teaches you to work under pressure. But it doesn't tell you how to handle those difficult people called colleagues and employees, and that is the most essential skill in business."
    Because it ignored the human side of business, Mr Bowkett said, the MBA tended to make graduates arrogant—as if they need not dirty their hands with the nitty-gritty of personal relationships.'
17. Boyatzis, R.E. and Renio, A. (1989) 'The impact of an MBA programme on managerial abilities' in *Journal of Management Development*, 8 (5), 66–77.

18. The quote is from a spin-off from the RSA—the 'Higher Education for Capability' initiative—in *Capability News*, 11 (February 1993), 1.

19. There is a huge (and growing) literature on competences. Much of it is repetitive, unanalytical or based around unevaluated cases. Some of the best sources of discussion on competences include the following: Myer, C. and Davids, K. (1992) 'Knowing and doing: tacit skill at work', *Personnel Management*, (February), 45–47; Iles, P. (1992) 'Centres of excellence? Assessment and development centres, managerial competence and human resource strategies', *British Journal of Management*, 3, 79–90; Stewart, J. and Hamlin, B. (1992) 'Competence based qualifications: the case against change', *Journal of European Industrial Training*, 16 (7), 21–32; Burgoyne, J. (1990) 'Doubts about competency', in Devine, M. (ed.) *The Photofit Manager*, London: Unwin Hyman; Holmes, L. (1990) 'Trainer competences: turning back the clock?' *Training and Development* (April), 17–20. I have also discussed these issues elsewhere: see, for example, Cunningham, I. (1987) 'Management training: patterns for the future', *Banking and Financial Training*, (Autumn) 26–30.

20. Hofstede, G. (1980) *Cultures Consequences*, London: Sage; and Trompenaars, F. (1993) *Riding the Waves of Culture*, London: Economist Books.

21. Quote from Carr, I. (1984) *Miles Davis*, London: Paladin.

22. *MCI Guidelines—Certificate Level*, National Forum for Management Education and Development, London.

23. Wittgenstein, L. (1953) *Philosophical Investigations*, p.583.

24. Day, M. (1988) 'Managerial competences and the charter initiative', *Personnel Management*, (August), 30–34.

25. Senge, P.M. (1990) *The Fifth Discipline*, London: Random House.

26. Keeney, B.P. (1979) 'Ecosystemic epistemology: An alternative paradigm for diagnosis', *Family Process*, 18 (June), 117–129.

27. Bateson, G. (1972) *Steps to an Ecology of Mind*, London: Paladin.

28. Szent-Györgi, A. (1964) 'Teaching and the expanding knowledge', *Science*, (4 December), 1278.

29. Cleveland, H. (1989) *The Knowledge Executive*, New York: Dutton.

30. Schumacher, E.F. (1977) *A Guide for the Perplexed*, London: Jonathan Cape.

31. Eliot, T.S. (1944) *The Four Quartets*, London: Faber & Faber.

32. Mead, M. (9178) *Culture and Commitment*, New York: Columbia University Press, p.63.

5   Holism

Introduction

In discussing wisdom and capability there is a tendency for many people to see these concepts as implying a largely mental/cognitive activity. I also see them as involving:

- feelings and emotions
- physical aspects
- issues of values, morals and spirituality
- social factors to do with relationships with others.

This perspective has been labelled 'holistic' and I shall try to give my view of how this concept can be applied to good learning.

As well as basing comments in this chapter on practical experience and on authors quoted, I have also drawn on research conducted on CEOs and other top managers. This research was carried out in the USA and the UK with a view to developing fundamental, cross-culturally usable concepts and models. I shall not continue to make tedious reference to the research, but there are some published papers emanating from it to which you can refer if necessary.[1]

Feelings and emotions

Let me first comment on 'emotional learning'. Mike Dixon, a columnist on the *Financial Times*, once commented to me that, in management, 'thinking is embedded in feeling'. This phrase struck a chord. Managers think out of an internal context of feelings and emotions: thoughts are not produced from other thoughts. We think what it is possible for us to think as a result of the other dimensions of ourselves (as mentioned above—the emotional, the physical, the spiritual and the social).

Keutzer[2], drawing on the work of Paul MacLean and others, suggests that neurophysiological evidence supports the view that evolution of the neocortex has produced a split between the archaic (emotional) structures of the brain and the 'thinking cap' that governs rational thought. Emotion is the older partner—and, it is suggested, the more powerful. Thus, given the inevitable conflicts between reason and emotion, the reasoning part is 'compelled to provide spurious rationalizations for the senior partner's urges and whims' (Keutzer, p. 79).[2]

Bramley,[3] from her experience as a student counsellor, argues that many students cover up emotional problems in unbalanced intellectual development. However, if we take Keutzer's hypothesis. seriously, we can see that this is misguided. As Bramley comments

> When and if a student realises, on attainment of a good degree, that his intellectual ability cannot give him love and security for which he yearns, he may become very ill indeed, and certainly several suicidal young people whom I have known come into this category.

All this was, of course, well known in ancient wisdom, and in many cultures. To take one example from the Middle East:

> Your reason and your passion are the rudder and the sails of your seafaring soul. If either your sails or your rudder be broken, you can but toss and drift, or else be held at a standstill in mid-seas. (Gibran)[4]

But the lessons have not been learned in the managerial world—or they have been forgotten or driven out in the learning environments of business schools. I shall quote just one example. The *Boston Globe* of 13 October 1986 wrote up the 25-year class reunion of the Harvard Business School 1961 MBAs. While it noted that there were positive comments about Harvard's role in making participants successful, significant concerns were raised. Edwin Stanley (chairman of Stanley Investment and Management Inc.) said that 'Business School did us a disservice with a compass locked on true north'. His criticism was of a narrowly focused driving ambition for success. Amos Hostetter (chairman of Continental Cablevision) went further when he claimed that his personal life had been 'subliminated' to business success. 'I was being a coward and afraid of intimacy,' he commented. One of the wives present criticized those who were raising these concerns. She said, 'I feel sorry for you guys. You shouldn't expect Harvard to teach you how to be human in your professional lives.'

That response was undoubtedly unfair. Business schools claim to equip people for managerial roles and if they pretend that personal feelings and values have no place, or if they force the sublimination of these in a pseudo-rational analytical atmosphere, then they do deserve to be criticized. La Bier's clinical research on young managers[5] produced clear evidence of this problem. He found that there were managers who superficially were climbing the corporate ladder with apparent consummate skill and who behaved in ways that were totally 'normal'. However, from an in-depth clinical study he found that they were, to use his words, 'quite sick'. He described them as 'dominated by irrational passions of power lust, conquest, grandiosity and destructiveness or, conversely, by cravings for subjugation and humiliation'.

On the other hand, he found another group who seemed to display some neurotic symptoms but were psychologically normal. These he saw as growing up through learning about and struggling with the difficulties of corporate life. This could be painful, and they sometimes showed it (e.g. through anxiety feelings or sleepless nights). The problem—to which William Temple alluded earlier this century—is that we are taught to think together and feel separately, whereas we need to think separately and feel together. That is the mark of good collaborative practice, such as teamwork.

Evans and Bartolomé[6] discuss these issues, drawing on writers such as Vaillant and Schein. They agree with the latter that 'the distinguishing characteristic of a top level executive is not his skill or ability but his emotional competence'. They show how, for instance, a successful manager may have to do an unpleasant task such as firing someone. They may feel bad about it, but will nevertheless confront it and do it. In other words, they experience negative feelings, but they deal with them appropriately.

Metafeeling

The term I use to elucidate this emotional sophistication is *metafeeling*; that is, the emotionally mature person may feel bad but will feel OK about feeling bad. He or she knows that life has its ups and downs, and accepts it. The mature person experiences crises, but works them through.

Metafeeling, then, is about how we feel about how we feel. People go to sad films, cry a lot and say how much they enjoyed it. They feel good about feeling sad. However, a person could experience some difficulty in life (e.g. loss of job), feel sad about it (reasonably), then feel bad about feeling sad. This can lead to a downward spiral of depression.

Some Buddhist monks have a routine each morning of thinking of all the problems they and others have or could have, then laughing out loud about them. They recognize problems and the negative feelings around them. They are not covered up or pretended away, but are put into perspective. (If you have to address a problem, try the Buddhist technique. If you are driving to a tricky meeting and worrying about it, recognize the worries, then laugh out loud about them. You might be pleasantly surprised at the result!)

Bio-rhythm evidence suggests that we go through cycles with ups and downs. It is suggested that we inevitably have emotional highs and lows, irrespective of what is going on in the world around us. While I am not sure that the wilder claims about bio-rhythms are not too fanciful, it seems undeniable that people do experience patterns of internal change, e.g. hormonal, which have an effect on our emotional states. If we accept this then we can metafeel OK—we can know that we will not be on top form every day of our lives and that these variations are not to be blamed on anyone— least of all ourselves.

Connectedness

One of the important aspects of good learning seems to relate to *connecting*. This includes *internal connecting* which integrates

- thinking
- feeling
- physical (body)
- believing/valuing (including spiritual beliefs).

These internal processes need to come together. Holistic learning is not about developing each aspect sequentially. When we learn, in the best sense, we have *feelings* about what we *think* and we integrate these in our *value/belief* systems. A useful concept in explaining this connection is *centredness*. We also engage in *external connecting*—that is, we interact with the world around us. *Grounding* is the concept I shall use to explore this (see Table 5.1).

I'll take the two concepts of centring and grounding in turn. They both came from Eastern thinking and are most visibly used in martial arts training, but are best seen as 'learning for life' in its broadest sense.

Centring

In some approaches to learning developed in China and Japan (such as Tai Ji and Aikido), the concept of the Centre is

Table 5.1   Connecting

Process	Internal connecting	External connecting
Links/integrates	Mind Body Feelings Values/beliefs	Self to world and world to self
Way to achieve it	Centre	Ground

important. It can be viewed as the centre of a single person, as the centre of gravity around which the body revolves (not literally!). It can also be seen that a person's Centre is the centre of the universe from that individual's point of view. It is the place from which to connect to others (people, things, animals, etc.), therefore it has an ecological sense. The Centre is the harmonizing focus of energy fields and patterns of relationships.

This can all sound pretty flaky, esoteric stuff if the language and way of thinking is new. But it is highly practical. There is a demonstrable difference between centred and uncentred people. Let me elaborate some features of centredness.

Harmony

'Harmony is an attunement of opposites, a unification of many, a reconciliation of dissentients' said Theon of Smyrna. Harmony is not, in music, unison. It is the aesthetic 'centring' of difference (different voices, different instruments). We each have these differences within us. Some psychologists and psychotherapists refer to our different parts as 'subpersonalities'. Berne,[7] in developing Transactional Analysis, used the idea of 'ego states' which he labelled 'Parent', 'Adult' and 'Child'. Irrespective of their theoretical base, there is much agreement among psychotherapists that they are in the business of helping a person integrate or harmonize or come to terms with these differences.

In terms of developing a holistic sense, the harmonizing required here is of head, heart and guts. Particularly as applied to centred managers, we are thinking of the person who

- demonstrates harmonized energy;
- shows congruence and coherence in integrating theory and

practice (in doing this, the person would bring together 'theory-in-use' and 'espoused theory', as Argyris and Schön[8] suggest);

- is able to work with difference and ambiguity, and has the self-awareness to do this;
- 'listens to the inner voice'—which is a term Bennis[9] uses about highly effective leaders (the influence on Bennis is from Ralph Waldo Emerson's essay 'Self Reliance'); the inner voice, if it is to be heard and believed, comes from the Centre;
- is able to be inside and outside at the same time—(Postman and Weingartner[10] call this 'the anthropological perspective', meaning someone who can understand the rituals, norms and culture of the group or organization—the insider perspective—and is able to stand outside, examine them and operate out of the inner voice);
- has personal theories and meanings which may not conform to the textbook (see McLean *et al*[11]).

Balance

Centred managers may not always feel 'in balance', but they are aware of the value of balance. They recognize polarities and dualities and address them as such. However, we can get inappropriate balance as in the suggestion that the balanced middle manager has a chip on both shoulders! Without a centred way of operating, and attention to some of the factors above, balance on its own is insufficient.

I shall spin through some polarities that are relevant here, but they are not exhaustive of all the possibilities.[12]

DOING/BEING

Centred managers are aware of what they *do* and who they *are*. The verb 'to be' is often used in their language (e.g. 'I am ...').[13] This balance is a mirror of the capability/wisdom balance since the former is associated with doing, the latter with being. (Like most of the issues in this part, I shall show in the next how a self managed learning approach can develop this balance.)

A related polarity is

PROACTIVE – REACTIVE

Proactivity is usually lauded as being better than reactivity, but it is clear from my research that this criticism is of the wrong kind of reactivity. Wise reactivity is at the heart of the best customer care practices—flexible, thoughtful, caring response to customer requests and demands. Proactive organizations, which push their technology onto the market with little reactive wisdom in their responses to the market, tend to suffer the consequences eventually.

Another related balance is

EXTROVERT – INTROVERT

This factor focuses on the individual personality. The common assumption is of a linear one-dimensional scale as in Fig. 5.1(a).

(a)   One-dimensional spectrum

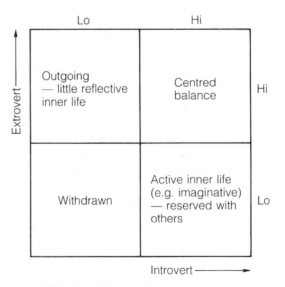

Extrovert   Introvert

The usual psychometric tests place a person at a point on this scale

(b)   Two-dimensional

Figure 5.1   Extrovert–introvert

However, as shown in Fig. 5.1(b), there is an alternative two-dimensional mapping. While such a mapping helps to challenge uni-dimensionality, it is not a truth. The harmonizing of extrovert and introvert aspects of the person is complex. Another mapping might be a double helix (comparable to DNA) with introvert and extrovert characteristics interweaving in three dimensions.

However I do not doubt the evidence of my research[12] which showed that effectively functioning people possess both characteristics. Taoists use instead the polarity

YIN – YANG

which is often translated as yin (feminine) and yang (masculine) but the concepts are looser and more sophisticated.[12] They can, for instance, be seen as subsuming proactivity (in yang) and reactivity (in yin). Taoists emphasize the complementarity and interpenetration of these apparent opposites. The Taoist principle of mutuality suggests that it is not possible to have one pole without the other. The analogies are that there is no night without day, no light without dark and no valley without hills.

Learning process

In the above I have elaborated some outcomes of 'good learning'. Learning to be centred provides a basis for effective managing *and* effective learning. It is therefore also part of the *process* of learning. Fiol and Lebas[14] suggest that there are a range of balanced outcomes necessary from a learning programme and that the *process* of the programme is the significant factor in bringing about change. They researched a senior management programme in a French bank, studying participants before, during and after the programme. They interviewed in depth all participants before the programme to identify each person's profile on a series of polarities. These included:

Short term	— Long term
Abstract	— Concrete
Backward looking	— Forward looking
Individualistic	— Collectivist

The process they adopted was:

- *First*—connect with the person's strong area. Thus an auditor might typically be strong on backward looking, (as his or her job role focused on past records) but weak on forward looking. Or a strategic planner would be strong on forward looking (as his or her job role focused on the future) but weak on backward looking. This connection to the person provided a base for the next stage.

- *Second*—help the person to balance; create opportunities to redress their weaker side.
- *Third*—help the person to develop both sides synchronously.

They focused on the *process* of the learning programme as a way of developing this balanced progress. Individuals were not taught the weak side, for instance. They undertook activities which encouraged this development. I shall indicate some of these activities in Chapter 6.

The Fiol and Lebas approach makes a link back to some earlier themes. For example, the balance of Dynamic and Systematic. Figure 5.2, shows how this can be translated into a map of learning approaches. The suggestion is that competence-based learning is too narrowly Systematic whereas approaches which emphasize only self/personal development may be too overbalanced towards Dynamic. In Chapter 6 I shall suggest that self managed learning provides an optimum balance.

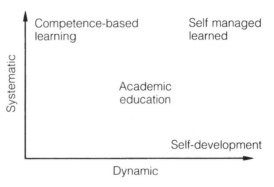

Figure 5.2   Learning

Theory/practice   This is a classic polarity which often surfaces in discussions about management. Business schools justify an overweening interest in theory by quoting aphorisms such as 'There's nothing so practical as a good theory'. In their turn managers attack academics. Two 'question and answer' pieces indicate this.

1. *Question*: If you push the Professor of Marketing and the Professor of Finance off the roof of the University, which one hits the ground first?
   Answer: Who cares?
2. *Question*: Why are academics buried 30 feet under the ground?
   Answer: Because deep down they're OK.

A root cause of these divides is indicated in Table 5.2.

Table 5.2   Theory and practice

Theory	Practice
Generalization	Experience, wisdom
Classroom	Job
Solution	Problem
• Specialization	• Person
• Subject	• Pattern
• System	• Process

This dichotomy postulates two 'worlds'. Firstly, a world of theory which tends to be concerned with teaching generalizations about management in a classroom. Such teaching gives managers *solutions* to apply to their problems. They tend to be taught *specializations* (HR, marketing), *subjects* (economics, sociology) and *systems* (IT, OR). This 'S' world can also include precise *skills*, and often particular *structures*.

The world of practice is where managers learn most of what they need to learn (research suggests 80–90 per cent of the abilities of successful managers have come from this world). Managers learn by experience and from received wisdom (bosses, mentors, etc.). The learning is job based and is often a response to live *problems*. For example, if a new IT system is installed, managers have a problem if they do not know how to use it. So they learn. Such learning is very *people* oriented; it is often about changing *patterns* of work and learning new *processes*. The 'P' world is readily recognizable by managers.

There are two difficulties with these two worlds. Firstly there is the 'S to P' issue. This is where managers are taught solutions and then have to find appropriate problems or people to use them on. Or, even worse, they distort the problems to fit the available solutions.

As an example, I was trained initially as a chemist. At one time I was offered a job as a research chemist in a pharmaceutical company. If I had taken that post, I might have been presented with the problem of alleviating or even curing a particular mental illness (say, depression). The solution I was trained to provide was a chemical one. Presented with such a problem the *only* solution I would conceive would be a new drug. My training had convinced me to look for chemical solutions to such problems. Some years after leaving the world of research chemistry I became involved in the field of psychotherapy. Here, presented with problems of mental illness, the therapist will commonly talk to the patient/client. He or she will look for solutions to the problem within the confines of the particular theoretical framework in which he or she has been trained. What the therapist will not usually do is search for a chemical solution to the problem, just as the average chemist would not think of refusing to search for a new drug and suggesting psychotherapy instead. Mental illness presents major problems in Western countries. It is arguable that developing apt solutions to these problems is hampered by the inability of the various professions involved from being able to talk to each other (and this problem seems to worsen as the subject boundaries are strengthened through increasing specialization).

This issue affects the managerial world quite broadly, and in training leads to difficulties such as 'the transfer of training' problem (a trainer euphemism for 'we taught them things that are no use in their work and therefore they don't apply them').

A different issue from the 'S to P' syndrome is 'P' only. This is where managers say 'I've learned all I need from experience. I don't need to explore new ideas being promoted by a bunch of ivory tower academics.' The difficulty with this approach is that experience is all about the past. If, as we assume, the future is not going to be like the past, this makes experience-only learning very limited.

As Fiedler[15] has shown in his research, highly experienced managers/leaders function well in situations that require little or no learning. These especially include high job-stress situations such as fire-fighting. Someone leading a group of fire-fighters will draw on experience very heavily. They will not, while fighting a fire, stop to think about learning issues. They work to well-rehearsed grooves, and stopping to think could be a dangerous activity. On the other hand, Fiedler's (and others) evidence suggests that in the low job stress world of the average corporation, intellectual and creative ability is more likely to predict good leadership performance than experience. Note that I say that the average corporation has low 'job stress', not necessarily low 'interpersonal stress'—i.e. managers may not get on with each other (hence producing interpersonal stress) but their jobs are not inherently stressful (e.g. dangerous, as in fire-fighting).

The two dangers I have identified, namely 'S to P' and 'P' only, need addressing. The answer seems to be 'P to S', that is going from *problems* to *solutions*, or from *people* to *systems*, etc. The point is that experience cannot be the only teacher. New ways of doing things are needed. There is a value in the expert, the professional, the academic. But each should be more in a role of responsiveness to the needs of people, problems, patterns and processes than is often in evidence. This example shows the need for balance to be driven more from one direction. That, however, is not to deny the need for balance. And sometimes the back-room boffin will offer a solution to a problem that no one knew existed (or which was downplayed).

Grounding

I have emphasized so far the idea of centring, and I have suggested the importance of internal balance and harmony. However, this is not enough. For instance, I quoted Bennis on 'listening to the inner voice'. But suppose the inner voice is coming from some disconnected, crazy place? At worst it could be a schizophrenic delusion.

Also, centred managers can be lively, creative entrepreneurs, but without connection into the wider society they may go off at tangents. The managers who are centred *and* grounded have a sense of these wider connections. They are the people who take environmental and ecological issues really seriously. They do not just see their roles as complying with the law or avoiding bad publicity if they pollute rivers. They see themselves as integrally involved in the planet and all life upon it.

Grounding can be grounding in

- *spiritual and religious beliefs* which provide a well worked out faith
- *professional values*—a sense of belonging to something bigger than the organization. (As one civil engineer in a public organization said to me: 'If my employers were to ask me to build something I thought might be unsafe or unwise, I'd refuse because my professional values override my loyalty to my employer.')

- *family and community*—a feeling of belonging and of intimate connection to others.

Grounding connects the inner to the outer worlds (and vice versa). It provides a solid base from which the manager can operate. Grounded managers are not pushovers. This is literally true. I often demonstrate this in groups by using Ki Aikido techniques to show how if people physically ground themselves they literally cannot be pushed over. If, on the other hand, they are not physically grounded, they can be knocked sideways with a moderate push on the shoulders. People in organizations often intuitively recognize these differences. They recognize who's a lightweight and therefore easy to roll over in a conflict—and they recognize who not to take on in a fight.

Centring and grounding need to be brought together. Grounding without centring can lead to inertia and lack of change: centring without grounding can lead to burn-out.

Morality and ethics

Rushworth Kidder[16] was the first Western journalist to visit the Chernobyl nuclear power plant after the accident there. He discovered that the accident had occurred because two engineers conducted an unauthorized experiment on reactor number four. In order to do this they had to override *six* separate computer-driven alarm systems. Now these engineers were highly competent, highly able men. The accident did not occur because of human error, in the sense of someone making an unknown mistake.

As Kidder commented, the accident was 'not a question of technology. It's a matter of ethics.' By this he meant that he saw the engineers' actions as requiring 'an ethical override'.

The question I have from this is: What was missing in their development and learning that left out ethics (or at least this kind of ethical issue)? Another incident points to this same problem. Richard Grabowski was, by all accounts, a brilliant aerospace engineering student. He was offered jobs with two prestigious companies, both of which would have involved designing weapons systems. On 16 October 1985, while considering these job offers, he committed suicide. His suicide note read:

> If I were to live out my potential, I would only destroy life .... I have such unbounded respect for the practical application of physical ideas that I would go so far as to murder humans .... I am incapable of love. I am incapable of compassion. I can only

respect rational, physical ideas. It is for this reason that I must die. If I were to continue living, I would only prolong my death. I cannot 'live' by any sense of my imagination producing weapons. (Quoted in Skolimowski[17])

That is pretty terrifying stuff. What, again, was there in this person's learning and development that created this awful end for him? We can guess that examination of morality and ethics—and the struggles we need to make with moral and ethical choices—was missing. But in an era where old certainties no longer exist, where post-modern views of knowledge encourage a nihilistic relativism, new bases for action are necessary. This points to a moral basis for managerial activity—and therefore the need to learn to make moral choices.

I do not want to preach a particular moral position. That discussion, to do it full justice, belongs in another book. My point is about learning. It is possible to argue that rather than seeing ethics as an interesting option in the business school curriculum, we need to *start* managerial learning on a base of examining issues of morality, ethics, values and social responsibility. The decision of what is right and good for a manager to learn must start from rightness and goodness being treated as moral questions.

There is much debate at present about what a good company is, or should be. Many, myself included, would say that the 'bottom line' is insufficient justification for the existence of a company or for measuring its success (goodness). Struggles with moral dilemmas, such as the interplay between the need for profit, the needs of employees, and the needs of the planet, are at the heart of the strategic learning that is needed in business. And moral development is

(a) a learning issue and
(b) learnable.

Indeed, in Iris Murdoch's statement that 'learning is moral progress'[18] we have a clue on how to proceed. She points out that good learning develops wisdom and subtler visions, and diminishes crass egoism. This kind of learning does not come from didactic preaching; it comes from individuals working openly with colleagues in exploration of moral dilemmas. Haste[19] suggests that moral development comes from two factors:

First, a caring community of which the individual feels a valued member, where mutual respect and justice are enacted, not just preached. Second, an environment which continually encourages reflection on the wider implications—including personal responsibility—of everyone's actions.

We come back, then, to the needs of a learning business, and we see the emphasis on the autonomy of learners. This will be the starting point for Chapter 6 in Part Four.

Summary

These two chapters have explored facets of 'good learning', largely through the discussion of key concepts. While it has overlapped into the wider field of what makes a good manager, I have tried to keep the analysis within bounds. Hence there is much more that could be said about issues only alluded to here.

Notes

1. My colleague Graham Dawes contributed to the research in the USA. One short paper which provided a background piece is: Cunningham, I. (1988) 'Patterns of managing for the future', *Industrial Management and Data Systems* (Jan./Feb.), 18–22.
2. Keutzer, C.S. (1982) 'Physics and consciousness', *Journal of Humanistic Psychology*, 22, 3 (Spring), 74–90 (esp. p. 79).
3. Bramley, W. (1977) *Personal Tutoring in Higher Education*, Guildford, Surrey: Society for Research into Higher Education, p.16.
4. Gibran, K. (1972) *The Prophet*, London: Heinemann.
5. La Bier, D. (1986) 'Madness stalks the ladder climbers', *Fortune* (1 September), 61, 64.
6. Evans, P. and Bartolomé, F. (1980) *Must Success Cost So Much?*, London: Grant McIntyre, p.155. See also: Schein, E.H. (1978) *Career Dynamics*, Reading, Mass.: Addison-Wesley; and Vaillant, G.E. (1977) *Adaptation to Life*, Boston: Little, Brown.
7. Eric Berne wrote a number of books. The most interesting in this context are probably: *Games People Play*, London: Penguin (1964); and *What Do You Say After You Say Hello?*, London: Andre Deutsch (1974).
8. Argyris, C. and Schön, D. (1974) *Theory in Practice*, San Francisco: Jossey-Bass.
9. Bennis, W.G. (1989) *On Becoming a Leader*, Reading, Mass.: Addison Wesley, p.34.
10. Postman, N. and Weingartner, C. (1969) *Teaching as a Subversive Activity*, London: Penguin, p.17.
11. McLean, A.J., Sims, D.B.P., Mangham, I.L. and Tuffield, D. (1982) *Organization Development in Transition*, Chichester: Wiley.
12. I went into some detail on these issues in Cunningham, I. (1984) *Teaching Styles in Learner Centred Management Development Programmes*, PhD Thesis, University of Lancaster.
13. I have analysed language issues in Cunningham, I. (1992) 'The impact of who leaders are and what they do' in Clark, K.E.,

Clark, M.B. and Campbell, D.P. (eds) *Impact of Leadership*, Greensboro, NC: CCL. This chapter also analyses 'doing/being' matters.

14. Fiol, M. and Lebas, M. (1992) 'A conceptual model of management leading to the development of a professional management learning tool', Paper to EFMD workshop *How Managers Learn?*, Tampere, Finland (October/November).

15. Fiedler, F.E. (1992) 'The role and meaning of leadership experience' in Clark, K.E., Clark, M.B. and Campbell, D.P. (eds) *Impact of Leadership*, Greensboro, NC: CCL.

16. Kidder, R.M. (1992) 'Ethics: a matter of survival', *The Futurist* (March/April), 10-12.

17. Skolimowski, H (1986) 'Destruction through education', *The Scientific and Medical Network Newsletter*, 31, 1.

18. Murdoch, I. (1992) *Metaphysics as a Guide to Morals*, London: Chatto & Windus.

19. Haste, H. (1993) 'Guilt and the struggle to teach right from wrong', *The Guardian Education* (March), 2–3.

PART FOUR

SELF MANAGED LEARNING

This part of the book moves from the general issues discussed into more specific ideas and approaches for learning. Self managed learning was outlined in Chapter 1 through two examples of programmes. The three chapters in this part elaborate SML principles, strategies and tactics.

6   Self managed learning: principles

Introduction

This chapter follows from the previous ones. It shows how a self managed learning approach is strategic for organizations and individuals. (Hence exemplifying a strategic learning perspective.) SML is a key part of developing learning businesses as the approach synchronizes managing and learning, so that they are not artificially separated (as in bureaucratic educational and training approaches). SML is a *process* by which people engage in 'good learning', hence showing practically how ideas covered in Part Three can be achieved. In Chapter 7 I shall show more specifically how SML designs work out, and I shall elaborate on ideas discussed in this chapter.

Much of what has been raised in the earlier chapters is lauded by other writers. Organizations are exhorted to do better by a wide range of commentators. Here, I want to suggest that we have to move beyond exhortation into practical, usable methods that achieve the ideals many espouse.

Comments on SML programmes

Before getting into the ideas, let me give a range of quotes from people who have been on SML programmes. The quotes allude to some of the issues I shall discuss, as well as mentioning ideas from earlier chapters.

> The really important knowledge that managers need is constantly changing. So the results of knowledge-based courses—even so-called leading edge programmes—are quickly obsolete. The key thing for me is learning how to learn—and learning a way of thinking that enables me to take on and manage new knowledge as it develops.
>
> *(Philip Smart, Channel Tunnel Project Manager,*
> *Railfreight Distribution)*

Everybody has their own learning style and the strength of this [SML] programme is that it allows me to express and expand my own ways of operating. This has been the key benefit for me.

All my learning during the programme proved immediately valuable and usable back at work. During the programme I moved into a new board level role. The programme had a great effect in changing the way I interact with my colleagues as well as helping me develop a new way of looking at the business.

As a result, the European team in which I work operates much more effectively. I am able to contribute at a strategic level and make contributions across different disciplinary areas.

I've learned all the knowledge and skills of a traditional MBA. But I've changed. I'm different. I have more wisdom.

(Dick Wood, Director of Customer Services,
System Integrators Europe)

The strength of self managed learning is that it encourages you to get up and take action to solve problems. Working in small groups helps by ensuring we push each other to get things done. The result is a programme that is much more rigorous than distance learning.

(Paula Stewart, Company Secretary, Leica UK)

The approach is flexible in the way it can be tailored to the participant's personal and company requirement, making it a truly individual programme. The learning contract requirement within the self managed learning format creates this unique approach. This is enhanced by operating in a learning set. These features encourage the manager to develop learning which can only be of great advantage in an increasingly complex business environment.

I believe good general management moves beyond the rational approach of business disciplines and recognizes broader inter-relationships both inside and outside the company; takes longer term views; develops congruent visions for corporate aims and harnesses all interests in working towards common goals. Inherent in this is the individual manager's willingness to be open to learning, to increase self awareness and focus on personal development issues.

I believe my experience has improved my managerial ability, broadened by outlook and enriched me as an individual and in doing so has increased my overall worth and contribution to my company.

(Paul Kraus, Personnel Manager, Yorkshire Water)

I find meeting once a month provides a regular and convenient structure, without interruptions to my work schedule. The regular meetings are also a constant motivator to keep up with the work and preparation required to make progress.

Self managed learning has proved a highly efficient way of learning that integrates theoretical background with practice. Developing my own syllabus was a useful exercise and is the most appropriate way to learn in the middle of one's career.

(Jörg R. Janke, Applications Localization Manager,
Oracle, Germany)

Self managed learning is a unique and powerful approach that is about solving problems in a more holistic way, rather than emphasizing narrow competences. The freedom to set one's own learning goals is marvellous, but that does not make self managed learning an easy option. Drawing up the learning contract is a challenging and rigorous process.

(Terry Piper, Internal Management Consultant,
British Gas)

What has this [SML] course uniquely provided? The content is devised to suit my individual needs. It has forced me to confront issues that, given the option, I would have ignored. It has taught me skills in personal relationships that I would not have developed easily in any other way. It has taught me how to work effectively as a member of a team. Most important, I have discovered a method and style of study which is effective for me. Self managed learning has had a more profound effect on me than any other single learning experience.

(Peter Maher, Deputy Headteacher in East London)

Response to comments

The kinds of things people say about SML programmes exemplify some of the points made in the previous chapters. They comment on being able to do more—not just in a disjointed way, but linked to their own and their organization's needs. They show developed wisdom. They rarely use the word 'wisdom', but they do show that they are able to operate more wisely. Comments also show the balanced development necessary (e.g. theory and practice) and people often talk in more holistic terms. More important, probably, than participants' words are (a) their actions and (b) the response of others around them (colleagues, bosses, subordinates, etc.).

An example of the evaluation by an organization of SML is that by the BBC. Their senior personnel staff found the following benefits from an SML programme for new personnel managers:

- 'They learned how to learn.'
- 'They ask more questions' (than previous trainee personnel managers).
- 'They are more tolerant of ambiguity.'
- 'They are able to get their *own* jobs.'
- 'They are more open and accountable.'
- 'They emerged more self assured, more enterprising.'
- 'The culture we are trying to create is that it is as important to help others succeed as it is to succeed yourself. SML helped us to put this across in a relevant way.'
- 'The SML approach enabled the BBC to reduce the length of the personnel training scheme from two years to one— while increasing its effectiveness.'

Achieving these results is not easy. Merely to tell people to shape up and take charge of their own learning is ineffective. Even when one has a sophisticated, well-designed SML programme, it is not a smooth, comfortable process assisting people's learning. And, given the objective of linking learning to organizational strategies and culture, programmes can be complex to operate.

This chapter makes the case for autonomy, personal responsibility and self-reliance. It continues with pointers on how SML has evolved in order to meet these requirements. There is then some discussion of aspects of SML designs before moving into more concrete, specific issues. The next chapter goes into more detail on precise practical applications.

Autonomy, responsibility, self-control, choice

Although these concepts are linked, I shall first consider responsibility.

Responsibility

Sheila Corrall,[1] director of Library and Information Services at Aston University, wrote about her experiences on two SML programmes. She included in her comments the following:

> Sceptics may say this 'DIY' approach is simply a management cop-out! I am convinced that this approach genuinely offers a realistic way forward, a means of empowering staff to achieve their full potential. Individuals must be prepared to take responsibility for their own development; they are the people best placed to analyse and assess their past experience, and to define their own priorities and future career goals.

Self-development starts with self-awareness and requires sufficient self-knowledge to diagnose what has to be developed, but once this diagnostic work has begun—and it must be seen as a continuous process—the individual will be in a much better position to identify and take advantage of development opportunities as they arise. . .

The key issue in Corrall's piece is that of *'responsibility for'*. The SML position is that

the learners must be responsible *for* their own learning.

However,

others have a responsibility *to* the learner.

'Others' might include:

* *Colleagues* who may accept responsibility *to* the learner to be supportive and understanding in their struggles to learn.
* *Bosses* who may accept responsibility *to* people who report to them to allow them to learn, to coach them as needed, to facilitate access to learning resources, etc.
* *Professionals* (HR staff, trainers, teachers, etc.) who accept their responsibility *to* learners to work with integrity, to provide access to resources, to respond to requests for help, etc.

Hence there can emerge a collective responsibility *to* support learning. But the person always retains responsibility *for* his or her own learning. A learning business cannot operate under any other conditions. This has important ramifications for individual learners and for the organization. Some of these will be discussed in this chapter, and later chapters cover the role of professionals and the need for good contexts for learning.

Self-control

Under this heading I shall also consider the linked concepts

* self-influence
* self-regulation
* self-monitoring
* self-reliance

and the overarching idea of

* self-management (i.e. I take self-management to include all the above).

The basic argument, from much research literature, from experience and from matters of principle, supports the centrality of these issues.

Goodwin[2] reviews research which suggests that 'changes which are self attributed are maintained to a greater degree than those which are believed to be due to external causes'. He argues that improvement through successful self-reliance is more easily renewable.

Manz[3] reviews an impressive array of literature as well as drawing on his own work. He counterposes assumptions of external control through performance standards, appraisals, reward systems, etc., with self-control processes. He shows that individuals use their internal self-control systems to self-evaluate, to set personal performance standards and to self-reward. As he says, 'organizations provide organizational control systems that influence people, but these systems do not access individual action directly. Rather the impact of organizational control mechanisms is determined by the way they influence. . . the self-control systems within organization members' (p. 586). He does not deny that external factors influence people, but he does reach the conclusion that 'the self-influence system is the ultimate system of control' (p. 586).

This perspective on self-control must be a facet of a learning business. We know, as the saying goes, that you can take a horse to water but you cannot make it drink. Individuals often need help in identifying what is needed to be learned and how to learn it. But they must control their own learning. This flies in the face of standard assumptions about education and training which erroneously assume that external controls are the main determinant of learning. Hence standardized courses assume that what is taught equals what is learned. The reliance on a predefined curriculum assumes that learners will be externally controlled and that their internal self-control systems are relatively unimportant.

Autonomy

The issue of controls links to the case for personal autonomy. The self-control case rests more on practical and behavioural grounds, whereas the case for autonomy is a matter of fundamental principle. However, they come together in the self managed learning approach.

When I say that fundamental principles are involved here, I am drawing on the views of educational philosophers who suggest that autonomy is *the* underpinning value in learning that is, learning to be autonomous is the most valued outcome of learning activity. David Aspin[4] included within personal autonomy

- critical thinking
- being a master of one's own situation
- making informed judgements
- planning courses of action for oneself.

His views were expressed in a conference group which included two other eminent professors of educational philosophy. They concurred with his formulation. As a member of this same group I suggested that if this was an outcome, the *process* of learning should mirror it, since we know that there is the need to integrate means and ends. If we want to develop autonomous people, that could not come through an authoritarian process. The other people in the group (all educationalists) could not accept this. They asserted (without giving *any* basis for this assertion) that autonomy would just come about by people learning theories and ideas from teachers and academics. I confess to being unable to understand this argument. It seemed, rather, that the individuals, like so many other professionals, wished to justify their existence by irrational assertions about the importance of their role, while ignoring the incongruence of a role that was achieving the opposite of their espoused outcome.

Young people coming out of schools and universities have often maintained a level of personal autonomy through bucking the system. Many successful business makers, such as Virgin's Richard Branson, did not go to university. Companies such as British Airways have been turned round by people who did not go to university (in their case Lord King, when chairman, Sir Colin Marshall as CEO and Gordon Dunlop, who was finance director of BA).

It is clear, then, that people do develop autonomy in varying degrees, and often through self-managing their careers (and the learning that has gone with it). In my own research into successful CEOs, I found that they talked a lot about learning, but it was usually learning they had initiated, and very little came from formal educational or training activity.

The issue of autonomy has, however, a wider impact than for the person. There is the role for a learning business in providing more autonomous working in order to foster good learning. We know that lack of autonomy increases stress and other dysfunctional characteristics (see, e.g., Broadbent[5]). It also inhibits learning, and makes the 'good learning' already referred to difficult, if not impossible.

People, of course, can trap themselves. They can create low autonomy for themselves as a 'security blanket'. This links to issues of responsibility. People can deny responsibility for their actions on the grounds that they were following the rules or obeying the boss. In its extreme, individuals who wish to deny responsibility for their own lives do find SML difficult. But the extreme is rare.

Choice

Stewart[6] has suggested a framework for looking at managers' jobs. She suggests three categories:

1. *Demands*. These are the things the manager *has* to do: what absolutely *must* be done. She excludes from this 'oughts', e.g. what another might think the manager *ought* to do.
2. *Constraints*. These can be external or internal. They put limits on what is allowed to be done.
3. *Choices*. These are activities the manager chooses to do.

Research suggests that less successful managers see themselves as having less choices than a neutral observer might identify. These managers often infer from situations that there are demands or constraints which, if tested, prove to be false. But many do not test. The successful, creative, entrepreneurial-type managers tend to be the ones who see more choices. Partly, this links to beliefs about autonomy—the person who feels more autonomous will push the boundaries of the role farther; partly, it requires that individuals have good 'maps' of the 'territory' in which they operate (and I shall cover this issue later); and partly it requires the learning business to create a culture where people are encouraged to break out of their self-imposed strait-jackets.

Self managed learning encourages managers to seek more choices for action (including for learning) through providing a level of autonomy and appropriate linkages into the wider organization. It also provides choice of *processes*. For instance, managers can choose the mode of learning that suits them. This gets over the problem that people have different learning styles and different preferred modes of learning.

Some history

It may help here to outline the history of the development of self managed learning. SML is the integration of various ideas and methods. Some aspects are original; others not. However, we have found that this integration is more than the sum of the parts. So although I am showing the roots of SML in other approaches and ideas, it is not merely a throwing together of these approaches and ideas. I shall start with my personal experiences and then move into more general issues.

Early experiences

School and university were disappointing for me from an educational point of view. However, my experiences pointed to things that I saw needed changing. These included:

- *issues of authoritarianism*—I found I learned best when I decided what I needed to learn.
- *subject divisions*—I was intensely frustrated by the subject divisions that were for the benefit of academics but not learners. For example, I was reprimanded by my professor of physical chemistry for asking 'what is an electron?'. I found Quantum Theory exciting and challenging but also confusing. My professor said that I was asking philosophical questions and this was not allowed. I knew I was asking philosophical questions, and I felt that they should be taken seriously.
- *disconnection from the world*—What I was being taught seemed unconnected with real problems affecting ordinary people. I had chosen to study chemistry at university because I thought it would be practical and useful. I found that, at graduation, employing organizations were going to have to show me what it was really like to do practical research and development.

I used my time at university to engage in student union activities, ending with two years as a part-time member of the National Union of Students Executive (1966–68), and then full-time National Secretary (1968–70). The first sit-in in Britain was in 1968, so I was around during an eventful period in the student world. The focus of much of this activity was more outwardly directed. Even inside higher education institutions the effort of students was addressed to structural and power issues: student participation, etc.

This had its place in the changes that I saw as necessary, but apart from the art colleges, few of the militant activities were addressed at fundamental issues of the nature of education. It did not seem to me that merely getting students onto committees would change what went on in the lecture theatre, and most students had little idea of an alternative to replace what we saw as a discredited educational system.

However, a few insights were creeping in. Summerhill, A.S. Neill's so-called 'free school', attracted attention, and there were outcroppings of Summerhill copies. But almost none survived, and radical alternatives in the state system were quickly squashed. In seeing why Summerhill survived (and flourished) where others failed, it was clear that the sloppy, disorganized, pseudo-egalitarianism of late 1960s hippies was ill suited to the rigours of making a school work. Neill's success was due to his clear, tough-minded leadership, his wisdom in developing appropriate structures and his capability in relating to young people. Neill was a visionary who could also make things happen. He stood his ground when the going was sticky (and when less resolute and less able people gave up).

These lessons were all important for the development of SML.

Training

When I started my first training role I had a chance to apply my ideals. The move to providing learning that was practical and not subject-dependent was not difficult. The training world is not bad at that. Also, the courses I was involved in were more participative in nature than my university experiences, and a lot more fun for all of us (participants and trainers). However, I was concerned about a number of factors:

- Transfer of training to the job did not go smoothly.
- Learning seemed shallow—and people slipped back.
- Participants did not have a say in course content.
- Doing more training did not seem to have much impact on organizational performance.

Regional management centre

In joining a regional management centre I had a chance to design longer programmes that were problem based. In the early 1970s these seemed quite radical. We designed a Diploma in Management Studies in 1972/73 which, instead of having subjects taught in the standard way, was problem based. There were thus modules on decision making, the environment of the organization, managing change, etc. Each of these was handled in an interdisciplinary way, often with team teaching around live cases. I find it fascinating that, 20 years later, some business schools are thinking of making what, for them, are radical shifts into working in this way. I would like to say to them that it does not go far enough.

Teachers still wanted to teach, so participants on the programme still had little say in course content. Also, the modular nature of the course still broke up what is a holistic activity (managing). The problem-based divides were just as arbitrary as subject divisions.

Independent study

In 1973 I joined the team that was developing the School for Independent Study at North East London Polytechnic (now the University of East London) on an 80 per cent secondment from the regional management centre. In 1974 we launched the two-year full-time Diploma of Higher Education as an independent study course (shortly followed by a degree programme). The approach was totally new in British higher education.

There were no entrance requirements beyond motivation to study and some understanding of the course. We had some students who had been expelled from school, some who had been rejected by other institutions, and some who had never passed any exams (as well as some who had). There were no course objectives; there was no syllabus; and there were no end of course exams. Students entering the programme were allocated a tutor group. They used this as a base for planning their programme of study. They had a 'planning period' of six weeks in which they wrote a statement of what they would do for the remainder of their two years. They split their time between specialist study in their chosen fields and group work, where they worked on projects they chose, in order to develop competences that required such collaborative activity. At the end, assessment was based on the two parts of the programme.

The great success of the School for Independent Study was that it showed that:

- people could design their own courses and set their own learning goals;
- the success rate was similar to traditional courses—despite supposedly lower entry standards;
- people grew in self-confidence and wisdom—they did not just develop competences;
- it was possible to provide a structure within which individual differences were respected—and get high standards.

However, while independent research confirmed the above, it also showed problems. Firstly, some students complained of isolation—not having anyone to talk to about their work. This especially applied to students who had chosen not to attend lectures or seminars, but rather to pursue a wholly individualized programme of study (apart from their group project work).[7] This linked to the problem of students making choices—they struggled because often they did not really know what they wanted to learn.

Research also showed up the tension between what was labelled:

Structure v Freedom[7]

This dichotomy was an interesting example of how the interplay of language and thought about these issues produced confusion. For me, there is no necessary clash between structure and freedom. What happened on the programme was that some students wanted more *structure*, more *support* mechanisms (for example, to overcome isolation). Staff interpreted this as a need for more *direction* and *control*—and some became more authoritarian as a result. Structure and direction can be relatively independent variables. Indeed, in the programme, staff who became more directive did not, in the process, provide better structures. Isolation continued, but students were now pushed more in particular directions or controlled through the assessment process.

The solution to better structures lay in lessons from action learning, which I shall mention shortly. Also, action learning addresses another weakness of independent study, namely the tendency for students to stay within the institution for their learning (and hence not tackling problems of usefulness and practical application).

Action learning

Shortly after taking up responsibilities in the School for Independent Study I became involved, as a consultant and as a set adviser, in action learning programmes. These programmes were like independent study in

- having no fixed curriculum;
- responding to individual learners' needs.

They differed in being

- for managers;

- more action oriented—requiring managers to work on live issues in real time;
- problem based and open ended—addressing problems which did not have a predefined solution;
- more supportive of learners through the use of 'sets' of about five learners and a set adviser (to help the set to function and to assist individual set members in their learning).

These latter positive features give clues as to how independent study programmes needed to change to be more effective. However, I also observed problems in action learning and these were subsequently confirmed in research I conducted.[8] The problems included:

- Some nominators of participants on action learning programmes were only interested in action (problem solving) and did not support learning.
- Links into organizational needs varied—at best projects carried out by participants were integrated with strategic changes in the organization—at worst they were invented projects just to provide something for the participants to do.
- Projects were often imposed on participants and proved poor vehicles for learning.
- In the absence of any pre-planned learning objectives, learning could be random, haphazard and not meshed with organizational needs.
- Participants often did interesting analyses of problems and then presented recommendations for action to, for example, their board or their boss. As there was no implementation, proper action learning did not occur.
- The idea of a 'project' could constrain the learners—they would be hemmed in by the definition of a project and were not able to explore other avenues of learning.
- While Revans and other proponents of action learning argue that Q (questioning knowledge) needs integrating with P (programmed knowledge), these two were often separate and unintegrated. So Q would be pursued in the set and P provided as an add-on in lectures, seminars and workshops. Theory and practice became disconnected again.
- Course participants usually had little or no say in the programme design. If there were workshops and seminars, these were imposed by programme organizers.
- Constituent members of a set were not the sole repositories of wisdom on issues around the projects being tackled—but

often sets 'closed in' on themselves and did not seek other perspectives.

Many of these problems were overcome in the very best examples of action learning that I saw. However, it seemed to me that there were potentially some structural and design possibilities that could more easily overcome the downside of action learning.

Self-directed learning/person-centred approaches

In my research on effective management developers,[9] two names were given more than any others as influences on people's professional practice: Reg Revans and Carl Rogers. Rogers was especially influential in the 1970s through his book *Freedom to Learn*[10]. Rogers provided a passionate and well-argued case for a person-centred approach to learning which respected the individual learner and removed authoritarian controls on individuals. His argument for 'facilitators of learning' rather than didactic teachers struck a chord with many, and numerous experimental programmes were established in the wake of his influence. However, like the free schools, few survived. Rogers himself acknowledged the problems in his follow-up book *Freedom to Learn for the 80s*. Allowing for these, Rogers was able to quote credible research[11] in schools which showed the following kinds of positive results from person-centred courses:

- greater gains in learning conventional subjects
- students more adept at using higher cognitive processes such as problem solving
- more positive self-concept in students
- less discipline problems
- lower absence rates.

Other writers in the 1970s espoused a learner-centred approach referring to the concept of 'self-directed learning'. Many management trainers and educators were convinced, in the post-1960s euphoria, of an inevitable move in this direction. Except that it did not happen. Most programmes collapsed because:

- Staff suffered burnout in their overzealous desire to respond to whatever learners asked for.
- Lack of structure in courses produced too much mess for traditional universities and company training departments.

- Some learners complained about not getting their needs met in these highly open-ended learning programmes; for example, sometimes the basis for any activity was simply being able to shout the loudest or made the most aggressive demands at meetings.
- Those programmes that succeeded did so because of the staff: when staff moved on, the programmes became diluted or were closed.
- The times changed. The 1980s were more materialistic, less open to experiment: humanistic ideals were submerged in instrumentalist career management (from both managers and academics).

Experiential learning This 'catch-all' phrase became popular in the 1970s and 1980s. Some used the ideas of David Kolb[12] and his learning cycle model as a basis for planning learning activity which drew on managers' direct experience as a way of developing general- izations for future action. Others saw experiential learning as covering project-based approaches (which again drew on live experience). Another group equated experiential learning with T groups, encounter groups and other intensive group-based approaches. Finally, there were those who saw 'experiences' occurring in lectures and through reading books as well as from projects on T groups. Here the notion of 'experience' is particularly linked to non-cognitive aspects (such as emo- tions).

Given that most now associate experiential learning with the 'learning cycle' model, I shall discuss this specifically. The advantages of this approach include:

- direct challenge to academic theory-based learning
- use of live problems for managerial learning
- encouragement of a 'practice to theory' link, that is, not a-theoretical
- ease of use—managers understand the model and usually accept it (though Kolb's instrument linked to his model is less user friendly).

The problems with an over-balanced enthusiasm for this approach include:

- Experiences can be unhelpful in providing a basis for learning; for example, the person who learns (from experience) to hate snakes can develop a dysfunctional phobia through generalizing from one experience.

- Not only is direct experience of work problems an experience, but also reflecting on experience is an experience, theorizing about experience is an experience, and so on. It is not possible neatly to compartmentalize 'experience'. It is also a problem to know if you have had an experience if you do not have concepts and theories (maps) to help you to identify it.
- Experience is always past—we can reflect on *memories* of that past and generalize therefrom, but there are dangers in applying such generalizations to future events, for example, the world may change.
- There are a lot of things that are best *not* learned from experience; for example, the effects of putting your hand in the path of a circular saw, the effects of AIDS, and so on. *Most* learning that is of use to us is probably *not* experientially based; we rely a great deal on the experience of others.
- People operate out of deeply grooved patterns: just reflecting on and analysing these will not necessarily lead to change.
- In management much of the feedback from our actions takes a long time.
- Strategic decisions may take many years to come to fruition and before we can reflectively analyse the pros and cons of such decisions.
- Experiential learning (of this variety) is very 'first order' oriented: second-order learning comes from reflecting on our reflections, theorizing about our theories and experimenting with our experiments. It is a meta-level process requiring a leap out of existing learning patterns.

Self-development

Pedler[13] suggests that 'Action learning starts with the person going out into the world, whilst self-development begins with retreat from it' (p. 56). He goes on to suggest that in reality action learning and self-development can come together, and that there is no need to postulate a rigid dichotomy. Hence, a programme can have the label 'action learning', but move closer to an introspective mode in sets. And 'self-development' groups can dwell a great deal on action issues. In this respect 'self-development', as a popular idea in the 1980s, became a over-arching term to cover a range of non-curriculum based, learner-centred approaches to management development. One benefit from self-development was the emphasis on the 'self'. This promoted a holistic, balanced approach to learning. However, many people came to feel that the worst kind of self-development degenerated into solipsistic navel gazing disconnected from organizational life. Hence some advocates of self-development have become more associated with developing ideas about learning organizations/companies.

Holistic education/confluent education

These terms were popular, especially in the USA, in the 1970s. Confluent means 'flowing together' and I link it with holistic education as both labels were used to cover approaches that moved beyond the cognitive. So in schools which adopted these ideas, young people addressed emotional, spiritual and physical development. At best this assisted people to learn the kind of qualities described in the previous chapters. At worst it produced distortions of educational activity and did nothing to redress teacher authoritarianism. To be told to meditate is not fundamentally different from being told to write essays.

Open and distance learning

These terms became popular in management development in the 1980s. I lump them together because their advantages were similar, namely:

- the development of more user friendly materials (audio tapes, video tapes, nicely designed packages, etc.)
- the opportunity for learners to choose the time and place of learning.

Their disadvantages are similar to standard taught courses:

- pre-fixed goals and learning methods
- if there is assessment, it is unilaterally controlled by academics
- rigidity and disconnectedness from the live problems of managers
- heavy cognitive bias to learning.

Self managed learning

In SML my colleagues and I wanted to pull together the best practices from the above approaches. Also, we did not neglect the fact that traditional universities had within them experts who could be used, though we did go with the Civil Service notion that experts should be on *tap*, not on *top*. (The role of experts ought to be to engage in dialogue with managers and to answer questions formulated by managers, not to distort the needs of managers to fit their expertise.)

In drawing together best practice I only had a way of judging 'best' because I had a vision of what learning could be and ought to be. I glimpsed examples of incredible learning in some of the approaches mentioned, but these were isolated examples or were not sustained. Therefore, the micro designs and methods that appealed did so because they contributed to a vision of a total architecture; and, in order to complete the picture, new facets had to be added.

Before moving on to Chapter 7 to give an overview of the total architecture of SML, I shall summarize the main aspects of what SML draws from the approaches discussed in this chapter.

Summary

1. There is no need for a predefined syllabus to a learning programme; indeed, it is constraining and unhelpful.
2. Learning should start from the needs of the learner and the organization—individual differences need to be recognized.
3. Personal autonomy is a means and an end of good learning. Means and ends both need integrating.
4. Holistic ways of working are also means and ends— learners engage head, heart, guts and more in the process of good learning and the outcome is a more integrated person.
5. Learners need to play an active role in learning; passive reception of knowledge encourages passivity in management (an undesirable outcome).
6. Learning needs structuring and supporting, it does not just happen. Liberating people from the constraints of traditionally taught courses does not necessarily produce good learning.
7. Learning in collaboration with others is crucial—again means and ends must mesh. If we want collaboration and mutual support in the organization, the learning process must mirror this.
8. Resources need to be provided to support learning—but these may not be of the traditional kind.
9. Leadership is important: organizational leaders need to model good learning, and leaders of organized learning programmes need to accept their responsibilities *to* learners (while learners retain responsibility *for* their own learning).
10. All learners are able to draw up statements of their learning needs and negotiate these with their organizations (as 'learning contracts'). This negotiation, if done

well, can ensure integration of personal learning within the wider organization.

11. Learning by individuals and within organizations needs to connect to wider issues outside the organization. A developed sense of ecology demands that we feel part of the planet and become involved in what is going on in the wider world around us.

12. The results of learning need to be assessed and evaluated, but such assessments must be initiated by learners and not imposed. However, self-assessment needs checking with others—again to encourage collaboration and sharing in the organization.

13. Managing and learning must be integrated; processes of learning must match processes of managing.

14. The roles of those assisting other people's learning are crucial. Helping someone to learn is not easy, and this process also needs to be learned.

The next chapter will continue the task of putting these ideals into practice.

Notes

1. Corrall, S. (1992) 'Self managed learning: the key to professional and personal development', in Foreman, L. (ed.) *Developing Professionals in Information Work*, Circle of State Librarians, London: HMSO, p.13.
2. Goodwin, L.R. (1981) 'Psychological self help: a five step model', *Journal of Humanistic Psychology*, 21, 1 (Winter) 13–28 (esp. p. 24)
3. Mantz, C.C. (1986) 'Self leadership: towards an expanded theory of self-influence processes in organizations', *Academy of Management Review*, 11, (3), 585–600.
4. Aspin, D. (1983) Contribution to 'Education Challenge' Conference, Salford University (April).
5. Broadbent, D. (1987) Quoted in *Personnel Management* (February), p. 13.
6. Stewart, P. (1982) *Choices for the Manager*, London: McGraw-Hill.
7. Percy, K. and Ramsden, P. (1980) *Independent Study: Two Examples from English Higher Education*, Guildford, Surrey: Society for Research into Higher Education.
8. Cunningham, I. (1991) 'Action learning for chief executives', in Pedler, M. (ed.) *Action Learning in Practice*, 2nd edn, Farnborough, Hants: Gower.
9. Cunningham, I. (1984) Teaching Styles in Learner Centred Management Development Programmes, PhD Thesis, University of Lancaster.
10. Rogers, C.R. (1969) *Freedom to Learn*, Ohio: Charles Merrill.

11. Aspy, D.N. and Roebuck, F.N. (1974) 'From humane ideas to humane technology and back again many times', *Education*, 95, 2 (Winter), 163–171.
12. Kolb, D.A. and Fry, R. (1975) 'Towards an applied theory of experiential learning', in Cooper, C.L. (ed.) *Theories of Group Processes*, London: Wiley.
13. Pedler, M. (1984) 'Action learning and self development: the knight and the monk', *Management Education and Development*, 15, 1 (Spring), 55–58.

7 Self managed learning: strategy and designs

Introduction

In this chapter[1] I shall pick up the threads from Chapter 6, and start with a model which expands the view of SML as part of a strategic approach to learning. I shall then elaborate some of the strategic choices available. SML can be used as an umbrella strategy which allows for considerable choice beneath it. However, there are some givens and non-negotiables within the idea of SML, especially around autonomy and responsibility, as outlined in Chapter 6.

I shall be emphasizing, as elsewhere, the use of SML for managers. However, in other programmes SML has been used with non-managers. The assumption that SML is only suitable for the more senior or the more able is not supported by research. For example, Gruber and Weitman's research[2] showed no correlation between the ability of people to take responsibility for their own learning and intellectual capacity or previous education.

A model for SML strategy

The historical analysis in the previous chapter emphasized practical issues. I would now like to return to the more strategic dimensions and integrate these with practice. I want to reiterate that self managed learning provides a strategic approach to learning. In this context strategy is for individuals and for organizations. Strategy is organized activity over the longest time horizon that the person and/or organization wishes to project. So a person may want to think long term about their career and the organization may wish to project ahead to address its vision.

I want to distinguish strategy from tactics. Tactics are short-term activities designed to meet strategic goals. What is common to strategy and tactics is that they are organized and time bound: the main difference is the time horizon. Figure 7.1

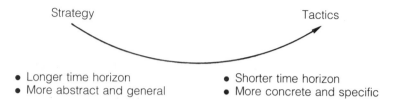

Figure 7.1   *Strategy and tactics*

suggests a relationship going from abstract, longer term to more concrete, shorter term.

The purposes of learning, discussed in Part Three, feed into strategy. Strategy is the practical working out of purposes. So purposes are more abstract than strategies. Purposes are also expressed in timeless terms and are not worked out as organized plans. The 'good learning' I have argued for (autonomy, wisdom, capability, holism, balance, centring, grounding, etc.) is elaborated in just such terms—that is, timeless, generalized, abstract. This is indicated in Figure 7.2. Thus the *strategy* of SML is the way of operationalizing 'good learning'. The strategy is more concrete, planned and specific (compared with purposes).

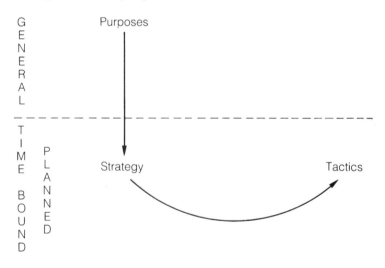

Figure 7.2   *Purposes, strategy and tactics*

A further addition can be made to the model in Figure 7.2. Tactics lead to action, to purposive human behaviour to make things happen. The *action* level is where real live learning takes place. So Figure 7.3 represents a more fully worked out model.

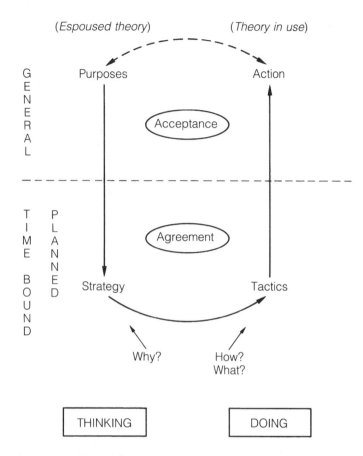

Figure 7.3   U model

The model in Figure 7.3 contains a number of important features.

Flow

The U shape indicates a flow from abstract to concrete, as shown in the arrows going anticlockwise.

Relationships

There are horizontal relationships. At the top, *purposes* and *action* are generalized; that is, purposes have general applicability—they are not context or time specific. Indeed, many of the ideas expressed about good learning come from the ancient China of the Taoists and from ancient Greece. The way we act is also not fixed by time or context. Hence, in pursuing learning the kinds of actions people can undertake (using experience, listening to lectures, reading books, meditating, etc.) are possible to carry out in any time frame or (almost) any organization.

At the bottom of the U, strategy and tactics are more bounded. SML is a specific response and it needs to be designed to suit the circumstances of organizations and individuals, including their time constraints.

Another distinction between top and bottom in the U is the mode of dealing with learning. At the bottom there needs to be collective *agreement* on strategy and tactics (in a learning business). Objectives need to be negotiated and the resources and design of programmes need to be agreed. However *purposes* and *actions* need *acceptance*. There may not be collective agreement on these issues, and it may not be sought. So if organizations are serious about empowerment they will recognize and *accept* that individuals will learn in different ways. They will be more interested in whether the person learns what needs to be learned than in precise hour-by-hour behaviour.

Coherence

In order to move round the U and check for coherence, particular questions can be used. To go from abstract to concrete (anticlockwise) one asks *how?* or *what?*. So if I say that I want to develop autonomy (purpose), I can be asked how? and the answer should be *strategic* (through an SML programme). If I am asked *how* the SML programme will work, the answer will be *tactical*. So I would indicate particular aspects of the design of the programme showing *how* strategy is implemented in tactics. Lastly, I could be asked *how* the tactics will work out, and I can respond with reference to precise *actions*.

An alternative is to go clockwise round the U. If you observe me doing something (for example, asking a question of someone in order to learn something) you may ask *why* I am doing that. My answer would be, to explain the tactical basis of my actions (for example, the person is my mentor and I am going to feed the responses I get into my set). If you ask *why* I am using a set and a mentor to assist my learning, I can reply strategically (for example, this is part of an SML strategy, and sets and mentors are tactical designs for implementing this strategy). If you ask *why* I use the strategy, I may reply that the programme is improving my capability (a purpose).

Divisions

There are vertical divisions in the U. Roughly, the left-hand side is associated with *thinking* and the right-hand side with *doing*. Also taking the top left and top right, these encompass Argyris' distinction between espoused theory (purpose) and theory in use (action). The dotted line at the top shows that there should be congruence here. If, for instance, I am developing autonomy (purpose) and I show by my actions that I am not behaving autonomously in my learning, then there is an incongruity to address. This, then needs second-order learning: I have to step outside the model to explore the incongruity. So the model is only a map to aid thought, analysis and integrated action. I should also 'step outside' at any time if I consider it to be necessary.

Change

'Ease of change' goes from top to bottom. By this I mean that changing fundamental purposes or changing action and behaviour can be more difficult than changing strategy and tactics. Individuals become wedded to purposes and patterns of action. A great deal of effort can be needed to make changes at this level—and it is often second-order (not first-order) change that is required. However, strategic and tactical plans usually need only first-order change. For instance, a tactic may be to offer a course on some topic. If it proves unpopular it can be scrapped or modified. There is some effort required to achieve this, but it is not comparable to the effort necessary to change some fundamental organizational purpose or principle. The thesis, then, is that the most abstract dimension (top left) and the most concrete (top right) are the most resistant to change and the most embedded. The middle ground of strategy and tactics is easier to work with.

Strategic learning and SML

Figure 7.4 shows, diagrammatically, linkages from purposes through to SML as strategy. The strategic role of SML bridges between overall purposes, and tactics and action. I shall describe in this chapter some key strategic processes which provide the basis for this bridging.

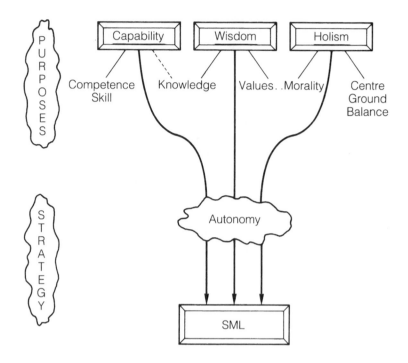

Figure 7.4   Strategic learning: linking purposes and strategy

There are four over-arching processes, namely:

- preparing
- resourcing
- collaborating
- judging

These are all deliberately formulated as verbs. There are subprocesses under each of these four headings, and these shall also be outlined. The four main processes roughly follow in sequence, although it is normally not as neat as this in practice. All four are core processes for strategic managing, and the basis of SML is the mirroring of managerial processes in learning.

Preparing

Preparing can be subdivided into other processes including:

- mapping
- diagnosing
- planning
- contracting.

The nature of preparing in this context is preparing to learn. Of course, this itself is a learning process. This self-reference is both a strength and a difficult complexity of SML. As with all other processes discussed here, these four subprocesses provide a basis for the *content* of learning—that which usually looks like a syllabus or curriculum or timetable or set of objectives. But the *process* of learning in this way provides the basis for learners to develop this process ability—in this case the ability to prepare themselves for action—and I would argue that this process ability is of a higher value. However, it can be less easily recognized because of its verb form in the English language. We tend to make processes into nouns in order to give them status—a pretend concreteness. So managing becomes management and as such it provides a basis for 'management' to become a subject within which other subjects (formulated as nouns) are studied (economics, psychology, statistics, etc.).

SML provides a way of addressing this issue by its process focus. However, this is a weakness in that, culturally, processes (verbs) are less acceptable as a basis for learning. Our noun–verb–noun syntax predisposes us to expect sentences of the form: 'Jim (noun) learned (verb) economics (noun).' 'Jim learned preparing' does not sound quite right because of the conventions of the English language. But English grammar is only a convention—and one that, in this context, gets in the way of clear thinking and sensible action[3].

Having made a case for this process orientation, I would now like to show the rationale for the four subprocesses under this heading. Figure 7.5 shows diagrammatically how these processes link up.

Essentially, mapping is the process of the learner using knowledge of 'the world out there' in order to prepare for learning. Diagnosing provides self-knowledge—developing a

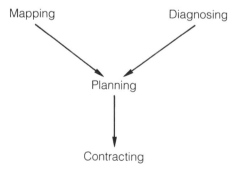

Figure 7.5   Preparing

sense of 'the world in here' (who the learners are and what they are able to do). These processes come together to provide a basis for the learners to plan their learning (including objective setting, programming, etc.). This then provides a basis for contracting—for agreeing with others the necessary basis for learning and for negotiating appropriate arrangements. The artificial separation of these four processes may imply greater complexity than in fact occurs. The processes flow together and occur in the same time frame. The separation here is for the purpose of analysis and exploration only. In practice it is important that they integrate.

Mapping

This process, like all the others described in this chapter, is a way of assisting a person to develop

- capability
- wisdom
- holism
- autonomy.

People who are better able to map their world and use the maps of others enhance their *capability* and their *wisdom*. Such mapping can facilitate *holistic* integration and balance, and can help the individuals develop *autonomy* through their increased ability to journey through more 'territory'. Rather than tediously repeat the above for each process described in this chapter, I shall leave it to you to make the necessary connections. The key question is to ask yourself if you would contribute to developing 'good learning' through each of the processes described.

I shall devote more space in this chapter to mapping than to any other process. This is partly because of its importance, but also because I am aware that it is less well understood and less valued than some of the other processes.

The nature of maps

When I first came to London, as a child, I believed that the maps of the London Underground system on tube trains were an accurate representation of the tube lines—that is, that they ran in straight lines and smooth curves. My naive belief was not a hindrance as I could find my way around the system, and work out where to change stations. When I discovered that tube lines were more complex, it was an enlightening discovery, and it enhanced my capability to find my way around above ground.

I suppose this was one of the earliest experiences that made me realize that 'the map is not the territory'. A map became, to me, something I could use but it clearly did not necessarily show everything that was going on.

Schumacher made a similar point. He found, when visiting Russia (during the Cold War), that churches were not shown on official maps, yet when walking around he could see them. As he said, it was not the first time in his life that a map failed to show things of importance.

> All through school and university I had been given maps of life and knowledge on which there was hardly a trace of many of the things that I most cared about and that seemed to me of greatest possible importance in the conduct of my life.[4]

He commented on how this perplexed him and that the breakthrough for him was to stop suspecting the sanity of his perceptions and instead to 'suspect the soundness of the maps'.[4]

Mapping in practice

When we launched the first SML qualification programme in 1980, we described our stance on knowledge and mapping in the following terms:

> In management education, there has been a move away from teaching the traditional academic disciplines (for example, psychology, sociology, economics) into teaching based around perceived management functions (marketing, personnel, etc.). Some would see this as progress in that the teaching is built around supposed needs of management (as opposed to subject disciplines). However, what now seems to have happened is that these new areas have become (for teaching purposes) subjects in their own right and we have once again lost sight of the possibility of responding flexibly to managerial needs. Marketing, personnel, etc., all now have the barriers around them that the 'classic' subject disciplines have (for example, separate journals). The trouble is that management problems do not crop up solely within the boundaries of, say, 'marketing' or 'production'. These artificially defined subjects meet the needs of *teachers* but not of *learners*.
>
> Teachers can develop their subject knowledge within a field, and feel secure about their competence within the boundaries of their subject. However, managers have to tackle problems on

their merits—they cannot be controlled by the limitations of teachers.

We went on to say:

We will initially help learners to:

a. identify their needs and

b. understand and make use of existing conceptual maps of the field of management.

Thus the programme of study of each individual will come out of an interactive process of comparing needs with existing conceptual maps. Each person will then be able to identify a tentative programme of action around some generally defined goals for them.

We believe that the process of making explicit to students existing conceptual maps in management is important. The student needs to be aware of the existing body of knowledge in management so that they can choose from it what is relevant to their needs. We use the term 'conceptual mapping' to draw the analogy with the geographical process of mapping. We can show the learner existing models and theories of the territory of management. These models and theories are themselves built on concepts which the learner needs to be aware of.

To take the example of the body of knowledge encompassed by 'organization development' the learner needs to know of the concept 'change agent', before they can make sense of theories of change which use change agents. If they know of the basic concepts of organization development (OD), they will be able to make sense of the body of knowledge encompassed by OD. Hence, if they become concerned about organizational change, they can evaluate whether OD has anything to offer them. If it might appear to do so, they can then explore the territory more effectively with the help of the conceptual map provided by OD.

To take the 'map' analogy further, learners will in essence need to pick a route across the territory of management, and the map will aid them. Naturally once they have an outline route they will see where they need a more detailed map of parts of the territory. In a sense, we as staff will initially provide a broad map in outline only. We will show the main features, but not the detail. Once the learner has an idea of a route, they can then get fine detail filled in.

The analogy should not be stretched too far. Our main point is that the learner needs to know (in outline) what they don't know in order for them to make choices. Without such knowledge, their choices may be based at worst on random guesses or prejudice.

Mapping and teaching

In the above we wanted to make a distinction between mapping and teaching. Teaching has been associated with a view that the teacher is imparting objective knowledge for the learner to absorb. Even in approaches such as the case study method, the teacher tends to suggest to learners the correct and incorrect ways of doing things. Also in business school courses, the assessment and examination process provides a control on what is legitimized knowledge.

Mapping is about showing people maps, and helping them to become cartographers. Experienced managers will always come to a course with existing mental maps. These mental maps give them a basis from which to find their way around. Faced with, say, a selection interview to carry out, they will have a mental map of what to do (for example, prepare for interview, send job description, read person's application form, set aside one hour for the interview, etc.). These internal instructions are vital to our everyday activity. If we did not have mental maps to guide us we would go crazy trying to create procedures for everything that came our way.

However, people's maps are always limited, and the mapping process at the start of an SML programme assists people to

- see other people's maps
- evaluate their own maps
- create new maps.

In offering other people's maps to learners it has to be done as an *offering*, not as an *imposition*. In organizationally based programmes, middle managers need to know the public maps of top management. They need to know maps that are articulated as corporate objectives, corporate culture and strategic directions. Newcomers to organizations are especially in need of maps. These are often offered in the form of organization charts, company policies and information on markets, technology and products. In offering mapping devices to newcomers, I have never come across an organization that does this in order to produce clones of existing staff. It is recognized that newcomers need to know how things are done around the organization, but that each person will have a level of uniqueness in his or her style of doing things. Hence the maps help the person to make choices, but do not dictate every element of the person's behaviour.

Limits to maps

Barber and Broad[5] suggest

> Maps are one of the greatest illusions known to man and yet we instinctively put our faith in them.

I do not see this as necessarily instinctive, though mapping (in the literal sense) is common to all major cultures. However, I do agree that the faith we put in maps can be problematic. Here I shall outline a range of limitations to maps, and use the example of the organization chart to exemplify this. Figure 7.6 shows a typical example.

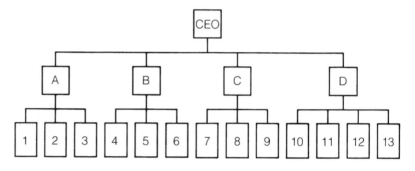

Figure 7.6   Organizational mapping: the organization chart

1. Generalizing

Maps generalize. The organization chart shows a generalized view of the organization, but it does not show specifics.

2. Distort

The organization chart is a distortion of how people actually relate to each other. Each line does not represent the same process. Manager A may relate to their direct reports in quite a different way to manager B.

3. Delete

The chart leaves out a lot. It does not show who is friendly with whom, nor does it show the politics of the business.

4. Suppressed

Information can be suppressed by the map maker. The chart is unlikely to show who is more vulnerable to being fired or who is expected to get the next promotion.

5. Lack of neutrality

Whoever draws the maps is not neutral in organizational processes. Organization charts can be created for political purposes. They are also based on assumptions, beliefs and cultural norms. The chart shown in Figure 7.6 shows a classic pyramid with the highest status person at the top (the CEO). This is a cultural norm ('up' is of a higher status than 'down'). If we invert the pyramid this challenges cultural norms—and some organizations have done this precisely to try to show a new cultural development (for example, where customer care initiatives suggest that front line staff should be at the top as they deal with customers, and the CEO is at the bottom because that job is to support them).

6. Limits of representation

We can only put on to a map what can be represented on it. In the case of Figure 7.6 this is a two-dimensional map, and it can therefore only show relationships in two dimensions. This problem has bedevilled proponents of complex matrix structures because if you go to four dimensions it becomes impossible to show it on a page, or a computer screen (three dimensions are possible, but not as neat as two).

7. Metaphor

The metaphors we use in mapping limit us. I have mentioned the pyramid metaphor. Some talk of 'organizational trees' and apply that metaphor to the organization chart. Whatever is used creates certain meanings and excludes others.

8. Outdated

In modern fast-moving businesses maps such as organization charts and phone directories rapidly date. People move upwards, sideways or out, and the map becomes inaccurate.

9. Strip and context maps[6]

Figure 7.7 shows a strip map for a person's reporting relationship.

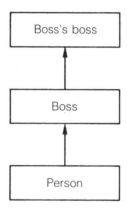

Figure 7.7   Strip map

A strip map shows just the main route. Motoring organizations often provide these to show how to go from one town to the next. They may not even be shown visually but rather give verbal directions. Furthermore, if you ask someone for directions, that person will tend to give you a strip map—for example, 'go down this road until you reach the traffic lights, turn right then take the second left . . .'. A strip map provides choice points, and marks a route. It has the advantage of simplicity and clarity, and it leaves out confusing detail. However, strip maps also leave out detail that might be useful. In Figure 7.6 this *context* map might help a newcomer who fits into box 4 to know that there are others at the same level in the hierarchy, and there are other senior people in addition to their own boss. Context maps fill in more detail and can help the person have more choices.

To return to road maps, it can be useful to know not just the main route from A to B, but also side roads to use in case of a road blockage. Hence, context maps are more empowering and give the user more opportunity to make a better judgement about action.

Choices in mapping

Learning to recognize the limits of maps is a starting point to moving into doing one's own mapping. In SML a key phase in learning is making this move. Learning about others' maps is first order learning. It is valuable, but has its limits. Creating one's own maps needs second order learning. It needs the ability to step out of the maps of others and make one's own choices.

The first aspect of choosing is choosing purpose. We need to be clear about our purposes in order to make choices. Why do we want the map and what will we use it for? In management some of the reasons include developing

- wisdom—being able to make wise choices of action
- capability—having more choices through enriched maps (for example, *context* in addition to *strip* maps).

A key role of staff is to assist learners to make these second-order learning shifts. (This will be explored more fully in later chapters, especially Chapter 9.)

Maps in SML

As individuals develop richer, personally owned maps they become more *centred* and more *grounded*, as described in Chapter 5. This allows them to dispense with guides. If we do not have a map of a territory, we may be reliant on a guide who does. In an organization this can be a boss, a trainer or an expert of some kind. Hence enriched maps for individuals can be a threat to the insecure (uncentred, ungrounded) person who is in the boss/trainer/expert role. That person can find it difficult to move from being a guide, in control, to being a companion walking alongside the other person. (This is one reason why SML approaches may not be implemented in organizations.)

Diagnosing

Another part of 'preparing' is the process of 'diagnosing', which matches 'mapping' and usually in SML programmes occurs within the same time frame. Diagnosing is more internally focused than mapping. While it has association with a medical model (e.g. diagnosing illness) it tends to be a commonly used verb in the development field. There is not a verb 'self-awarenessing' though 'self-knowing' might do. All I mean by the term 'diagnosing' is finding out sufficient about yourself to provide a basis for learning.

Much of the methodology and technology is well known—as is the value of the process—so this section will be shorter than the last. However, there are a few facets of the process which need to be emphasized in an SML context.

Firstly, there is the issue of balance. If we are to project into the future in planning a learning programme, then this needs balancing with a past orientation (as shown in Figure 7.8).

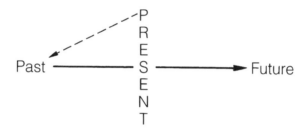

Figure 7.8   Balancing past and future

An aspect of my research on effective CEOs is relevant here. Mostly I found that they talked about time and in specific ways. If they faced a current problem they tended to progress in the manner shown in Figure 7.8; that is, they looped back to past experience from present issues. They might, for instance, check their own experience to see if they had faced a similar problem in the past. They would then project that past experience back through the filter of current circumstances in order to plan future action. This seemed to provide an excellent preparational base for action.

The value of this is important. Many managers want to leap straight into planning, goal setting, etc., without exploring their own history. Yet when we have urged people to explore previous ways of doing things they have often identified patterns in their behaviour which they were about to repeat; they were wanting to base objectives on deeply ingrained mental patterns that emerged from the past. So exploring the past is not self-indulgent time wasting but, if focused on needs for the future, is essential to effective planning.

The process encourages learners to think about the way they think (have thought) and hence promotes second-order learning. Diagnostic activity can raise issues of personal strengths and weaknesses, but if the learner merely produces a pedestrian list without critically examining it, then learning can be superficial (though not valueless). Also, there is an initial tendency for managers to take a 'doing' focus in diagnosis. They may say 'I can do X, but I can't do Y' and focus then on learning to do Y. A balance to this is a 'being' position. As well as asking the person to say what they can and can not do, it is important to ask them who they *are*. Answers to this question are different from the 'what they do' domain, but both are important. Doing answers give more of the basis for capability development: being answers assist the person to see ways of increasing wisdom. I have implied, though, in the above that there needs to be the outside question-asker. As the Chinese saying goes: 'The eye cannot see its own lashes.' In SML the role of others in assisting diagnosis is crucial, and will be explored more fully under the heading 'collaborating'.

Finally, while much of the standard technology of assessment centres, psychometric tests and appraisal interviews provides certain kind of data, it usually needs to be elaborated, modified or even toned down or rejected. A problem with this standard technology is that the process is 'outside in'—that is, judgement is provided from someone else's perspective. In SML the focus is on the learner driving the process.

Planning

The five questions approach mentioned in earlier chapters is a valuable planning tool. Figures 7.9 and 7.10 show the basis of this. However, it is only a tool. There are other ways of planning. The issue is for learners to engage in a planning process. Specifically it engages people in a holistic look at themselves and the contexts in which they operate. It is not meant to be a hurried, mechanistic process. For instance, in addressing Question 3, individuals have to consider their own values and ideals, and in the process they may need to re-evaluate these: deeply held career goals may need re-examining. Those who set their minds on becoming CEO by 40, or making their first million by 30, might have to re-assess the realism and validity of such goals.

As with 'diagnosing', this planning process is best carried out with others. It needs engaging with fellow travellers through life who also have to grapple with their values and ideals. The collaboration is, however, not for people to copy each other, but to learn to improve their own processes.

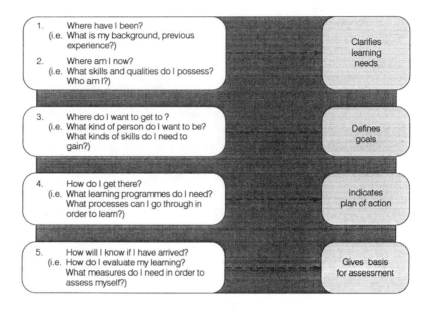

Figure 7.9   Planning learning in SML

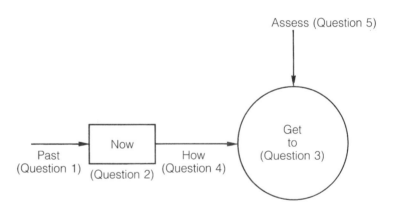

Figure 7.10   Problem solving and learning: five questions

I have indicated above the use of the metaphor 'life is a journey'. This is a common metaphor in our culture[7] and provides a readily understandable basis for planning. From this metaphor we assume that:

- people are travellers
- purposes are destinations
- means for achieving purposes are routes
- difficulties are impediments to travel
- staff on programmes are guides

- progress is measured by distance travelled or destination achieved
- landmarks gauge progress
- choices are crossroads.

Like all metaphors, however, this enriches meaning and at the same time constrains and closes in. Life is not a journey: it is just life. But we tend to feel we need ways of making sense of our lives and in Western cultures we want to be more in control. We may look down on, say, the Hindu as too fatalistic. But perhaps our metaphors become too entrapping. In planning we need to balance attempts at control with serendipity and a recognition of non-controllable events. In learning it is good to plan and also good to welcome and recognize unplanned learning. In SML programmes people say that they benefited from setting objectives and trying to achieve them. They also say that they learned much more that was not in their plan.

Often the learning that comes in the unplanned category is 'being' level. People say that they *are* different, not just that they do different things.

This balance issue is reflected in the way the five questions can be tackled. I have already mentioned the balance of past (Question 1) with future (Question 3). Also in addressing these questions learners can balance

- concrete and abstract (in Question 5)
- rigour and creativity (in Questions 3 and 4)

and so on. This balance also leads to the need to link individuals to their contexts and reflects the value of contracting.

Contracting

Planned learning can be encapsulated in a 'development plan', but such a plan can so easily abstract the person from the context. In SML we suggest people develop a learning contract as a basis for creating their learning within a wide context. Hence the contract needs to be negotiated and agreed with others (a plan may not be). Such agreeing will typically be with fellow learners and with those in authority in the organization. Those in authority may be those authorized to provide resources (especially money) or to allow the person to use time to attend set meetings, for example. There may be a third party to the contract if an outside organization is involved (for example, in providing set advisers).

The negotiating of a contract is another aspect of the rigour of SML and its integration into the life of a business. If contracting works well it weaves together relevant threads to enhance the benefits of learning for all involved. However, it is often not quite so smooth. Organizations that are not moving in the direction of being a learning business still see learning as detached from core business issues. So we find that a boss may authorize a person to go on a course, with fees paid, but take little or no interest in what the person is learning.

This is one of the major challenges for the development of SML. We know that people can go on SML programmes and develop enormously, but in too many situations we have found the newly developed capabilities being under-used because significant authority figures have not taken an interest in the person's development.

The other main challenge in contracting is to make the learning contract live. It must not become a dead document to be followed mechanistically. It must be possible to renegotiate it, and especially to improve it as time goes by. The contract can act as an umbrella document in showing how tactical learning elements are encompassed in an SML strategy. And it can enhance coherence and realism.

The learning contract will need to spell out the resource implications of a person's proposed learning, and this is discussed in the next section.

Resourcing

The previous section covered issues of mapping, diagnosing, planning and contracting. This *preparation* has to be matched with resource considerations.

There is not a great deal that needs to be said under this heading. Resourcing issues are part of managing—and are mostly to do with getting resources (money, materials, etc.) and working with limited resources. (With unlimited resources, lots of managerial problems disappear.) A major difference of SML from traditional education and training is in the control of resources. Participants are usually given significant control over resource decisions such as budgets. A typical programme will provide for individuals or sets to have a budget for learning purposes, and the learning contract is used to justify resource use. If a person wishes to buy a book or attend a workshop, then that person may be able to spend money from his or her budget (subject to its being in the learning contract).

As with other aspects of this chapter, Chapter 8 will show some more concrete (tactical) activities under this heading. It is important to emphasize here, though, the high priority a learning business needs to give to strategic decisions on resources for learning.

Collaborating

I have already indicated in the preceding sections of this chapter the importance of collaboration in learning. Also in an earlier chapter I referred to a personalistic stance which transcends individualism and collectivism. In SML by allowing people to be themselves and in legitimizing their right to speak solely for themselves, it encourages a personalistic collaboration. People hear each other—in depth and about fundamental issues. As a result they are more able to see their connection to others. In sharing joys and fears, needs and desires, values and beliefs, people come to see each other's humanness in situations where they may previously have felt disconnected and isolated.

A problem is, though, that connection to others is sometimes seen as creating uniformity and insipid compromises. Mutual support is characterized as being counter to individual freedom and individuality: it is seen as creating sameness and not allowing difference. In SML, collaborative modes such as the set are important as vehicles to encourage *oneness* and *difference*. Each individual is pursuing a personal programme, but other members of the set learn to care about the goals of others and their struggles towards those goals. So a collective entity exists where each person is encouraged to manifest his or her own uniqueness, while at the same time being at one with others. There is equality *without* conformity.

People often find this confusing at the start. Some want to copy others—for example, one person talks of his own interests and others may want to (inappropriately) copy that, as a means of security (rather than develop their own thinking). This results from the pressure for conformity and sameness that institutions such as schools promote.

A crucial problem for people in a set occurs where assessment is involved. Some find it difficult to cope with the idea that their assessment is unique: they want comparators: they want to measure themselves against others rather than against specific goals. This is an example of the compete/conform polarity emerging: either we compete to beat others or we conform. We need to dispense with the polarity altogether. It is not about choosing to compete or to conform: it is about each person choosing his or her own route and yet supporting others in their own chosen paths. Not competing *or* conforming—*neither* is useful. We may learn from others—listening to ideas that others offer—but a slavish conformity means that the ideas are only introjected without being absorbed. They do not become part of *us*, but a bit tacked on at the side. There is a difference between refining and enlarging one's own cognitive maps and swallowing undigested part of a map belonging to someone else.

The two can be compared as in Figure 7.11.

Connection versus Introjection

a. Connection

b. Introjection

Figure 7.11   Connection versus introjection

Thus in the set, each person has to learn how to learn from others, and at the same time how not to impose on others. The set adviser must assist in this at times, especially in halting any attempts to force ideas onto a person by someone else.

The set is not the only collaborative forum in SML programmes. The wider community of learners is also important, as is networking into other parts of the organization. Mentors can play a significant role in making these links, and they often assist in taking the learning from SML beyond a defined programme. This latter aspect is important as a structured SML programme is best seen as the *start* of a person's continued development, not as a separate distinct event. In evaluation of SML programmes ex-participants often comment that they have applied more of their learning after the programme than during it.

Judging   This is the fourth of the major strategic processes in SML. Like the others it is an aspect of effective managing. Managers have to judge courses of action and make decisions on the basis of judgement. It is rare to have all the information one needs such that a decision makes itself. Mostly decisions are made in the absence of full information and therefore rely on good judgement.

In SML the judging process can be subdivided into

- assessing and,
- evaluating.

Judging occurs at various stages:

1. Before an organization decides to use SML it has to *assess* if it is to be of use and perhaps *evaluate* previous experiences of development activity (for example, has management training been of value in the past?).
2. If an organization decides to go ahead on the basis of a well-considered judgement, individuals need to *assess* if SML will help them.
3. On joining a programme, the diagnostic activity at the start requires judgement. Participants have to *assess* their previous learning and make judgements about their current abilities (and hence about learning needs).
4. During a programme, participants need to judge if they are on track. Are they meeting the objectives they have set?
5. At the end of a programme participants need to *assess* their learning.
6. After the programme there is a need for *evaluation*. Did the programme work? Was it cost-effective? Is it worth continuing with?

In all of these processes collaboration with others is crucial. Prior to a programme there is a need for dialogue between relevant parties, and for collective decision making. In examples mentioned earlier, such as Hiram Walker and Shell, it was essential to have discussions in top management with staff providing the programme so that a fair evaluation could be made of the validity of the approach. Part of the evaluation could come from information. We could, for instance, provide examples of previous programmes, but the judgement to go ahead or not involves other non-rational elements (such as *feelings* about this kind of learning approach).

This process of judging at the start is repeated through the programme. There is always an intertwining of information/ facts and response to the information. SML makes this more open than is often the case in managerial decision making, and in the process helps improve strategic decision making in organizations.

The end point assessment is also unusual in organizational programmes. Many organizations now engage in judging *prior* to a programme—for example, through the appraisal process or through the use of assessment centres—but then do not encourage assessment down the line. Individuals may leave an assessment centre with development plans to focus on learning things that have been identified as weaknesses. They are then left to solve their problems, often without proper support and without any process at some future date to assess their improvement, if any. When this happens it seems that assessment centres (even if called 'development centres') are low on cost-effectiveness.

Another crucial difference in SML from traditional assessment processes is that the learner drives the assessment. The learner makes self-assessments which are tested on peers, bosses, programme staff or any other relevant person. Eventually this produces a consensus which, by virtue of such collective agreement, has greater power and effectiveness. If all relevant parties reach a consensus (and this is normal in about 99 per cent of cases), then the base for future action is extremely solid. Many appraisal schemes are now moving in this direction, especially with the emphasis not just on self assessment but on getting the views of others (for example, subordinates) on performance.

In judging activity and learning, this has to be placed alongside processes of feedback. In earlier chapters I emphasized two kinds of feedback:

- primary—sensory based, direct
- secondary—verbal judgements, not direct.

Secondary feedback, in some respects, comes between primary feedback and judgement. Primary feedback is unadorned data; for example, a sales person has sold X amount of a product. Secondary feedback might be a boss's response to this—for example, 'I'm not happy with this'. The judgement process then may follow; for example, assessing the implications of the situation and making a judgement about future action.

A danger in some SML sets is where participants want to stay at the level of comfortable, low-judgement feedback. This might include such comments as: 'That report had X and Y good features, but it needed a bit more work on section Z.' Eventually such generalized feedback needs shaping up. Learners need to move from asking for such feedback to a situation where they can say: 'I set A, B, C goals in my learning contract. This report is meant to demonstrate these. I feel I surpassed these goals for X, Y, Z reasons. Do you agree?' Responses can then be sharpened into, 'Yes, I agree and these are my reasons' or 'No, I don't agree. You met goals X and Y in my judgement, but not Z. And these are my reasons for saying this.'

Judging is a central process in management. It is a continual process in the life of a manager—and hence can be missed. Self-judgement is also part of judging. Managers have to judge whether they are up to a particular job or not, what career moves to make, and so on. All this requires the ability to assess and evaluate oneself. Hence a strategic learning approach needs to develop this capability through the *process* of learning. Sitting people in classrooms and putting them through exams encourages them to leave judgement issues to others. This can be a problem in SML, particularly with young new graduates from university who have been successful in the traditional education process. If they come from a prestigious university with a so-called 'good degree' they naturally tend to feel that judgements by others are OK. The down-side of this reliance on others is that they often make poor self-judgements, especially around career decisions.

Those who do full-time MBAs in their 20s also suffer from this; hence, the criticisms from employers about the unrealistic expectation of young MBA holders. Also, there is the situation of the seemingly successful MBA holders suddenly facing an existential crisis in their 40s when they realize that they have unthinkingly followed an inappropriate career path. Their self-judgements in early career have proved to be poor.

In SML, therefore, this emphasis on self-judgement can initially be uncomfortable. Learners want external validation, but time and again in evaluation of SML programmes people say that the final assessment was a high point of the programme. Rather than submit themselves to the judgement of others they had to struggle with developing a realistic sense of themselves and their capabilities. And they had to engage in open judgement of colleagues. All this benefits their later ability to select people, make career choices, and work effectively in groups with others.

This links to a moral issue. For me it is immoral for managers to accept the status, power and rewards of their positions (which include judging others) if they are unable to judge themselves. I would never wish to place people in positions of responsibility unless they were prepared to judge themselves. This is not to say that they have to do it perfectly; that is not possible. Just to do it is the issue. And if we realize that we often do it inadequately, we should be very humble about our judgements of others.

Summary

This chapter has outlined SML strategy. The U model provides a basis for linking purposes, strategy, tactics and action. I then discussed four strategic processes

- preparing
- resourcing
- collaborating
- judging

These intertwine with each other. Also, learning through these processes assists effective managing by using them so explicitly. It is like DNA—a spiral interweaving of some complex processes. It provides a model of the life of managing and learning and, like DNA, allows for replication and growth.

Notes

1. This chapter draws on the work of Bateson and his followers, specifically Bandler and Grinder (see Bandler, R. and Grinder, J. (1975) *The Structure of Magic*, Vols I and II, Palo Alto. CA: Science and Behavior Books).
2. Gruber, H.E. and Weitman, M. (1962) *Self-Directed Study: Experiments in Higher Education*, University of Colorado: Boulder.
3. Gregory Bateson was the best writer on this issue (see Bateson, G. (1973) *Steps to an Ecology of Mind*, London: Palladin). He points to the split in Greek thinking at the time of Pythagoras, and how the latter had a more process-oriented view of the world which was lost in the dominant thinking of other philosophers after Pythagoras. Noun/thing thinking also dominates other Western (occidental) languages, hence providing a powerful force to maintain these conventions.
4. Schumacher, E.F. (1977) *A Guide for the Perplexed*, London: Jonathon Cape, p. 9.

5. Barber, P. and Broad, C. (1993) *Tales from the Map Room*, London: BBC Books, p. 8.
6. Fiol, C.M. and Huff, A.S. (1992) 'Maps for managers: where are we? Where do we go from here?', *Journal of Management Studies*, 29, 3 (May), 267–285. These authors review a range of literature and provide an excellent exposition of the importance of maps. The whole issue of the *Journal of Management Studies* (29, 3, May 1992) is a valuable collection on mapping for managers.
7. See Lakoff, G. and Johnson, M. (1980) *Metaphors We Live By*, Chicago: University Press.

8   Self managed learning: tactics and practice

Introduction

In this chapter I shall show some ways in which the purposes, principles and strategic processes of SML can be implemented. I shall not go into great detail on precise methods and techniques as these matters will be covered in a separate book; however, I shall quote from participants about aspects of SML programmes so that there is some concrete information about practice.

A particular emphasis in this chapter will be on structures used in a wide range of SML programmes. However, although I shall point up these programmes, SML and its place in strategic learning is broader than this. Figure 8.1 indicates how programmes fit strategically.

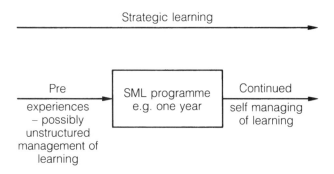

Figure 8.1   SML programmes in context

People will have already managed their learning to some extent prior to getting involved in SML. What SML does is to sharpen, focus, organize, and perhaps re-frame, the existing management of learning. Also, after a structured programme, people continue to manage their own learning for the rest of their lives.

Programmes, by definition, introduce structure and precise processes into learning. Hence, while there is in SML the highest possible flexibility in terms of content of learning, structures limit flexibility in process, but such limits are necessary to provide boundaries within which to exercise freedom and choice. The analogy (taken from Taoist ideas) is the cup. It is a rigid, unbending structure within which the user is free to put in any desired liquid and in any desired amount (subject to the size of the cup). Taoists[1] point out that use comes from space that is bounded. But it must be tightly bounded in places. A floppy cup would be no use. A wheel needs to be solid and rigid but it is useless without a hole at the centre to put the axle in. Although the structures of SML seem initially unusual, people can rapidly integrate them into their overall patterns of working and learning. Let me give two quotes from people on a two-year post-graduate diploma programme.

> How has it worked for me? I initially accepted at a cognitive level the theory of self-determination of learning objectives and methods. I had had some short experiences of unstructured courses which I had found very exciting in learning terms. It seemed to make perfect sense to me that if managers were being asked and paid to determine their own work needs and routines and that of others, then they were equally capable of determining their own learning needs and routines. I was also strongly committed to the necessity of management learning to be as relevant as possible to individuals' situations. Busy managers have enough to worry them in their working lives without overloading them with unnecessary information either at a cognitive or affective level. I was therefore quite shocked at my own reaction to the realization in the second term that I was apparently losing sight of where 'work' ended and 'course' began. So deeply ingrained in me was the conditioning that formal education should be something extra academically removed from reality, that I began to worry that I was not doing something which was, in my perception, on a different plane from my work. I took the problem to my set who eventually helped me,
>
> 1. to understand what I was saying and therefore to reconcile my acceptance of the theory of self-managed learning with the practice, and
> 2. to see that what was in fact happening was that I was working at a more advanced level. I was actively seeking and taking on work from which I would hitherto have shied away.
>
> (Liz Atkins,[2] p. 8)

A normal management course would have taught me a lot of things I don't really need in my career. On the other hand, the self managed learning diploma allowed me to concentrate on just what I needed to learn. It was very useful working with other people in a group, because they helped me see what my weaknesses were. It was the first time I'd been able to sit down with a peer group of people prepared to listen to my personal development problems. Indeed, the group members found it so useful that they still meet regularly every six weeks, even though their course finished more than six months ago. They still find they can help each other tackle current job problems.

(Rob Holmes, quoted in Clutterbuck[3])

Both managers found that learning and working merged, and that the learning approach carried on beyond the programme. And structures such as sets and learning contracts continue to be of value. However, one of the problems with the possibility of using SML structures quite widely is that they can be used in a way which is not self managed learning. Programme organizers can say 'We're using sets and learning contacts, so it's the same as SML' or 'Within our course we give participants freedom to choose a project—and therefore it's SML' It is not. Figure 8.2 shows two distinctions.

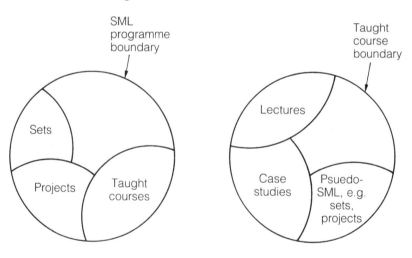

(a) SML strategic programme   (b) Taught course strategy

Figure 8.2   SML as strategy not tactics

Figure 8.2 suggests that SML provides a strategic frame within which individuals may, because of the needs of their learning contract, attend a standard short course. This latter is then a *tactical* means towards achieving *strategic* ends. SML allows for almost any choice of tactics. The example of pseudo-SML is where within, say, an MBA, participants do some self-development or undertake a project. But assessment stays controlled by professors, and the general curriculum is determined by the faculty. This kind of programme has nothing to do with self managed learning.

I have found myself criticized by others who see my stance as too rigid. They suggest I am being too purist and that compromises are necessary. I am with Toyota in their slogan:

'Compromise is the enemy of achievement'

Having a bit of SML in a programme is equivalent to being a bit pregnant—impossible. Either managers are managing their own learning or they are not. Also, the issue of purity is interesting. The opposite of pure is impure, and in this respect I am not for impurity.

Compromises on quality are just that—they reduce quality and produce second rate learning. I am not suggesting that SML is a perfect Utopian strategy. But if I knew of anything better I would do it.

SML programmes

At this point I shall outline a basic design approach for SML and later I shall discuss some of the elements of SML programmes. Some of these have already been introduced in earlier chapters, and here some of the earlier themes will be pulled together.

Designing

Chapter 10 indicates the role of designing in SML programmes. The key to successful design is to get a good basic macro design, so that micro elements can evolve to suit learners and their organizations. I remember one CEO criticizing his trainers for over-elaborating designs. They had done a good basic job for him, and then wanted to gold plate it. As a result it lost contact with his needs.

In any design there will be aspects which are non-negotiable. These need to be made as clear and as explicit as possible. Typical non-negotiables might include:

- resources available, such as budget
- time—length of programme and off-job time possible
- use of certain structures such as learning contracts and sets.

In SML the negotiables typically include:

- location of set meetings
- content of learning contracts
- criteria for assessment.

Robust design: the idea

Allowing for these variances in negotiables and non-negotiables, there is a good basic robust design for SML programmes. The ideas of a robust design is an analogy with, say, the Boeing 747. This aeroplane has been enormously successful because it has a basic robust design. Robustness comes from the ability to modify the basic design to respond to a wide range of customer needs. Airlines have been able to specify to Boeing a wide variety of needs within the basic framework of the 747. Table 8.1 shows a comparator between some feature of the Boeing 747 and a robust SML design.

Table 8.1   Robust design

Boeing 747	SML robust design
Able to stretch or contract length of aircraft (within limits)	Able to stretch or contract length of programme (within limits)
Possible to furnish interior differently	Possible to have different content to programme
Possible to vary seating arrangements	Possible to vary arrangement of elements
Possible to vary power supplied—engines	Possible to vary resources supplied

Such analogies should not be pushed too far. A programme is not a physical structure like an aircraft, and cannot be treated in the same way.

A robust design for SML

Figure 8.3 shows diagrammatically a robust design for SML programmes. It shows the processes discussed in Chapter 7, and specific activities along the bottom of the diagram. The essence of the design is a first phase which uses a start-up event and set meetings to assist the learner to produce an

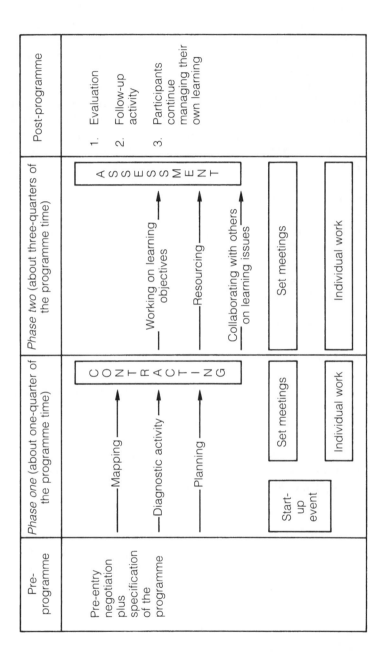

Figure 8.3   SML robust design

agreed learning contract. The learner will also be doing individual work such as writing the contract.

In phase two the contract is put into practice using live work experience and regular set meetings. This leads to an end point assessment. The diagram also alludes to the importance of pre- and post-programme activity.

This design is not intended to represent all the possibilities for SML programmes. Rather it shows one design that can be modified to suit a wide range of possibilities. For instance, in Shell the ten-month programme leading to a Certificate in Management Studies (CMS) had the following features from Figure 8.3:

- a start-up event of two days
- set meetings over ten months (one day per month)
- learning contracts developed and agreed in the early set meetings (phase one)
- final assessment for the CMS
- individual work on learning objectives
- collaboration with others in the set and in the company
- resources allocated to sets to meet learning needs and workshops to support learning.

Additional features not in Figure 8.3 include:

- mentors for programme participants (these were arranged during the start-up event)
- group and individual projects during phase two
- a hand book for participants to provide basic data, guidance notes on resources and an explanation of the programme
- access to a 'learning community', that is, when sets came together on common issues.

Elements of SML programmes

Figure 8.4 shows how the strategic processes in Chapter 7 are delivered as tactical elements of programmes. On the left are the processes and on the right examples of tactical elements. An asterisk marks elements that have already been identified as part of a robust design.

Start-up event

In a typical programme within an organization one or two days might be allocated to a start-up event. Activities within this can include:

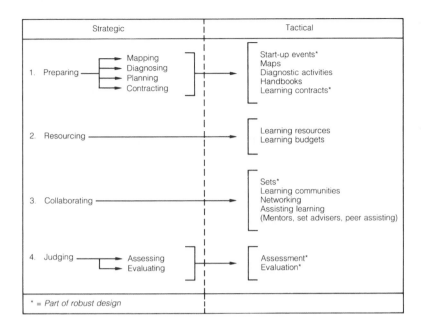

Figure 8.4   Strategic processes to tactical elements

- explaining SML
- explaining the programme
- locating the programme in the organization's strategies
- introductions—participants to each other, participants to staff
- agreeing ground rules for working.

Much of this would be expected in any significant management development programme. The key difference is the need to get people into the SML process. Also, typically in a start-up event there is the need to form learning sets of around five or six persons in each.

Maps

Chapter 7 discussed the value and importance of mapping. In translating this to practice some issues are important. Firstly, in an organizational programme there needs to be an organizational map. This might include:

- strategic directions, mission and vision statements, etc.
- competence lists, if the organization uses them

- organization charts
- HR/personnel policies
- technology, products, markets, etc.

Many organizations are now using competence lists for selection and appraisal. If this is so, it is likely that these will 'map' the views of HR or top management on development issues. I have already indicated the severe limitations of competence maps, but if they are being used, then people have to respond to them. Managers might be joining an SML programme following an assessment/development centre and come with a competence map given to them as a result of feedback from the centre. They often need help in making sense of the map and of the diagnostic information accompanying it.

Competence lists imply that they cover the territory of management. However, it can be useful to expose managers to other maps to help them to make choices about learning. A typical map is the standard curriculum of an MBA. This can then be broken down into subjects (HR, strategy, finance, etc.).

Instead of presenting maps it can be valuable to pursue two alternative methods:

1. Help learners to map their existing knowledge and hence see what concepts and theories they currently work with.
2. Use a questionnaire to ask learners about their knowledge of standard methods and techniques in management. Table 8.2 shows part of a strategic management questionnaire. This questionnaire (or rather the full version of it) can be given, in advance of a workshop, to participants; it can then be collected, analysed and used as a basis for a workshop session.

An alternative to using standard maps is to show a different approach to mapping. I prefer to use process maps (rather than content maps) so that managers can insert their own content. Examples such as the triangle model (linking Why?, What?, How? and Who?) and the U model shown earlier in this book have been used on SML programmes to develop strategic leadership.

I also like to 'nest' models and maps inside each other. The analogy here is with, say, a map of the world which can be broken down into maps of a country, regions in the country, towns and districts. A district map is 'nested' inside a town map, inside a regional map, etc. An advantage of nesting is that it improves ease of use. This is especially so if one applies

Table 8.2   Exhibit: basic strategic management ideas

Issues/methods	Know and use	Know well but do not use	Know a little	Don't know
BCG approach				
Contingency planning				
Environment scanning				
Forecasting, e.g. Delphi				
Mission statements				
Porter's model				
Scenario methods				
SWOT analysis				
Visioning				

Miller's theory[4] of short-term memory. Crudely, Miller suggests that we can hold in short-term memory 7 ± 2 chunks of information ('chunks' may be concepts, words, variables, etc.). If we take the lower limit of short-term memory (5 chunks) then one 'chunk' is used to process and link other concepts. Hence, it is desirable to restrict models to four variables if they are to be remembered (and hence usable). You will note that in this book I have generally followed that theory; for example, in Chapter 7 I discussed four basic processes and then subdivided these (nesting subprocesses where needed). The U model and the triangle model also have four basic variables (chunks) in each.

Diagnostic activity

To balance the mapping processes learners need to acquire information about themselves, their strengths and weaknesses, values, interests, and so on. Often there is considerable data available, but it may be in a poor state of analysis. Managers can often draw on:

- appraisal data about themselves
- day-to-day feedback
- assessment centre feedback
- psychometric tests and instruments
- colleagues' views
- subordinates' views
- data from family and friends
- data from career counsellors, etc.

The trouble is that data may conflict, may be missing key dimensions, may be poorly presented, etc. Sets can be of enormous help to individuals in assisting them to sift and sort data. This is especially so in low trust cultures where it is not possible for the person to test data in the organization.

Handbooks

Over time we have found it valuable to produce handbooks for significant SML programmes. These have varied from guidance notes about the programme, contact points in the organization, etc., to more lengthy documents which include diagnostic instruments, handouts (to assist in mapping), etc.

I mention this detail here to exemplify the need for good structuring devices in SML. These devices look different from those used in traditional programmes, and hence often need thinking through carefully.

Learning contracts

The first point to emphasize is that by a learning contract I mean a document written by an individual specifying that person's learning proposals. Some writers use the term 'learning contract' to mean a set of ground rules agreed in a group.

For example, Lee comments:

> The first session was introductory, getting the students to talk about themselves and their expectations, trying to establish rapport and build up a *learning contract*. The basic messages were:
>
> - this is a low threat environment in which we can learn together;
> - you will have control over both content and process, I will be here to help;
> - we are all responsible for this course, it will be what we make it;
> - I do not consider myself in charge. (Lee,[5] p. 33)

I would accept that this has an element of contracting to it, but it is better characterized as a 'process contract', not a 'learning contract'.

In order to indicate how learning contracts are used in SML I shall quote from three programme participants. Firstly, Michael Skilton, a housing manager:

The contract requires an honest self analysis of one's present position and identifies how that position was reached. The contract also requires identification of the progress the writer wishes to make, an analysis of what must be achieved to obtain that progress and a checklist of anticipated indicators that one has arrived at one's objectives. The other fundamental aspect of the contract is that although it is negotiated and written at an early stage of the course it need not be a rigid document and can at any time be renegotiated. My contract identified eight projects needing to be achieved. For instance, I have been looking at how computerisation can help the working of the department, at internal training and at problems identified in involving tenants in management.

Now, at the start of my second year, I am renegotiating my contract. My work in the first forced me to take a close and critical look at the way I applied myself to some of the problems I was currently experiencing. I became aware that, although my knowledge of housing was reasonably good, my understanding of some basic concepts was lacking. Further, it is now clear that when I started the course I had not been able to identify properly my requirements in relation to what I was trying to achieve. A major difference between this course and more conventional courses is that part of the process of learning is to reach an understanding of why you are learning, which helps you to identify what you should be learning. This is not available in traditional courses, for once you have embarked on them you are committed to either completing or abandoning the process of learning.

(Skilton,[6] p. 4)

Nigel Boldero, a policy analyst, commented as follows:

The first term (out of a total of six) was spent in small groups (or 'sets') considering the content of members' contracts—these documents set out the areas to be studied, skills and experience to be acquired and methods for so doing. The development of these statements of an individual's needs were supported by a series of 'taster' sessions on the range of disciplines and approaches which form the core of the term 'management'. The contract also included arrangements for assessment (the contract and these arrangements are negotiated and agreed within each set and with the external assessors).

I found this period useful in enabling me to look fundamentally at my career pattern to date. As a result I had a clearer idea of my future intentions and the *skills* and *experiences*, as well as the *knowledge* I would need to acquire to achieve these.

With the help of fellow set members (which included a course tutor), I identified four main areas of work:

- management accountancy;
- organizational behaviour and development;
- operations management (including operations research);
- a range of communication and other interpersonal skills.

(Boldero, [7] p. 292)

Peter Maher, a deputy head teacher, commented on the value of working with others:

> I learnt a lot from discussing other set members' contracts as they are interested in topics beyond my own experience. The process of negotiating the contracts was just as edifying.
>
> (Maher,[8] p. 8)

The positive comments above are in keeping with the research evidence in Malcolm Knowles' book on learning contracts.[9] Research that he and others have analysed suggests the following benefits:

- more effective integration of theory and practice
- greater sense of ownership of own learning
- increased ability to define and set measurable goals
- enhanced self concept
- greater self-motivation to learn, participate and achieve more realistic attitudes towards work and career
- enlarged awareness of individual strengths and weaknesses.

Steiner[10] makes a point of comparing contracts with legalistic contracts. As he points out, they need to meet at least three criteria:

- Mutual consent—there has to be explicit, clear agreement on all sides that the arrangements are voluntarily accepted. Also there is the understanding that there will be mutual effort to meet the contract.
- Consideration—meaning that, for instance, a learner may pay an educational institution for a course and expect 'education' in return.
- Lawful—a contract must not violate any laws.

In SML there are extra features of a contract, especially given the involvement of a range of parties (for example, the learner, set colleagues, the learner's boss, etc.). Figure 8.5 shows the range of influences on a learning contract.

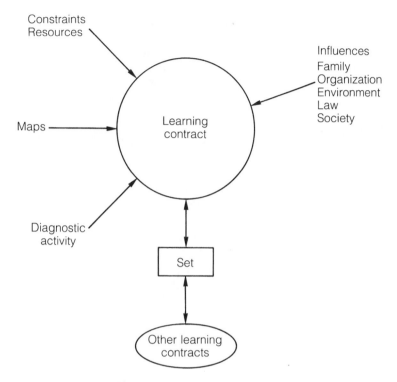

Figure 8.5   Learning contracts

Learning Resources

Access to a range of learning resources is crucial in SML.
However, an advantage of the SML approach lies in liberating
learners from the constraints of traditional learning modes,
and in encouraging learners to be creative in their choice of
methods. Here is another quote from Nigel Boldero:

> There are a range of mechanisms available for managing the
> contract. My programme has drawn upon:
>
> - a specialist seminar group on finance, including a tutor and
>   financial managers from both the public and private sectors;
> - library and video resources available in the Management
>   Centre (computing facilities are also available);
> - specialist tutorial assistance from a work colleague on certain
>   management accountancy techniques (my contract includes an
>   emphasis on projects which are centred upon 'live' work
>   activities);
> - training sessions/workshops on particular skills—so far there
>   have been three residential weekends aimed at developing a
>   variety of 'interpersonal skills';

- a 'learning set'—the same set which helped develop the contracts is now taking on the role of monitoring progress on them, resolving particular learning problems, considering approaches to projects, supporting and confronting individuals' work and a forum in which developing skills can be 'tried out' and discussed.

(Boldero[7], p. 292)

The following is a list of some of the learning modes used on SML programmes:

- Work experience—work itself
  —culture
  —boss
  —colleagues
  —other employees
  —projects
  —secondments
  —mentor/coach
- Outside organization
  —travel
  —courses—employer sponsored
            —adult education
  —therapy/counselling
  —reading
  —TV/radio/cassettes
  —family/friends
  —retreats
  —museums
  —libraries
  —art galleries
- Internal courses
- Team development/organization development.

Learning budgets

In SML it is important that participants are able fully to realize their responsibility for learning. This ideally includes some control over budgets for financing the kind of learning activities mentioned above. In some programmes, individuals have been allocated a personal budget to spend money to meet the requirements of their learning contract. Thus the person writes into the contract where financial assistance will be required with particular activities. The organization, in agreeing to the contract, agrees to the financial and other resource needs.

In some programmes the budget is allocated to the set, and they have to justify, collectively, to those in authority how they wish to spend their budget. This responsibility passed to participants not only ensures ownership of the learning, but also adds the dimension of the concomitant duty to the organization to be working within resource constraints.

Participants usually show great care in handling budgets, and the process does not throw up any issues not already present in budgetary systems in organizations.

By providing individuals with the budget they come to realize the costs involved in activities, and develop a real sense of cost-effectiveness. For instance, where participants collectively agree that they want to learn something, they may decide to hire an eminent professor. When they discover what the professor will charge to do a one-day workshop, and compare it with the cost of the professor's book, they may elect to buy the book instead! They may not, of course. They may want the interaction with some famous guru, and decide it is worth it. Hence, they may economize on other activities.

I have also found that when participants on a programme are given budgetary responsibility they become quite frugal in their use of resources. They will negotiate with speakers to keep fees down; they will invite company people to provide sessions (so that they do not have to pay for them); they will see the value of less expensive resources such as audio tapes and print material.

All this contrasts with traditional training approaches where managers often feel happy to apply for expensive courses, without a thought about cost-effectiveness, because it is out of someone else's budget. Many HR development people would like managers to see that training courses form only one learning mode among many. However, if they insist on holding the training budgets, and do not encourage people to take responsibility for their own learning, then they will continue to be unsuccessful in getting a shift in attitudes.

Learning sets

Learning sets are central to SML operation. However, because in SML they are used in rather unique and particular ways, it is often difficult to describe their value and their function. I shall begin with a lengthy quote from a piece written by a woman who was a member of a set with whom I worked in the 1970s. Out of the many examples I could have chosen, I felt hers is interesting because it shows her own growing strategic sense. It is also an example of someone—who was not a manager—struggling to establish an independent self-employed status (which she achieved). I have only lightly edited her comments in order to keep it to what she wanted to say, and in her own style.

When I went to the set I had not heard of the theories of self managed learning and for some weeks I had no clear idea of what was going on. I heard the explanation of how the group was expected to plan their course but it was like listening to a foreign language which I had learnt but before my ear had got attuned to the sound of the words spoken by a native of the country. I was confused and unclear about what each person wanted to achieve and only gradually saw that other members of the group were also confused. It then became clearer that the group discussions were the process of clarification being worked through together. What was new to me was the idea that I could design a programme to meet my own personal needs and it took me a long time to grasp this and experience that idea in a way that I could feel it belonged to me. And that this groping towards solutions together was a learning process in itself which we were each experiencing for ourselves as well as observing it in each other. The idea that I could focus on my own personal needs and requirements for training and education; that I could decide for myself what these were; that I could plan how to get them and not fit into someone else's programme was so new and alien it took a long time to recognize what this meant as an experience. My degree had seemed to be a task and a programme of work set by someone else and I had then squeezed myself into a shape that would fit their requirements and expectations like an Ugly Sister distorting herself to fit into Cinderella's shoe. Now I was free to create my own programme and I didn't know that I was free. I had always had that freedom, but I had not been able to use it because I didn't recognize that I had it. The moment of realizing this was full of excitement for me and I felt warm and loving and grateful to each person in the group for the way in which our working together had produced this feeling as an experience of release. It wasn't something which happened suddenly and easily however but was the product of many hours thrashing out problems together. The essential change for me was the transformation from knowing something with my head to experiencing what I knew with my emotions.

The way we worked in the set was that we were each responsible for asking for the time that we wanted and for deciding for ourselves what the area was on which we wanted to work. At first I considered only practical questions but as I became more confident in the group I began to bring up personal questions because that was what was the most important focus for me at that moment. In the past I would not have considered that appropriate to bring into a study group, and, as at college, I would have thought only academic problems were legitimate questions to bring up. Neither would I have thought of approaching a tutor to discuss an emotional problem. I made the assumption that he was only concerned with my academic progress. It gradually became clear that our academic progress was linked with our personal development and that personal issues often stood in the way of making academic progress. And these were what needed working through first. At the end of each meeting we set ourselves goals to be reached within a time limit, often before the next meeting.

These goals were not always reached and that focused our attention on how we were not keeping our agreements with ourselves. We challenged each other's justifications or rationalizations for failure to keep a contract and the work in the set was often centred on the areas in which we were blocking ourselves. I saw that, as we got to know each other, a caring and supportive relationship built up between us where I could be open about my own feelings and frank in my response to others. I came to feel accepted and supported no matter how challenging the set response was to me. The challenge was not presented in terms of advice or help but more in terms of questioning what was going on in my life and then of us sharing with each other our own experiences. The tutor and members occasionally gave specific information and suggested directions in which to move, but mainly the aim was to assist us in reaching our own decisions to suit our own needs.

This meant being clear about what these needs were. In my case I wanted to plan my life and my means of earning money in a way which satisfied me. I didn't know clearly how I wanted to do this and the set became a place where I learnt to explore that question more effectively as well as to learn to know myself better. These two aspects were closely linked.

My position at this time was that I had worked in public relations and had qualified as a teacher before bringing up three children who were then aged 4, 9 and 11. To return to teaching seemed an obvious solution. I would be earning money and it had been a job that I'd found challenging and interesting. However, I wanted to work where I felt fully committed and invested in what I was doing and I did not want to do a job only because it was convenient through lack of making a clear choice on the matter. I wanted to make a conscious decision to do whatever I did because it was what I wanted—and convenience might be the deciding factor—but I didn't want to slip into a convenient situation without choosing to commit myself to it. The manner of working in the set, encouraging each other to become more autonomous and self directed, increased this feeling and also gave me the confidence to act and plan a freer life, which was what became clear was my preference. So eventually I chose to work freelance in several different areas. I could equally have chosen freely to work full time in an establishment, but decided that it suited me better not to do that.

When I first went to the set apart from caring for a household of five people I was coaching in English part time, interviewing and writing articles for a career's magazine and attending a variety of growth groups as part of my wish to further my own personal development and also in order to gain experience to train as a group facilitator. My motivation was to earn money to supplement the costs of the family and the household and to re-establish myself as an individual with an identity outside the family. However, it was rather a chicken or the egg situation. I needed to develop skills and gain experience in order to develop the confidence that comes from doing something and at the same time I needed more personal development in order to go and do what I wanted. The set was a place where both these things could happen.

My sense of personal identity seemed to me to depend mainly on my roles as a wife and mother and both were defined relative to and dependent on very special relationships. After 10 years in these roles I didn't have a strong sense of personal identity.

I went to a wide range of groups through which I began to know myself better and to extend and challenge myself. The set provided a long term situation where I could go and discuss and make sense of this variety of experiences with members who also had experience of group work and who could provide an environment where I could digest and assimilate a fairly rich diet. The quality of the environment provided by the set varied for me. At first I was pleased to meet with friends who were open and welcoming and interested in my activities, as I was in theirs, but as time went on the very real sense of caring which we shared was very important as well as the feeling that I could turn to any person in that group at any time if I wanted a friend. And this was based on me as an individual and in no way was connected with my previous roles or dependent on them. The set became perhaps a different sort of family and one where it was alright to make mistakes and that was a great release to not have to be perfect all the time.

I realized just how much I was waiting for life to be interesting so that I could commit myself, and I switched to seeing that it was my responsibility to make it interesting for myself and only I could put in my energy and investment and not to wait for the activity itself to come up and grab me and in some way make it all magically work. This applied equally in personal relationships. I had always thought that it was my responsibility to make things work. I became much more aware of this as a personal experience and more able to put the idea into practice with an awareness of what I was doing, which I found strengthening. I was less fumbling along with a well meaning idea and more accepting my responsibility for making life work for myself and at the same time accepting that I was not responsible for making anyone else's life work. I then felt less guilty towards the family when I went out to meetings, and with my change in attitude I found that they became less resentful of my outside activities. What seemed to happen was that I accepted their anger and hostility as theirs and with accepting it the anger seemed to evaporate.

The set also focused my ability to give and to receive; that it was alright to give whatever I wanted to a group member and I discovered my ability to receive too so that when someone told me that through working with me they had found their own self confidence I could accept that and receive it and feel good. In the past one way I had reduced my self esteem was to disbelieve any positive feedback. Now I didn't need to believe it. I could just receive it and choose to either make myself feel good with that or undermine it by disbelief and feel I was being conned. Once I was aware of this I was less likely to cheat myself of something good and so reduce the quality of my experience.

The quality of Ian as the set adviser was most important to me. My experience of schools and of university had been of very hierarchical organizations where students were told or advised what to do and where on the whole the atmosphere encouraged the student to feel that authority knew best, and perhaps it is necessary for me to say that my own education had been very authoritarian. My experience of teachers and tutors had been that there was an absence of empathy and a large measure of criticism and judgement. I never felt criticized or judged at any time in the set by Ian or by anyone else, and I think that this atmosphere of detachment was a quality which came from Ian. There was also a caring and an understanding. This detachment was in no way a cold quality, and I felt I could expand and grow in this atmosphere that he encouraged. I also felt that I was free to make mistakes for the first time in my life—and again I didn't feel judged for this. The result of this for me was that I felt freer to be myself in the set than anywhere I'd ever felt before. I felt free to give and to take and to expose myself and be open emotionally in a way that I hadn't permitted myself to be before. He created a containing space where I could look at my abilities as well as my weaknesses. He showed no impatience, but waited for when the time seemed right, for each member, to challenge them when he saw that they were stuck and needed to do something in a particular area in order to move on. I never saw him push any one and my own experience was that when he challenged me it was very clarifying to have to confront myself at that point. I didn't feel reaction or resistance being stirred up and I think that this assisted my own developing and learning in the set.

All of these experiences seemed to apply to other members and from the first it was clear that the relationship between Ian and the student was person to person—which I now take for granted but which surprised me originally. There was no sense in which Ian suggested that he knew better than the students. Any information was given in the sense of sharing of his own experience or knowledge and he listened with attention and without ever dismissing or discounting a reply. He gave unstintingly of time and hospitality as well as of his own personal possessions, e.g. books and car. I found that to be given to so freely in this way was a tremendous form of being affirmed as a person and to be given to without any strings attached gave me a lot of pleasure and energy and a feeling of self esteem. This seems to be part of his personality. He gives totally of himself in terms of investing himself during a meeting. I always feel him as totally present and interested. He never encouraged us to make the set the only place where we could enjoy these experiences and it was from the set that we all moved out taking and using the results of our work with us.

I think that I have gradually changed from either resisting or submitting to life to more often creating what I want. I have moved from avoiding to confronting situations more readily. Confrontation is something I'm only just moving towards and see as my next step forward before the next and the next. None of which I know right now but which I look forward to with excitement.

Nature of learning sets

What I hope the piece shows is that a set is quite *unlike*

- a team
- a business meeting
- a syndicate or group discussion
- a therapy group
- a T group
- a support group (sets do more than just support)
- an action learning set (where the focus is more on projects)
- a seminar
- a group tutorial.

Table 8.3 shows a comparator between a less-than-ideal seminar and a good learning set.

I shall also quote here from the views of a student who had taken a degree by independent study, where she used tutorials as her main focus of interaction with others.

I have been involved as a participant in a set for a period of approximately one year. Prior to this, I received my 'tuition' in a one to one tutorial situation. Thus, what I want to do here is compare my experience of the use of a set and the use of a tutorial as methods of exploring intellectual and personal problems.

Table 8.3 Sets are not seminars

Seminar	Learning set
Ideas discussed are 'out there', i.e. they are someone else's *and* someone else's choice for discussion (usually the tutor's)	Ideas discussed originate from individuals. These are not separate from the concerns of the person. The person raises issues because they *mean* something
People often try to 'win' in debate, e.g. by knocking down others' ideas	People are not trying to win by debating. Respect is shown for others' ideas
• by pushing in to the discussion to create space for themselves	There is no need to push-in as each person has his or her own space
• by seeking approval, e.g. from tutor	Everyone assesses final work so tutor's approval is less crucial
• by trying to *look* smart (irrespective of whether they are being true to their own views)	People try (usually) to be true to their own beliefs
People are often thinking up the next bright thing to say, so they do not listen well to others	People are given space to struggle with ideas, so listening to others comes naturally
People are sometimes put on the spot in a Socratic manner. They then feel the need to defend ideas to the last, even though they may not care about such ideas (or even believe in them)	People are helped with their ideas. Questions are asked for the benefit of the person, not in order to put someone on the defensive. People's feelings are taken into consideration. Arguing is avoided as this usually serves to entrench ideas, not change or improve them

The tutorial

My first experience was of the one to one tutorial. I was able here to test out ideas and clarify areas of confusion. However, the ideas were being tested on one person only—an 'expert' opinion on matters. This immediately puts the student into a Child state and the tutor into a Parent state (in Transactional Analysis terms). I found that my way of coping with this was to try to 'wangle' my way out of doing things! More importantly, I think, was that I felt that I was producing work to please my tutor—not for myself. In other words, I was not taking responsibility for my own learning.

The set

The set was formed comprising myself and four other students. I found distinct advantages in this method of operating, for several reasons.

1. There is a more equal distribution of power. Every member of the set both gives and receives help thus setting up an Adult to Adult relationship.
2. I think as a direct result of the above, the responsibility for learning lies in the hands of the learner.
3. The *set members* have a responsibility to others as well as *themselves*. Therefore, I think, *they* are more likely to attend meetings.
4. The set members are answerable to other members of the set as well as the tutor and are thus less able to wriggle out of doing work. (It is embarrassing to admit to others that you have not done something you agreed to do!)
5. The students can test their ideas out on more than one person and therefore get more than one perspective on them.
6. Questions are posed to the student by other members of the set as well as the tutor. The questions asked by the other set members may have been overlooked by the tutor.
7. The members of the set are 'all in the same boat' and are perhaps in a better position to understand each others problems.

I think that I need here to mention how I perceive the role of the set adviser or tutor. Whereas in a tutorial I think the tutor's main function is to help the student by giving 'expert' advice, I think in the set his main function is to facilitate learning. More specifically, I think this includes asking pertinent questions, moving the set member(s) to explore problems at a deeper level, refraining from advice giving and directing communication to maximise benefit for the student(s) (eg bringing people in, shutting people up). In addition, he is also another member of the set who has a body of expert knowledge which can be 'tapped' by the students. To sum up, the one to one tutorial and the set are two methods of helping a student with their learning. The features of each situation as I see them are summarised below.

Tutorial	*Set*
Unequal power (Parent-Child relationship)	More equal power (Adult-Adult relationship)
Student gains opinion of expert	Student gains opinion of expert and laypersons
Student answerable to tutor	Student answerable to tutor and set members
Tutor as 'expert'	Tutor as 'facilitator'[11]

Factors in set organization

Some of the factors that impinge on the organization of learning sets include

Size

Five is the ideal number (plus set adviser). This, in a one-day meeting, allows everyone to get at least an hour's time if they need it. Also the organization of meetings is easier than with a larger number (finding time in people's busy schedules can be a problem). With only four in a set there is a problem if someone is absent. A set of three reduces the level and quality of interaction and can put more pressure on the set adviser to take part. Six works reasonably—it just puts a bit more pressure on the set to be well organized and pay attention to time. Seven becomes a strain (I have worked with a set of seven, but I was relieved when one person dropped out). Eight is impossible: people have too little time to explore issues in depth, and the process becomes too superficial.

Heterogeneity/homogeneity

Learning sets work best when there is sufficient commonality between set members to bond the set yet sufficient difference to produce creative tensions. Usually the latter factor is there without prompting it. So in helping sets to form I tend to encourage people not to consider personality factors and other aspects of potential difference. In sets of managers it can be useful to ensure that, in an in-house programme, people are not at highly disparate levels in the hierarchy. It is not possible to have the CEO and a junior manager in the same set.

Some other interesting differences include age, gender, nationality and colour, which are discussed in a later chapter on diversity and difference. The token woman or token black person may initially experience some difficulty in some sets. The set adviser must be able to raise these issues of difference, and get the set to recognize their impact (if they do not already).

Set formation

I prefer to have an open discussion in a start-up event about set formation. I encourage people to consider initially only two factors—time and location; that is, a set may form around people who can meet on certain days only, or in certain geographically defined locations. Usually most people have some flexibility on these issues, and therefore sets can group around these common factors.

Location

Sets can meet anywhere. I have held meetings in training centres, offices, board rooms, people's homes, hotels and, in good weather, out of doors.

Scheduling

An ideal is for sets to meet about once a month for a whole day over a period of at least six months. However, in Cable and Wireless a set of secretaries met every week for one hour, in their lunch break. It was not ideal, but they could not get time off work. The set still provided enormous value to these women and they made it work. If sets meet infrequently (e.g. at more than six-weekly intervals) there can be too much catching up to do—unless set members have known each other for some time, when two monthly intervals can work.

Sets often continue to meet after formal programmes. I know of one that is continuing 13 years after it was formed.

Learning set processes   To function well a set needs

- a reasonable level of openness so that set members will discuss genuine issues
- sufficient trust so that people will feel able to, for instance, share confidential information
- good listening from everyone
- set members to 'own' what they say, usually by using 'I' statements (e.g. I believe this, I am concerned about that, etc.)
- a preparedness for people to act non-defensively—to hear ideas without premature negative judgements
- space for people to reflect on what comes up—not pressure to rush on from item to item
- limited advice giving—too much is intrusive
- questions and comment made between participants designed to help people learn (not to play clever).

Guidelines for set meetings

A way of assisting a set to develop its processes of working is to have explicit ground rules agreed at the start. These ground rules provide a basis for agreed modes of operating. Even if they are violated, which they usually are at times, the explicit nature of the ground rules allows for the set rapidly to get back on track (by referring to the rules). The following is a list of ground rules that I have used in some sets.

1. Accept responsibility for your own learning—no one else is responsible for it. If you need help, ask for it. Other people are not mind readers.
2. Collaborate with others in their learning, but do not try to take it over for them.
3. Listen actively to everyone. If you find it difficult to follow someone—tell them.
4. Do not try to make people be like you—accept them as they are.
5. The detail of what happens in the set is confidential. However, general decisions taken will need to be communicated outside.
6. Try to be as honest and as open as possible, while being sensitive to the needs of others.
7. Everyone has the right to a reasonable part of the set's time for his or her own problems and concerns.
8. Do not pretend that things are not the way they are: try to present honest concerns.
9. Speak for yourself and avoid generalizing. Use 'I' rather than 'we', 'you', 'they', or 'one'.
10. Everyone has the right not to answer a question if that seems appropriate.
11. Set advisers are bound by the same rules—and they have trouble following them too!
12. The set adviser in a set is another *person*—he or she is not here to prop up the set or to take decisions for it.
13. Decisions that need to be taken are done collectively, by consensus.

In order to short-circuit needless discussion, I have tended to offer a list like the above for the set to consider. It is not imposed; it is merely a mapping device to help the set. The set can reject it, modify it or accept it as it is.

Structuring of set meetings

A typical structure might be:

1. Checking in

Set members each say a few sentences on anything that has happened since the set last met, or anything that might be an obstacle to their participation at this meeting. This process lasts perhaps ten minutes, but can be a valuable reconnecting device.

2. Agenda setting

The members, in turn, might suggest what they want to raise at this meeting, and how much time each might need. Also, there may need to be time available to discuss general set issues, e.g. dates and venues of future meetings.

3. Working through the agenda

Usually people need more time than they estimate. They might say that they need 30 minutes to raise an issue, but their colleagues may question them on it to a greater extent than they predicted. The agenda, therefore, has to contain some flexibility, but a problem can occur if insufficient time remains to discuss the last person's items. Hence, the set needs to develop time awareness so that this problem is minimized or eliminated.

There may also need to be a space between items so that individuals can record agreements, commitments and decisions, before continuing.

4. Checking out

A round of responses to the day can be of great value. People can express how they feel about how the set is going, or clear down unfinished items. This is usually a ten-minute process.

Comments on sets

I shall end this section with two more comments on sets, from participants on the two-year post-graduate diploma.

> SML is different from other courses: first was 'the set', a group of five fellow novices, a second year 'adviser' and a tutor also acting

in an advisory capacity. This 'set' of disparate personalities has helped plan my study programme and monitor my progress through the course. Initially they seemed to have nothing to offer me but within a short space of time my attitude had changed. While they had no right of veto over my work plan (or 'contract'), they put me through some hoops trying to justify it. Issues of my own personal and professional development were brought together to construct a learning contract that has become important to me.

(Maher,[8] p.1)

The most important element of the course for me has been the set. Without that vehicle, the problems I had would possibly never have been raised let alone so thoroughly and effectively worked on. The set becomes different things to different people, but, for me, some of those things are—a sounding board for ideas; a confessional for a variety of problems, many of which could not be discussed as fully at work for reasons of both vested interest and time; sometimes an uncomfortable put-on-the-spot experience where I have really had to face up to my own responsibility for my actions; and an invaluable support group. The other members of my set would have other perspectives, but we are all agreed that that experience has been the most powerful throughout the whole course.

The process is also about taking risks. The ethos is about change and change can only happen if you are prepared to take risks. The set helps you to take risks as indeed does the whole 'Community', i.e. the other members of all the other sets in both the first and second years.

(Atkins,[2] p. 18)

Learning community

The last sentence in the quote from Liz Atkins above leads us from sets into the idea of a learning community. Peter Maher comments:

The community—staff and students—exercises control over the way that the course develops. This forum, which now numbers fifty souls, is the arena for debate about any issue relating to groups or individuals. It also provides a resource for learning and allows participants with common interests or goals to learn together or share experiences.

(Maher,[8] p. 1)

The example above is from a programme in a higher education setting. But in-organization programmes also develop as a learning community, e.g. in Hiram Walker, Shell, BBC and British Airways. In all these organizational programmes participants did not just draw on their set for support, learning, risk taking and stimulation, they also used the wider community of all the sets in the programme. The use of this wider community is not essential to SML, but there is no doubt that it not only assists individual learning, but also supports the development of a learning business. As people see that they can draw on these wider resources for learning they start to reach out to others in the organization.

Hence, the notion of a learning community in SML ideally broadens to encompass the whole organization (though this is not easy to achieve). I want to emphasize that the learning community idea fostered in SML is not like a closed clique. It is to do with broader development. However, I have drawn on the ideas of others in developing the use of the learning community in SML. Pedler's review of the field is particularly valuable. His definition of a learning community is helpful. He says it 'involves bringing together a group of people as peers to meet personal learning needs primarily through a sharing of resources and skills offered by those present'[12] (p. 68). His paper elaborates the points in this definition and he shows how five activities are required, namely:

1. *Building the climate:* establishing openness, interdependence and mutuality.
2. *Sharing needs:* of all the persons present and the legitimacy of these individual needs.
3. *Providing resources:* both without but particularly within the persons present.
4. *Community planning:* to establish a 'programme' to meet needs, share resources, to learn and develop.
5. *Evaluation:* identifying criteria for success; looking at where we've come from, where to go next; resolving conflicts'.

(Pedler,[12] p.69)

In SML, in addition to the focus on personal needs, there is the linkage to organizational needs. Through the use of learning contracts and other mechanisms SML makes it easier for a learning community to work effectively. For instance, people work out their needs in a set such that their interactions with colleagues in the wider community outside their sets are more focused and clear.

Networking

The learning community can facilitate networking. Networking may be

- within the learning community
- outside it.

In either case SML encourages people to explore wider resources, and link with a range of people. Sets can be especially helpful in encouraging people to develop new contacts, and to use others to assist their learning.

Assisting learning   Part of the collaborative activity in SML is assisting others to learn. Sets and learning communities only work really well when participants see that they can

- assist colleagues in their learning
- ask for assistance for themselves.

Interestingly, in many organizational cultures asking is more difficult than giving. People can feel inhibited to ask for assistance if it implies a weakness. This is especially a factor in macho power cultures: you are a wimp if you do not demonstrate total self-reliance.

But SML is not about such individualistic modes of operating. A learning business cannot develop without asking and giving. Another imbalance is in social services, education and other 'helping professions'. So-called 'helping professionals' can exhibit a pathological desire to help others—to give unstintingly of themselves so that they smother other people. They can need as much assistance as the macho manager in recognizing the value of asking.

In order to get this balance (and to do many other things) SML programmes delineate the role of staff as 'learning assistants'. In sets the role is usually described as 'set adviser'. In one-to-one work the assister may be called a mentor or a coach, and in I shall discuss these roles more fully in Part Five. However, I would like to re-emphasize here the role of 'peer assisting'. In some programmes we have encouraged people to assume the role of 'co-set adviser'. In the post-graduate diploma already mentioned, second-year course members would volunteer to work with a member of staff in co-set advising a first-year set.

Liz Atkins indicates the value of this:

> There is opportunity also within the programme for course members to take the role of set adviser. I became a set adviser to a first year set in my second year as part of my contract was about improving my set advising skills. This was an invaluable

experience which has helped me at both the technical level of acquiring skills and at the personal development level of getting feedback from both the set and the set adviser on the way I function. I am continuing to act as set adviser for that set although I have finished the course and am continuing to grow and develop through it.

(Atkins[2] p. 18)

What Liz Atkins does not mention is the value to those in their first year. They have indicated, in evaluations, how helpful it can be to have someone present who can model being a self managing learner, and who can show how peer assisting can work. It is also important in the programme to show how the authority role of staff can be de-emphasized by trusting second year participants to work with staff in this way. However, to make this process work requires the development of co-set advisers. On the post-graduate diploma programme we held a two-day workshop every year for co-set advisers, we developed a pack of materials for their use, we held regular meetings of all set advisers throughout the year to review progress, and co-set advising pairs (staff plus second year) met after each set meeting to review their own working. Set advising does not just come naturally, and Part Five emphasizes the importance in SML of getting this activity right.

Assessment

Assessment in this context is about assessing learning. Specifically, in SML it is important for learners to assess if they have achieved the objectives identified in the learning contract. However, as indicated in the last chapter, individuals almost always learn more than is in their contract. This also may need recognizing. So at the end of an organized programme the learner, in conducting a self-assessment, may raise wider issues than those in the learning contract. Also a set may agree some common 'framing' goals, such as that all members of the set need to be conscious of their own learning and be able to make self-assessments. These framing goals are, as implied, a way of providing a frame or a series of parameters for assessment. They indicate what the assessment is about and in what context it is undertaken. A particular 'given' in SML is the expectation of collaborative assessment. This means that the person's self-assessment is checked with

- peers (usually the set)
- a set adviser
- those external to the set (for example, mentor, boss).

Also, in a programme for an educational qualification, such as a diploma or Master's degree, the role of external examiner/assessor/validator must be accommodated.

The basic issues of collaborative assessment are explored elsewhere,[13] and will not be repeated here. Rather, I shall refer to a few specific factors that affect SML practice as described in this book. Firstly, however, I shall present two quotes to set the scene.

> Finally the style of assessment. The parallel has been drawn between the set and jury trial. The jury, unusually, includes the defendant, who not only has an opportunity to frame opinion, but also has a vote! The assessment is no less rigorous for this. Past experience has shown that the harshest critic is often the very set member whose work is being assessed.
>
> (Maher[8], p. 1)

> Now, after two years of this learning experience I have accepted Self Managed Learning at an affective level. I have felt the process and lived with it and through it, and it is now becoming a way of life. I cannot accept that the final assessment is in any way final. It is to me merely a statement of where I have got to by that particular moment. I feel no more 'qualified' now than I was when I started. The programme has simply begun the process of opening up paths of learning and has helped me choose for two years the path to follow. It has also given me an internal mechanism to help me choose paths for the future by providing me with insight into how I learn and, therefore, how I should tackle my own learning problems. It has given me greater insight and understanding of how others learn and, therefore, I hope has made me more aware and empathetic in my work to the different needs of others. I accept total responsibility for my own learning—if it does not happen then it is my own fault.
>
> By the same token if I want things to happen in my life then I accept that I must make them happen and not sit around blaming others for lack of activity.
>
> Although from an assessment point of view I say that I do not feel 'qualified' I can honestly say that a very different person left the course from the one that started it. For one thing I am no longer a down-trodden, frustrated Training Officer for I achieved my objective of becoming an independent consultant. And what's more I was able to make the final leap into the unknown with a greater sense of confidence and knowing where I was going. The outside world, when I at last stepped into it, did not seem nearly so alarming and risky as it had once appeared. I very much doubt that I would ever have made that step without having followed the programme and I also doubt that I would have completed a programme which was more prescriptive.
>
> (Atkins,[2] p. 18)

Views of the collaborative assessment process

I have discussed with learners their views of the process. They have *all* said that this approach is preferable to any other (all of them have, of course, experienced traditional modes already, so their comparison is with those approaches). Many approach the assessment process with trepidation, but afterwards most agree that it was valuable and helpful. Some have even said that it was 'the high spot of the year' in that they could experience a culmination of their work in a context where they could get live feedback. Some specific positive points mentioned have been:

1. It gives face-to-face contact so that people are treated as human beings.
2. The person being assessed by others can comment on the judgements of others. There can be a dialogue which can resolve misunderstandings.
3. The individual has to justify his or her own work to others and confront his or her own judgement with those of others.
4. It is all open and above board.
5. When someone is presenting work which is not in the traditional mode (for example, creative work) then it can be most easily discussed in this context.

Some negative points have been:

1. It takes time to do it properly.
2. It does not necessarily reduce stress and tension. Some people still feel nervous facing their colleagues even when they have come to know them well.

Standards

On programmes leading to a qualification, people get concerned about issues of level or standard. They want to know what makes diploma or Master's level work. They are concerned about equivalence. As everyone is doing different things, how can each person be measured against the same standard? Addressing this problem forms a key discussion in sets. Learners need to recognize that in traditional educational programmes there is no guarantee of equivalence and similar standards applying across all courses. In the Minutes of a meeting of the Convocation of the University of London on Tuesday, 12 May 1981, the following exchange is recorded:

Question

What are the procedures whereby it is ensured, as far as reasonably possible, that the same class of degree is granted by the University for work of equivalent quality in different faculties and subjects, both at first degree and higher levels; and how is a comparison of quality made in relation to such different disciplines as, for example, Geography and English?

Answer

While the establishment of exact equivalence of standards in widely different fields may be a matter of legitimate aspiration, the University makes no claim that its procedures can achieve it.

This is the only honest answer possible. Even in the same subject area there is no guarantee of equivalent standards in research degrees such as PhDs where each person is doing something different. So an SML programme throws up no new issues in this area. What it does, however, is to make the subjective, messy side of assessment more transparent. It is exposed to scrutiny by giving set members responsibility for assessment.

Criteria

People normally find it difficult to come up with specific, measurable criteria by which to judge work. This is not surprising given that (a) most people have not been asked to do this before coming on an SML programme and (b) it is difficult to tie down criteria for everything one does. I think people can beneficially struggle with this issue, but it also needs sets to recognize that some criteria will be more readily measurable than others. I do not take the view that if it cannot be measured it cannot be important. The most important things in life often cannot be measured—like love or artistic ability. We cannot expunge these from organizational life just because they cannot be neatly tied down.

Evaluation

Evaluation is the other judgement process to set alongside assessment. Evaluation is of the worth and value of a programme or activity. SML programmes covering many hundreds of managers have been evaluated since 1980. I have, in this chapter, quoted from published comments of individual managers about the post-graduate diploma in management (by SML) at what is now the University of East London. I chose these comments because they have been published and are therefore accessible. Evaluation of SML programmes creates no different issues from evaluation in general, and I have commented elsewhere on evaluation research.[14] A model piece of research evaluating SML was carried out in British Airways.[15] I say it was a model because the perspectives of participants, managers, HR staff and mentors were obtained, hence drawing together a wide range of views. Also, the evaluation covered recent graduates from the programme as well as those who had finished a year earlier.

This latter point is important. Often we have had evaluation reports months after a programme where managers have said that they were only just appreciating the full benefits of their learning. A contrary situation has occurred in more than one organization where evaluation was carried out in the middle of a programme. In SML this can be a disaster. If participants have not seen through their learning contract, evaluation is of limited use. It is not like a modular course where it is possible to evaluate each module in turn after it has happened.

An aspect of evaluation which is often lost is the need to evaluate at different levels. Here the U model comes into play. A programme needs evaluating as to:

- *Purposes and principles*—are they appropriate?
- *Strategies*—have they worked?
- *Tactics*—have they worked?
- *Actions*—were they as planned, and appropriate?

From a range of studies, evaluation of purposes and principles is almost wholly positive. People say that they want the autonomy of an SML programme. They welcome the chance to own their own learning. The only negative notes have occasionally come from traditional, power-oriented senior managers who are less interested in organizational performance and more interested in controlling their employees.

On some programmes there have been concerns about strategy. In one organization participants were critical of the company for not integrating the SML programme into company practice. They felt let down by senior management. However, these criticisms grow less over time as organizations start to see the merit of a more strategic approach to learning.

Tactical evaluation is usually very positive. People like the concept of sets and they usually welcome the idea of learning contracts. However, at the action level a few concerns are expressed. About 3–5 per cent of sets struggle and never achieve high levels of trust and openness. At assessment, around 1–2 per cent of participants have significant problems. The percentage of those who fail is higher than this, at around 5 per cent: however, only some 'fails' create ongoing difficulties (that is, that they are unhappy with the outcome). While I always hope (and aim) for zero per cent problems, I am comforted by the fact that in evaluating appraisal systems and assessment centres, the levels of dissatisfaction are typically much higher.

Summary

This chapter has explored some aspects of typical SML programmes from a tactical perspective. I have indicated how the strategic processes in the previous chapter can be put into practice. The one area I have largely omitted is that of the role of 'staff', such as set advisers, mentors, etc. This issue will be central to the next part of the book.

Notes

1. Lao Tsu (1972) *Tao Te Ching* (translated by Gia-Fu Feng and Jane English), London: Wildwood House. (This is one of the most accessible translations, but there are many more.)
2. Atkins, L. (1983) 'Self managed learning at the Anglian Regional Management Centre', *Group Relations* (Winter), 7–21.
3. Clutterbuck, D. (1983) 'Cheating—and making better managers', *Observer Business*, (Sunday 28 August), 16.
4. Miller, A.G., Gallanter, E. and Pribram, K.M. (1960) *Plans and the Structure of Behaviour*, New York: Holt, Rinehart & Winston.
5. Lee, B. (1985) 'Learner-centred courses—a personal experience', *Management Education and Development*, 16, 1 (Spring), 31–40.
6. Skilton, M. (1982) 'Self managed learning—a manager's report on his management course', *LGTB Training Newsletter* (Nov./ Dec.), 4.
7. Boldero, N. (1981) 'Self managed learning: a personal view', *The Training Officer* (October), 292.
8. Maher, P. (1984) 'SML: it changed my life', *ARMC Newsletter* (February) 1.
9. Knowles, M. (1986) *Using Learning Contracts*, San Francisco: Jossey-Bass.
10. Steiner, C. (1974) *Scripts People Live*, New York: Bantam.
11. Maclean, C.A. (1978) *Sets and Tutorials*, North East London Polytechnic, Working Paper.
12. Pedler, M. (1981) 'Developing the learning community', in Boydell, T. and Pedler, M. (eds) *Management Self-Development: Concepts and Practices*, Farnborough, Hants: Gower.
13. My own writing on assessment has included:
    (a) Cunningham, I. (1991) 'Case studies in collaborative assessment', in Dove, P. and Brown, S. (eds) *Self and Peer Assessment*, SCED Paper 63.

(b) Cunningham, I. and Dawes, G. (1990) 'Is objective assessment rigorous enough', paper to Ashridge Management College Research Conference (January).

(c) Cunningham, I. (1981) 'Assessment and experiential learning'. Paper to Fifth International Conference on Higher Education, University of Lancaster (September).

(d) The above paper was modified and published (with the same title) in Boot, R. and Reynolds, M. (eds) (1983) *Learning and Experience in Formal Education*, University of Manchester: Manchester Monograph.

(e) There is reference to assessment in Cunningham, I. (1981) 'Self managed learning and independent study', in Boydell, T. and Pedler, M. (eds) *Management Self-Development: Concepts and Practices*, Farnborough, Hants: Gower.

I would also recommend, Heron, J. (1979) *Assessment Revisited*, London: British Postgraduate Medical Federation, for an excellent theoretical analysis of assessment issues.

14. (a) Cunningham, I. (1991) 'Action learning for chief executives', in Pedler, M. (ed.) *Action Learning in Practice*, 2nd edn, Farnborough, Hants: Gower.

(b) Cunningham, I. (1988) 'Interactive holistic research', in Reason, P. (ed.) *Human Inquiry in Practice*, London: Sage.

15. Fraser, J. (1988) *An Evaluation of Self Managed Learning in Practice*, Berkhamsted, Herts: Ashridge Management College.

PART FIVE

PRACTICE

The three chapters in this part cover some key practical issues. Chapter 9 discusses 'staff' roles and the role of assisting learning. The chapter emphasizes the role of the other person or persons in linking with learners. Chapter 10 discusses the learner in context. Chapter 11 concludes the book by looking at directions in strategic learning, including issues for organizations and for individuals. It also discusses directions for self managed learning.

9   Roles in learning and change

Introduction
Strategic learning, the development of learning businesses and the operation of self managed learning, does not just happen by saying it ought to. I realize that this would be taken as obvious by most people. Yet much of the literature on learning organizations and cultural change seems implicitly to assume that change will happen because someone says it should. Books and articles say it is a good thing, and gurus exhort managers to change through charismatic performances. Yet it is not obvious that these methods on their own bring results. I am not suggesting that the analyses of theorists and the expositions of gurus are valueless. They can energize people and inspire them to want change. But something more is needed—a lot more in fact.

One part of this 'more' is the role of people such as top/senior managers, HR/personnel professionals, management developers and consultants. Part of the change process is bringing together the strategic alliances mentioned in the opening chapters of this book. We need those:

- who can
- who know
  and
- who care

to work together to assist change to occur. It is clear if one analyses the situation in organizations against the above framework that specialists such as management developers cannot produce change on their own. (The wider dimensions of managing change belong outside this book.) So let us assume that top management has agreed to a strategic learning policy and wants self managed learning programmes. (Such an example was quoted in Chapter 1 on the

Hiram Walker Group.) What is now required to make it happen?

The thesis in this chapter is that specific people need to play particular roles in making it happen. These people may be all from personnel/HR departments, but this is seldom the case. The roles I shall describe could be seen as 'professional' roles and I am comfortable with the term professional if it is used in a loose way (and implies the opposite of 'amateur'). I am not comfortable with professionalism as an élitist, closed shop model of working. This latter model undermines strategic learning, and I shall comment on it later. Another term I have used earlier is 'practitioner'. This is looser and perhaps more user friendly.

The labels to try to describe all the roles are often inadequate, so let me, instead of labouring this, introduce the four roles that, from research[1] and experience, describe all that must be done and all that is needed to be done. These are:

- theorist
- designer
- manager
- assistant.

Theorists provide the theory for action.
Designers design programmes and activities.
Managers manage them.
Assistants assist learners to learn.

These roles can be played by one person (though rarely), by small teams or by a dispersed range of people. Let me explain each in turn before returning to the overall theory.

Learning theorist

The learning theorist (LT) role is essentially about

(a) creating and developing
(b) reviewing and synthesizing
(c) articulating

the theory underpinning any programme.

All programmes are based on theory: in this context theories of learning and theories of managing. (Burgoyne[2] provides a good analysis of the major schools of thought on learning which underpin management development programmes.) Often the basic theory is not made explicit, particularly in traditional management development courses. But a 'theory' is, nevertheless, there.

It is worth emphasizing that there are three aspects to the LT role. 'Theory creating' may be, in its full-blooded sense, relatively rare. However, 'theory review' and 'theory articulation' have to be more widespread. Every planning or development team starting up a programme needs to articulate theory. For instance, in SML there is an understood theory related to learning, part of which I have indicated in earlier chapters. In traditional management courses, when people say 'We should have a session in the course on X' they are implicitly saying something about a theory of managing (e.g., to be an effective manager you need to know X). The problem is that 'theory articulation' is often done implicitly, and one has to dig beneath the surface statements to understand the base theory.

In SML, underlying theory is more likely to be articulated in an explicit way. Indeed, it is often argued about in great detail in planning teams.

The issue of theory links back to earlier discussions of mapping. Theory provides the basis for mapping. If an organization is serious about becoming a learning business, developing sufficient shared maps becomes important. (I say 'sufficient' because it does not need total uniformity–nor is it possible.) The LT role is key to developing shared maps. Effective CEOs that I have studied have had clear theoretical bases to their work and have usually made these relatively explicit. They do not, however, tend to use academic language, so the point that they are good theorizers is often missed. For instance, they tend to communicate in metaphors and analogies or in visual models. A good theoretician CEO can provide a back drop for practitioners to develop specific theories about· learning and about managing. In SML programmes both are important. Managers need to develop an understanding of learning issues so they need a theory *of* strategic learning. They also need a theory *for* strategic learning, for example, theories of managing.

A theory *of* strategic learning includes issues discussed in earlier chapters, such as:

- first-order and second-order learning
- theories of good learning.

Theories *for* strategic learning include:

- the U model linking purpose, strategy, tactics and action

- the triangle model linking questions of Why?, What?, How? and Who?

Practitioners such as management developers and consultants working on SML programmes need to be able to work with such theories. They need to be able to use theories and models with comfort in planning programmes and in working with managers on programmes. This is not to say that such theories have to be articulated in the way it has been done here. Each practitioner will integrate theory and practice in their own way. This is the mark of the 'centred' practitioner.[3]

Learning designer

I take 'design' to be the process whereby the 'theory' is fleshed out in order to provide a basis for action. The learning designer (LD) role is often written about, but seldom analysed. Some of those who have commented on it usefully include Garratt, Harrison and Morris.[4]

The term is used in a metaphorical sense, since one does not literally design a product. I think this is a problem with the concept as it can give a false concreteness to the idea of 'a programme' which has been 'designed' by someone (and made by that person or someone else).

Despite the difficulties with the metaphor, I want to use it because

(a) it is what has been used by others, and changing the language is a problem
(b) I cannot think of a better term.

I want to define 'design' closer to Harrison's[4] use of the term than to Morris's[4] more restricted use. The latter talks of:

> trust-based negotiation, which aspires after the condition of a gentlemen's agreement, and design-based negotiation, which always seeks formal commitment on details. (It seems no accident that 'designing' and 'calculating' are applied to people that we do not feel we can trust!)

I believe that design can be a mutual activity: the staff and manager(s) can design a programme together. I do take Morris's point that tightly defined prestructured courses may be predicated on low trust assumptions, and I am not in favour of rigid pre-timetabled designs.

However, in my wider use of the term, no matter how loose the structure of the programme, it is a design. We can have a 'non-design design' as the designer (non-metaphorical) Massimo Vignelli suggests. Even to call together a group of managers and say 'choose what you want to do' is a design. (It might be labelled a non-design design, but it is a design.)

A useful distinction might be between macro design and micro design.

Macro design is related to the totality of developing strategic learning and the structure of activities to achieve it. So practitioners in an organization could design a strategy based on the strategic processes discussed earlier, namely:

- preparing
- resourcing
- collaborating
- judging.

The micro design of events within this overall strategy might be left more in the hands of others.

In the last chapter I have shown aspects of design such as:

- the use of sets
- the use of a learning community
- the use of learning contracts (as individual designs).

Each of these elements provides the basis for micro design work. A staff team may do this prior to launching the programme. Once the programme starts it is possible to work on the kind of trust basis that Morris suggests.

A learning contract is an example of micro design. While needing to be written in order that other set members can read it, it is very much taken on trust by each set. There is no pressure from staff for course members to produce a carefully set-out and immutable design; rather the set to which the person belongs needs to have some idea of what the person is aiming to do so that it can be of most help to the individual. Thus the micro design (by the learner) of a learning programme, which constitutes the contract, is seen as an attempt to think through ideas, but not as an immutable document.

In engaging in design activity, one draws on the following, in addition to theory:

- client needs
- economics—for example, cost-effectiveness
- social factors, including what is allowable in the norms of a society

- methodology available—that is, what can be done
- staff capability
- time factors

and so on. Designing requires considerable capability and wisdom, though I hope that the chapters in Part Four of this book can assist designers.

Design work generally tends to be done by 'professionals', for example, consultants and management developers. This makes sense. Designing for learning is not usually part of the capability of a line manager, except where we are involved in elements such as learning contracts.

Learning manager

If one articulates a theory and a design which could be the basis of a programme, in order to operationalize that theory and design, a programme has to be established and run. This is where the role of the learning manager (LM) comes in. I further subdivide this role into two: one I shall label 'Fronting' and one 'Back-up'. The spatial metaphor is reasonable to use if one perceives the programme as delineating a bounded 'learning experience'. It can be presented in diagrammatic form, as in Figure 9.1.

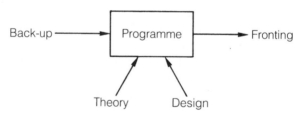

Figure 9.1   Managing learning

This shows that the theory and design provide the basis for the programme and fronting and back-up are in direct relationship to the programme.

'Fronting' covers the following kinds of functions and activities:

1. The initiator role, a term used in action learning, see Pedler.[5]
2. The leadership role, in terms of, say, leading a staff team which sets up a programme.
3. Most of Mintzberg's[6] ten managerial roles (liaison, figurehead, spokesman, negotiator, entrepreneur, resource allocator, disturbance handler, leader, monitor, dissemi-

nator) in so far as any of them would be relevant to a particular programme.
4. Political activity, specifically the preparational work necessary to set up a programme.[7]

Some of the above relates to setting up a programme (for example, initiating and planning) but other factors are relevant during the operation of a programme. This tends to be underestimated in the self-development literature, and may be a factor as to why there is sometimes little follow-through of programmes (for example, they do not tend to be recorded so it is difficult to know the extent of them).

Another factor in hindering programme efficiency is the lack of recognition of the 'back-up' role. This covers:

• administration—for example, getting material posted on time, etc.
• registry-type activity—admitting people to a programme (more relevant in institutional settings usually)
• finance/budgeting, etc.
• technical support—for example, with equipment such as VTR, computers, etc.
• premises organization—booking rooms, etc.
• learning resource back-up—handouts, materials, library facilities, audio-visual material, computer access, etc.
• secretarial—DTP, photocopying, filing, etc.

Some people have assumed that an SML programme implies that the boring administration is less relevant. They equate 'administration' with 'bureaucracy', which is not necessarily so. Bureaucracy describes a particular theory or style of organization: administration is necessary whatever organization theory one works upon.

In some cases, especially in educational institutions, much of this back-up role is passed on to other staff. However, in other programmes this is not so.

I shall refer to these two roles by abbreviation:

Learning manager (fronting) = LM(F)
Learning manager (back-up) = LM(B)

LM(F) has tended to be seen as the glamorous side of managing and LM(B) has been largely ignored in the literature. This may partly be due to the fact that it is relatively easy to see what skills and abilities are necessary to perform the LM(B) role. However, I think it is also related to the lower status given to non-academic/non-professional trainer staff in organizations. Hence, I suspect that some people would not even see LM(B) a part of SML work. I obviously disagree with this view.

Learning assistant

The learning assistant (LA) role is the aspect of SML work concerned with face-to-face interaction with learners. Set advisers and mentors come within this category. When one set advises, the role is defined through interaction with learners. This makes this role different from the other three (LT, LD and LM) as they do not *require* direct contact with learners. Learning theorists and designers do not have to see the learners for whom they have theorized and designed, though such theory/design activity would eventually become sterile without contact with learners. However, in relation to a *particular* programme, theorist and designer may rely on research evidence collected by others to get feedback.

Learning managers may also 'front' a programme to get it started and provide back-up facilities, but not meet course members. This may be especially so when a steering group has been set up to initiate a programme: not all steering group members need necessarily meet learners. So the LA role is uniquely defined as *requiring* face-to-face contact with learners, and, as I have defined the other three roles, at one level one can say: the LA does the rest. However, before saying something about the concept as a whole, I should perhaps say a little more about the 'assisting' process, as assisting is not a readily accepted concept. I take 'assisting' as a noble, valued, time-honoured process in human communities. Parents assist their children to learn; a person assists another person with a job that is too big for them; children assist their parents with housework and gardening. Someone assisted me to learn to drive; my accountant assists me with my finances. Note that I want to define professionals in general as 'assistants', as I wish to play down the power that they have accumulated to themselves. Negative aspects of professionalization include:

1. Changing processes to nouns. So instead of 'need' being a verb it becomes a noun. People have come to have 'needs' which have to be met by professionals, as in 'training needs'. In the process professionals redefine what a person wants to learn into their own language.
2. Successful clients are those who are able to satisfy the professional. In a well-known management college course participants were given a secret rating by trainers and this

was put on file for future reference. This rating was linked to the extent to which participants had learned what the trainers wanted them to learn.

3. Professionals define what are legitimate problems.
4. Management educators in business schools limit what can be addressed by the subjects they are able to teach.

Functional LA activity in strategic learning and SML is such that one can take categorization one stage further and identify:

• LA (problem/person based), i.e. LA(P)
• LA (solution/subject based), i.e. LA(S).

LA(P) is the set adviser-type role: the person who works with a group (but also possibly individuals) and works with them on their problems. The LA(P) is not there to teach or train in any standard sense, but to assist others with what is relevant to them, and in the process help them to learn.

LA(S) is a legitimate role. It is sometimes undervalued in the pendulum swing towards rejection of expertise. In the postgraduate diploma mentioned in Chapter 8, LA(S)s were called 'specialist tutors' and their role was to respond to the requirements of learners who wished to tap into their expertise. Thus in a set meeting a person may identify that they need to learn about accountancy. The set adviser (LA(P) may then help them to identify different ways of learning about accountancy. These might include: reading books, watching videos/films, listening to tapes, or using a staff member to tutor them on the problems that they have identified. The learner chooses the mode they want to use (or more than one mode if needed): many choose to go to tutors to get their advice. The sequence in this is (crudely):

1. Define the problem.
2. Look for the solutions (if necessary).

At stage 1, LA(P) *assists* in defining the problem; at stage 2 LA(S) *assists* with providing solutions. LA(P)s ask questions; LA(S)s answer them (approximately). Table 9.1 elaborates on this.

This process reverses the usual order in teaching/training, where the manager learns solutions (subjects) and then has to find problems to use them on.

In such a process one only needs one staff role, that of teacher, as learners are left to fend for themselves in finding applications for the knowledge and skills they learn.

Table 9.1   Learning assisting-roles

LA (P)s	LA (S)s
Assist learners as *persons* to define *problems* Assisting them to change basic *patterns* and *processes*	Assist learners to develop *solutions* to problems by drawing on *specialisms* and *subjects* or using *systems* Learners may also learn *skills*

It is worth noting that traditional teachers are well able to play the LA(S) role, but this is not traditional teaching. The learner goes to the LA(S) with their requirements, and ideally the latter responds to what the person asks for. This does not always work out that way, of course.

It is possible to argue that the LA(S) role does not require face-to-face interaction with learners. Certainly Open University type courses provide tutorial guidance for learners by mail or on the telephone, and in their context the 'expert' can operate at a distance. Also, people with expertise can make such expertise available by writing articles/handouts, making tapes, etc. In the context of SML activity I doubt that the expertise can be solely dealt with in this way. The essence of SML programmes is that managers should be able to pursue concerns of their own, which they may well conceptualize in their own language and not in that of the subject specialist. Hence, managers often find the written/packaged material produced by management teachers and trainers difficult to access.

Standardized material on its own without an efficient access system can be of low usefulness. Hence, face-to-face interaction is usually necessary as managers find it helpful to talk through their problems and have a dialogue with 'an expert' (LA(S)) rather than just passively absorb information. At its simplest level, the LA(S) can of course advise the individual on the standardized material (books, tapes, etc.) that would be useful in relation to that person's problems.

In the above, I have defined roles, not persons. One person may play both roles, as long as the roles emerge roughly in the order indicated (problem to solution). In the post-graduate diploma course we had a rule that the LA(P) to a course member could not also act as that member's LA(S) (that is, in an official capacity). That does not preclude a set adviser from offering knowledge to a set member, if needed, during the process of a set. We rejected the pseudo-Rogerian mode of the LA(P) merely making reflective or process comments. If I know something, and I am asked about it, I shall give an honest answer and not deflect the question onto another staff member.

Assisting and facilitating

Many see the set adviser as a 'facilitator' and draw on interpretations of the work of Carl Rogers to justify a particular facilitative stance in sets (and other learning environments). In its common, everyday use or in its dictionary definitions, there is not much wrong with facilitating. Making something easier for someone seems a good activity.

However, in the training profession, facilitation has become a noun and 'Facilitators' have gained a particular status. My concerns about the new profession of facilitation include the following:

1. There is a gross misunderstanding of Rogerianism around. Carl Rogers was seen as demanding therapists and counsellors to adopt a dogmatic non-directive approach, and this was linked to his ideas on facilitating learning. Brink comments:

   In Germany, all counsellor education consists of bureaucratically controlled training in non-directive technique. Rogers' offers to meet with the leaders and participate in training seminars have been declined. It appears as though he is seen as a threat. Here, in New England, a two-year masters' program in counsellor education drills its students in reflection skills. One of their graduates, a gifted young man, unusually warm, sensitive, bright, insightful, finished the program having been stripped down to an efficient echoing device; *he* had largely disappeared. Instead of the program having been a growth experience for him, he was diminished by it as a person and as a professional.

   (Brink,[8] p. 32)

   Rogers, in response to this, wrote:

   I totally agree with Brink in deploring the inauthentic, mechanical, wooden, dogmatic, client-centred therapist. In fact, I probably feel worse about such therapists than they do, because

I feel personally offended. But I equally deplore dogmatism and rigidity in any therapist of whatever persuasion.'

(Rogers,[9] p. 33)

2. Facilitators may attempt to deny responsibility *to* learners. They pretend to be just one of the group and deny that they have a specific role apart from 'non-directive' 'catalytic' remarks.

3. Facilitators can get over-obsessed with group process. Sets are there to assist learners to learn what they (learners) decide. Facilitators can overemphasize the set as an entity beyond its basic role. If the set is working well, 'process comments' are not necessary.

4. Learners can get 'facilitated' whether they want it or not. The worst excesses of this include the promotion by trainers of inappropriate secondary feedback. Note the following interaction reported in Clark *et al.*[10] (p. 37).

Trainer:	What are you doing, Jim?
Jim:	(Who has been silent and looks very tense) I'm thinking.
Trainer:	Tell me what you are thinking.
Jim:	I'm trying to find the right words to give Peter (another trainee) some feedback.
Trainer:	How about taking the risk of giving feedback using the wrong words?
Jim:	OK . . . Peter, I don't like you.
Trainer:	Are those the right words, Jim?
Jim:	Yes (smiling). That's what I wanted to say.

5. Facilitators can get into 'Rescuing'. This term has a technical meaning in Transactional Analysis, developed from the work of Stephen Karpman. James and Jongward[11] interpret 'Rescuing' as maintaining dependence under the guise of helping. Steiner[12] argues that Rescuers believe people cannot really help themselves. He suggests that Rescuing reaffirms and maintains inappropriate power imbalances. He proposed

(a) do not help without a contract to do so
(b) do not believe other people are helpless
(c) assist others to find their own power
(d) do not do most of the work (in an assisting relationship).

My own mapping of the relationship of the main approaches to helping people to learn is shown in Figure 9.2.

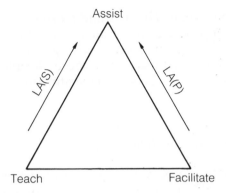

Figure 9.2   The assisting role: a map

The implication of this figure is that there are three major processes being used. I have argued in favour of assisting rather than teaching or facilitating. However, the boundaries of these processes are not neat. The teaching role shades in the direction of LA(S), as I've indicated earlier, when teachers give up teaching, in the didactic sense, and instead offer expertise and wisdom to learners in response to what learners ask for.

The facilitator role shades in the direction of LA(P) when facilitators see their role as helping learners to define their own problems and change their patterns of behaviour.

Assisting—Who?

Who assists learning is an open question. It does not have to be a designated practitioner. Sets encourage peer assisting. Bosses hopefully assist people who report to them.

Assisting—How?

There are many aspects of the how? of assisting (for a fuller analysis see my earlier research[1]). I shall indicate a few major ones here.

Legitimizing

Learners need their involvement in learning legitimized. If they leave their work place to attend a set meeting or meet up with a mentor, this has to be seen as a legitimate use of a person's time. The learning assistant, whether set adviser or mentor, can legitimize such time. This is especially necessary where an organization is moving away from the dominant use of training courses to a more flexible approach. Training courses tend to be seen as legitimate: other modes less so.

Supporting and stimulating

These two processes need to go together. There is significant research[13] to suggest that supporting on its own may lead to the learner feeling comfortable but not stimulated to learn. Stimulation only—the heavy pushing of someone to learn— can lead to burnout, stress and anxiety. Stimulating people to learn through challenging them can develop skills and abilities, but at a cost if there is little or no support. Figure 9.3 shows, simplistically, the linkages of support to satisfaction, and stimulus to satisfactoriness.

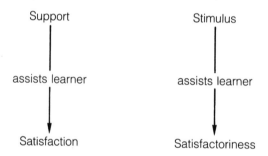

Figure 9.3   Support and stimulus

In other words, feeling good and performing well can be balanced. Balancing in this process can assist the kind of balance discussed in Chapter 5. Learners can be assisted in developing a 'both/and' rather than an 'either/or' view of the world.

Encouraging

The assistant encourages 'good learning'. This is not imposing on the learner, but helping people to open their eyes to new possibilities and to make these new possibilities real. Learners can see that they can become more capable, more wise, more centred and more grounded.

Modelling

The learning assistant can model 'good learning'. I am not saying that learning assistants are infinitely capable and wise, but that they are moving in this direction. They can show that it is possible to change through learning.

Trusting

The learning assistant needs to show appropriate trust. Set advisers need to show that they trust the set and the people in it. When they challenge learners it is not to try to take control, but to stimulate.

Linking

A set adviser can link members of the set to other learning possibilities. Set advisers may point the way to resources. A mentor may help someone to access other people in the organization in order to further their learning.

Intervening and responding

This is another balance. Some literature characterizes the set adviser as an 'interventionist'. The set adviser is viewed as making interventions in the set process, for example, to help the set to function better. This, like 'stimulating' discussed above, is a yang activity (in traditional Chinese philosophy); it is outgoing and active. However, as Taoist Chinese philosophers point out, this needs a yin balance. Yin is receptive, and open. So intervening needs balancing with responding. This is in fact confirmed in research. Set advisers will not just intervene, they will be asked questions and they need to know how to respond appropriately.[1]

Guarding

Set advisers are often in the role of guarding the principles of the processes used in SML. They may need to be vigilant to watch for any undermining of these principles—for example inappropriate controls creeping in. Also, senior managers who have promoted strategic learning may need to be continually monitoring progress and guarding against back-sliding.

Infilling

Often the set adviser's job in a set is to do what no one else is doing. If a set is very challenging and confronting, the set adviser's first role may be to show supportive behaviour in order to develop balance in the set. Similarly, a good boss will note those things that their direct reports are missing in their learning, and help them to find it. If a more junior member of staff is excellent at learning some things and not others, then the boss's attention may be focused on filling in the gaps.

Befriending

When someone is struggling with difficult and perhaps painful learning, maybe all they need at times is a friend—someone to talk to; a friendly ear. It sounds a simple remedy, but it is easily forgotten.

Meta-assisting

By this I mean assisting the process of assisting. Top managers do this when they create a culture conducive to learning, encourage senior managers to mentor their juniors, sponsor development programmes, etc. In an ideal world they might then be able to sit back and let it all happen. Except that ideal worlds rarely exist for long. The meta level processes need continual attention.

LA Style

Within the processes described there is the situation where each person has their own style of doing things. There are some common features and there are some differences. It can be interesting to study the different styles to recognize these similarities and differences. In my own research[1] I studied a number of people. In some cases I taped them talking about their style. Here are two examples for comparison.

Example A:

I try to tease out the task they (the learners) are working on—and sometimes help them to be aware of it from time to time.

I risk being disliked: I'm initially tough and difficult.

I confront personal difficulties between them and me.

I try to be silent a lot of the time—but it's difficult.

I try to be patient when they're struggling.

I share my understanding of what is going on at any time—test the validity of it. I'm prepared to be wrong sometimes.

I work when and where appropriate—I'm not likely to work in contexts which don't seem right.

I work by example as much as possible.

Example: B

My style is my predominant manner of working—what I do without thinking about it.

In groups this is what learners would say of me:

—remotish—warming up with time
—do rough work out loud
—tend to be obscure
—romantic
—belligerent and lethargic with bouts of excitement (intellectual and emotional).

My approach is to work towards shared responsibility—organizationally and conceptually (I prefer ideas that emerge rather than what comes from me).

I can easily (unhappily) slide to being directive—however mental untidiness and emotional unreliability saves the day—directiveness breaks down.

The two examples are edited from long tapes but they give a flavour of style issues.

Another way to explain this is through studying people who are particularly effective in special areas, especially sport. The advantage of sport as an arena of study is that results are generally quicker and more precise than in management. I can take as an example David Leadbetter, the golf coach, because the results of his students, such as Nick Faldo, are easy to see. Here are some quotes from an article on Leadbetter[14].

'He bases his teaching methods on the fact that no two players are identical.'

'You can't just say there is only one way to do it .... You tailor your instructions to the player' .... .

'David is a very introspective person, which may be to his detriment', Nick Price says. 'But if you disagree with something he encourages you to bring it up, to give him your opinion. He listens to you, tries to understand what you're saying and then guides you into an understanding of what he is talking about.'

Faldo cites Leadbetter's ingenuity in making practising more interesting .... Leadbetter is endlessly inventive in finding devices to help his pupils understand what he is trying to get them to achieve .... .

'I try to help players by getting inside their mind to see what they're thinking' Leadbetter says. 'Once you have established the ways in which you can help, the key is to explain them, give them concepts. But I always listen. I learn from these players. They are the greatest players in the world doing it under pressure. I want to know what works and what doesn't work'.

All of the above is *very* relevant to the set adviser, mentor or boss assisting someone else's learning in an organization.

Four roles: pulling it together

Figure 9.4 shows a way of linking the four roles. The four leaf clover shows how each leaf is part of one plant: the leaves do not have an existence of their own. The roles need to 'centre'

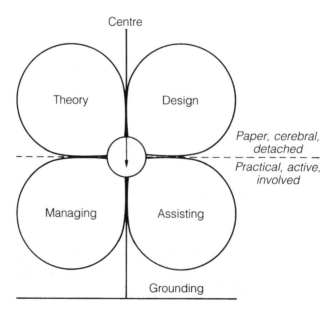

Figure 9.4　The four leaf clover

that is harmonize and balance, and then ground themselves (in values, in contexts, etc.). Figure 9.4 also shows that 'theory' and 'design' tend to be the more paper-based, cerebral, detached roles, and 'managing' and 'assisting' tend to be the more practical, active and involved roles.

The research evidence suggests that if the roles are played poorly then significant problems occur. Indeed, this is a major weakness of strategic learning and SML: it takes good people to make it work. It is much easier to run a learning/training activity on the reactive or bureaucratic models I discussed in Chapter 2. In standardized (bureaucratic) training procrustean tactics can force trainees into a fixed mould. Also, it is much simpler to ignore strategy and to muddle along. The challenge is that the tougher (strategic learning) route is going to be the one that ensures organizational survival and growth in the future.

Four roles theory

1. These four roles are all necessary even though some of them may be partially played out in absentia. This usually applies only in relation to theory and design—for example, learning managers may pick up and use theory and/or design already developed by others. However, someone will need to *articulate* the theory even if that person is not involved in its development. Hence, while someone may have done the theory *development*, if no one in, say, a planning group, is able to articulate clearly and accurately the theory upon which they are working, a genuine learning programme is unlikely. (How can someone design or plan (manage) anything without having a theory to base it upon?)
2. Roles are not necessarily fixed to individuals:
   (a) More than one person may be involved in playing a particular role; for example, there may be a team of LAs, a management team (LMs), etc.
   (b) More than one role may be played by the same person.
3. These roles are sufficient for SML programmes: one does not need any other roles to be played in order to run an effective programme.
4. These roles are interdependent: they do not stand alone. For this reason it may well be desirable for people to play multiple roles in order to ensure linkages. It seems to be a feature of effective practitioners that they are able to play multiple roles.
5. The roles need to be further subdivided. Specifically in LM, the fronting and back-up roles are distinctively

different. In LA, the problem/person-based (P) role is different from the subject/solution-based (S) role. Macro design is different from micro design.

6. People can play different roles and they can also play roles differently. The balance of roles played indicates something about

   Macro style

and the way the person plays a role says something about

   Micro style.

Thus one could say of someone that they are more interested and involved in theory and design issues than in managerial issues. This says something about that person's macro style. However, to define more clearly the person's style one would have to say *how* they played each role— for example, are they more theory creators (innovative, original); or more theory reviewers (good at synthesizing); or more theory articulators (good at understanding others' theories and seeing the relevance of a particular theory to specific situations); or all three?

All the above propositions are ones I have tested and they stand up.[1] The theory would need modifying or scrapping if such propositions were found to be invalid by others in future.

Learner involvement   Once a programme of learning has started there is the issue of the extent of learner involvement in the four roles. Let me run through them in turn:

LT   A programme is set up on the basis of a theory, and it seems difficult for learners to be involved in altering that theory. My research indicates that practitioners often tend to be quite fixed about the theory base of their work, and some explicitly said that if learners wished them to change the theory underpinning the programme into one closer to traditional management training, they would refuse to do it. This can be a source of confusion to learners who imagine that on an SML programme everything is open for negotiation. It is not.

LD   I have already stated that I think design should be relatively open for joint agreement. Learners often have problems with doing design; and in terms of design (as it affects a whole programme) I believe in joint action, where staff can contribute their expertise, but course members/learners have some power to say yes or no.

LM   The political aspect of 'Fronting' a course or programme tends usually to be played by staff, though learners need not be excluded from that role. Also, learners tend to prefer much of the tedious 'Back-up' work to be done by staff—for example, administrative work, resource acquisition, etc. In the mid range between these two, our experience has been that course members can be equally involved with staff. Indeed, in terms of strategic and tactical issues it is important that course members share in major decisions.

LA At one extreme there is the position which says that learners can and should do it all. Few people support this view. However, a key role for sets is to encourage learners to take on more responsibility in assisting others.

Value of the theory   I want to summarize here what I think is the value of the 'four roles' theory:
1. It provides a reasonably clear basis for categorizing practitioner activities.
2. It fits in with earlier theory I have discussed.
3. It does not prescribe the content of roles as they are variable and dependent on style. However, it does provide a prescription in terms of the need to consider the four factors.
4. As a result of the above, it provides a better basis for practitioner development.
5. It has been widely tested: it is neither armchair theorizing nor the result of a one-shot case study.
6. It provides an overview from which more detailed analysis can come—for example, the subdivision of roles already indicated.
7. It shows, in the model, the interdependent links, thus avoiding the notion of four separate distinct roles.
8. It provides a better way of characterizing the job of an academic in SML than the traditional administration/research/teaching split, especially by distinguishing LM(F) and LM(B) roles; by separating out teaching activity into LA(P) and LA(S); by showing where research (if it is for theory development) fits into the process; and by identifying 'design' as a key element.

Summary

This chapter has moved into the arena of implementation. It has made a specific case that four roles need to be played to make strategic learning and SML successful. It has also been acknowledged that programmes tend to fail if these roles are not carried out effectively.

Notes

1. Cunningham, I. (1984) *Teaching Styles in Learner Centred Management Development Programmes*. PhD Thesis, University of Lancaster.
2. Burgoyne, J.G. (1975) *Learning Theories and Design Assumptions in Management Development Programmes*, University of Lancaster: Centre for the Study of Management Learning
3. See: McLean, A.J. , Sims, D.B.P., Mangham, I.L. and Tuffield, D. (1982) *Organization and Development in Transition*, Chichester: Wiley. Also, see Cunningham, I.—note 1 above.
4. Garratt, R. (1983) 'The power of action learning', in Pedler, M. (ed.) *Action Learning in Practice*, Farnborough, Hants: Gower; Harrison, R. (1978) 'How to design and conduct self-directed learning experiences', *Group and Organization Studies*, 3, 2 (June), 149–167; Morris, J. (1980) 'Joint development activities: from practice to theory', in Beck, J. and Cox, C. (eds) *Advances in Management Education*, Chichester: Wiley.
5. Pedler, M. (ed.) (1983) *Action Learning in Practice*, Farnborough, Hants: Gower.
6. Mintzberg, H. (1973) *The Nature of Managerial Work*, New York: Harper & Row.
7. Cunningham, I. (1984) 'Planning to develop managers', *Management Education and Development*, 15, 2 (Summer), 83–104.
8. Brink, D.C. (1987) 'The issue of equality in the client- or person-centred approach', *Journal of Humanistic Psychology*, 27, 1 (Winter), 27–37.
9. Rogers, C.R. (1987) 'Comments on the issue of equality in psychotherapy', *Journal of Humanistic Psychology*, 27,1 (Winter), 38–40.
10. Clark, M., Phillips, K. and Barker, D. (1984) *Unfinished Business*, Farnborough, Hants: Gower.
11. James, M. and Jongeward, D. (1971) *Born to Win*, Reading, Mass: Addison-Wesley.
12. Steiner, C. (1974) *Scripts People Live*, New York: Bantam.
13. (a) See note 1 above
    (b) Smith, P.B. (1980) 'The T-group trainer: group facilitator or prisoner of circumstance?', *Journal of Applied Behavioural Science*, pp. 63–77.
    (c) McCrone, J. (1993) 'Is there a gene for genius?', *The Independent on Sunday*, 2 May, pp. 52–53.
14. Hopkins, J. (1992) 'The Mr Masterclass of golf', *The Independent*, 23 August, p. 24.

The learner in context

Introduction

This chapter focuses more on the learner. Firstly, I shall say something about the self managing learner, and then discuss issues of difference and diversity among people, specifically as they affect learning issues.

Self managing learner

Umberto Eco[1] in his essay *Reflections on 'The Name of the Rose'*, discussed how he came to write his famous novel *The Name of the Rose*, and his choices in the way he wrote it. He commented on the first 100 pages of the novel, which many readers had found tedious. These pages set the scene for the book's story of murder and intrigue in a monastery in the Middle Ages. Eco said that he wrote these pages in the way he did so that the reader could read what follows in the appropriate way. He wanted the reader to have to go at the pace of the monastery and to get into the spirit of the times. In short, he wanted to create a reader who could read in the way necessary to get the most from the book.

Eco's idea of 'creating a reader' has great relevance to our concerns here. In order to make strategic learning work we need to 'create learners' who can learn in appropriate ways. Learners who are comfortable with change, welcome it and see it as an opportunity to learn: learners who enjoy difference, like to visit other countries, welcome visitors from different cultures and like diversity in their organizations. Learners who can take calculated risks, but not stupid risks. Professional gamblers are those who know when to risk and when not. They prefer limited risks.

It is desirable to develop this learning pattern as early as possible in people's careers. A problem is that many graduates come from university with characteristics that make them poor learners in business settings. They have learned the ways of a distorted academia which values detachment, analysis, individualism (but not individuality), conformity and dependence.

I shall take as a text a paper by Indrei Ratiu[2] as this links to the other part of this chapter. He based his research on how international managers learn, and conducted an elegant study which is relevant to more general learning issues. His first step was to identify managers who seemed to be more 'international': people who were more interculturally adaptable. His study identified those people who were seen as particularly adaptable, flexible and open-minded in intercultural working. He then studied these exceptional performers especially from the point of view of key learning experiences.

This produced evidence of *patterns* which particularly distinguished international managers. These included:

- their views of what is 'international'
- their assumptions about the world and themselves
- their ways of dealing with stress
- their ways of making sense of new experiences.

The most international managers tended to talk of relations with individual people rather than with cultures. They took a micro view. They learned from experience through modes that were identified as intuitive, empirical, relational and immediate. Less international managers learned in ways that were described as analytical, conceptual, theoretical and withdrawn. You will note here that this latter learning style is closer to that valued in academic settings, and is characteristic especially of new graduates. (Ratiu's research is supported by others—for example, Harrison and Hopkins[3], who provide an incisive critique of university training in the cross-cultural arena.)

The more involved, personalistic style of good international learners correlates with effective learners in general managerial situations. My own research on CEOs produced results which support Ratiu.

Ratiu's research also showed that international managers worked on a subjective view of the world. They did not assume that they could find fixed, true knowledge. They were, in my terms, good cartographers. They went into new cultures with a rough map which they modified as they went along, responding to new information all the time. Less international managers had either fixed views which remained stable or poor maps which might stay that way.

Cross-culturally able managers seem to concentrate a lot on the need to map. They focus on *what* is going on in a new environment, and they assume that they will have to modify their maps accordingly. Less cross-culturally able managers get more concerned with *why* questions. They tend to lose sight of the data around them and perhaps reach premature conclusions. They are also less likely to deal well with their emotional responses to situations, perhaps by making judgemental remarks such as blaming others for problems.

The kind of research I've mentioned is consonant with evaluation studies of SML programmes. Managers learn how to learn better by integrating data and feelings, by developing wisdom and capability, by becoming more self-reliant *and* more able to assist others in their learning.

Self managing learners are not 'perfect' individuals. Rather, they see the value of changing; of re-patterning their existing abilities as well as adding new ones. Their continued desire to learn is because they recognize that there are still things to learn. They make mistakes—and use them as data to be addressed not explained away in rationalizations and excuses.

Self managing learners tend to *reduce* secondary feedback in order to allow them space to get primary feedback. They are less interested in the opinions of others and more concerned to get close to situations and learn from sensory-based data. At the same time they want to balance this with feelings and values. Among other features:

- They are active learners—seeking new learning, asking questions of others, learning from unusual circumstances (they may get insights into new ways of thinking from almost anything that happens to them in a normal day).
- They use formal situations for their own benefit. Self managing learners may go to lectures but they will do so with clear objectives or from a serendipitous perspective. Poor learners either take no notes or try to get the lecturer's ideas onto paper. Self managing learners note what they want in relation to their own maps, values and require-ments.
- They translate learning across contexts - but only if it does translate. They will test and modify as they go along.
- They take responsibility for their own actions, their own feelings, their own learning.
- They prepare for new circumstances through learning.
- They are strategic—linking big picture with little picture and macro with micro.

Much of what has been indicated above has been discussed earlier, so I shall not labour the points. Rather I want now to move away from universal and shared factors to the differences between managers, and diversity among people in organizations.

Difference and diversity

There are at least five ways of thinking about the process of managing:

1. *Universalist*
   This assumes that all managing is very much the same the world over. Or if it is not, it ought to be. This assumption has been the basis for much of the work of consultants going from rich countries to poor countries to offer advice. Poor countries are seen as 'underdeveloped' and in need of developing to be like rich countries. A similar view underpins the work of the majority of consultants and developers going from North America and Western Europe into Eastern Europe. Simple messages such as privatization are seen as part of a universal requirement for good management.

2. *National cultural relativism*
   Writers on cross-cultural issues base their work on the assumption of large, possibly unbridgeable, difference between national cultures. They may suggest that theories developed in the USA have almost *no* relevance elsewhere, that almost *all* US writing is ethnocentric and culture bound and that *no* methods developed in the USA should be translated directly into another culture.

3. *Organizational cultural relativism*
   Just as the above view has become increasingly prevalent in Europe, this third perspective has become a key feature of US literature. The argument is that organizations vary widely and that we may not be able to translate ideas from one organizational culture to another. As with 2 above, in the extreme some writers suggest that there are no universals, because each organization is so different.

4. *Individual particularism*
   This position argues that every manager is different, so we should stop generalizing. Psychological literature is used to show large-scale differences between individuals, for example, through psychometric tests.

5. *Subgroup diversity*
   In this stance subgroups in society are identified as a

source of difference (and often disadvantage). These include:

- women
- black people
- disabled people
- gay men and lesbians
- older people
- working-class people

It is argued that people within each group will have something in common which also creates a difference from other people. As indicated in Chapter 3, a learning business would welcome difference and diversity. A strategic learning approach recognizes the value of balancing all five perspectives. There are universals—such as the need for learning: there are national and organizational differences which must be accommodated strategically: each person is different and needs treating as such: and there can be sources of disadvantage which need to be tackled directly.

In Part Two of this book I discussed organization culture, so that issue will not be considered here. I shall begin with the issue of disadvantage and then move to national culture. SML addresses individual differences, as discussed in Part Four, so that will be taken as a base line for moving into these other domains.

Diversity and disadvantage: strategic learning issues

Most management development activity in North America and Europe is designed on the assumption that the customers (course members) are white, able-bodied, middle-class, heterosexual males aged 25 to 45. In the UK, this group is less than 4 per cent of the population[4]; in the USA it is an even smaller proportion.

Some of the simple ways in which these assumptions create problems for those outside this privileged group include:

1. If there is a social function to which partners/spouses are invited, how is the situation handled for gay people?
2. Courses tend to rely on visual communication. What does this mean for people with sight difficulties?
3. Cocktail parties and many group exercises can create problems for some people with particular hearing problems.
4. Tiered lecture theatres can create difficulties for those with mobility problems.

These are all practical issues which can be addressed in practical ways. More profound difficulties come in the course curriculum where, say, case studies assume managers are within the privileged group. This can alienate others. Even in flexible programmes which encourage people to discuss their own issues, black people, women and gay people comment that they find it difficult to raise issues of concern to them when they feel they are the only ones in the group who face particular problems. A black manager, for instance, had just experienced some racist attitudes before coming into a group. This deeply affected him and he underperformed in the group. He did not, however, feel able to say this to his all white colleagues.

The latter example raises the problem of denial. There is an expectation in many organizations that managers will deny aspects of themselves if they do not conform to the requirements of white, able bodied, middle-class, heterosexual male society. A successful managing director of a factory in the north of England was required by his chairman to attend a course 'to polish himself up' and rid himself of his blunt, northern, working-class ways. Women are expected to join in with men on a course, and deny any differing perspectives on managerial issues. Gay managers are expected to keep quiet about their sexuality. A lesbian training manager was reprimanded for going into the company shop with the child of her partner.

In SML we expect to be able to address factors of difference and diversity in a positive way. The design of programmes helps, but there is also a premium on learning assistants, such as set advisers, in recognizing and dealing with problems. There are certain aspects of SML *designs* that help these situations:

Sets

These provide a base for people to talk personally about themselves. Where a difference is visible (e.g. if someone is black or in a wheelchair) a capable set adviser can play a key role in creating an environment in which these factors can be opened up. However, some differences are not necessarily visible, for example, if someone is gay. We have found, however, that a gay person has valued a 'set' environment where they could open up. I have seen heterosexual managers benefit greatly from this, as often they have never had to talk openly with a gay colleague about sexuality issues. Many 'straight' men initially find it uncomfortable but gradually see this as part of their learning—their need to develop wisdom.

Although sets are of great value, we have, as staff, often encouraged women managers and black managers to form support groups to discuss issues of common concern. This itself can initially feel threatening in a learning community, but again the white males can gradually adjust to the situation and see that their feelings of being threatened are something to address for themselves.

Learning contracts

These provide a basis for anyone on an SML programme to create a curriculum to suit themselves. A woman of 50 commented:

> The course is excellent for a middle aged woman like me. I have realized that I could create a new future for myself—even at my age. I ceased to feel stuck and now I feel I'm escaping from stagnation. It's an amazing relief to feel young again.

However, this is also an example of the need for a set adviser to support difference. A Chinese manager, on the post-graduate diploma course mentioned in Part Four, expressed an important formulation of the problem. As she saw it, there was a danger in a set that white managers expected her to conform to their expectations of a good contract. This would also have affected assessment as she was going to have to present her self-assessment to her set for confirmation and approval. She characterized the potential problem as in Figure 10.1.

Her concern was that she would have to conform to an end point level that was inappropriate for her as a Chinese manager (managing a Chinese centre in London). She felt that the set needed to understand that she could develop a parallel track based on the requirements of her own culture. This needed the set adviser to assist her in raising these issues in an appropriate way in the set, and getting other set members to appreciate the problem. On the same programme a number of black managers put issues in their learning contracts that, to white managers, raised political matters. Again, this had to be worked through so that white managers could see these concerns, and learning needs, as legitimate.

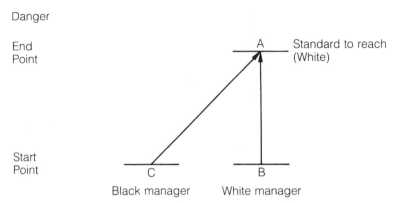

Danger

Path to travel for black manager (CA) is longer than for white manager (BA)

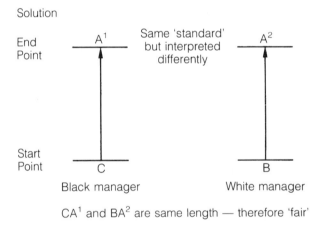

Solution

CA^1 and BA^2 are same length — therefore 'fair'

Figure 10.1   Levels and differences

Learning assistants

Learning assistants can play a key role, as already indicated. Mentors in organizations can be of great value. Many women on SML programmes have chosen women mentors to provide the support that they have felt was lacking from their male boss and/or their husband. Another way of addressing this issue has been to bring bosses and husbands/partners into the programme. We have often found that men have no desire to be explicitly unsupportive of a woman's learning; rather they have not recognized what was required and, with some guidance, began to see ways in which they could be of more help. The balance in a learning assistant team can be important. One cannot cover all the alternatives, but by being sensitive to the male/female, black/white balance in a staff team one can go some way towards modelling not just a respect for diversity but a positive valuing of difference.

Learning community

Learning community processes and structures can help to create a culture which supports difference and addresses disadvantage. The openness and trust that can be created in such contexts can provide the one place in which managers can really feel that they can be themselves without having to deny aspects of themselves. Men can also allow themselves to open up about issues they cannot raise in their day-to-day work. They can stop feeling the need to be macho and show other sides of themselves.

Strategic approaches

These show the need to address issues of the contexts of a development programme. For example, selection issues are important. Often they subtly discriminate against people, and development programmes end up with an imbalance of privileged white middle-class males. A strategic perspective requires programmes to be created in context, and these contextual factors to be addressed, such as: how do imbalances occur? and how can the problem be solved?

Cross-cultural issues

Some of the points made above can assist strategic learning

(a) to be relevant to managers from different national cultures and
(b) to assist managers from different cultures to learn well together.

Indeed, with the globalization of management we have no option but to consider how learning can occur across cultures. Ratiu's research, discussed earlier, gives us pointers. He, and Harrison and Hopkins, show that learning to work across cultures cannot be carried out in standard classroom-based courses. Managers need to become self managing learners to work cross-culturally. Also the obverse applies. By working cross-culturally, by travelling and by experiencing other cultures, people become better self managing learners.

However, all of this may need assistance—and we are back to staff/practitioner/professional roles and the need for good designs for strategic learning. We have found that managers from a wide variety of cultures can come together in sets and use SML methods. I have worked with managers from Europe, America, Africa and Asia and SML pro-grammes are starting to develop in a variety of countries. They, of course, have different styles and outcomes in different cultures. In the USA the natural tendency to self-reliant optimism has meant that managers easily pick up the basic ideas. Learning contracts have been used in the USA for a long time, though not necessarily in the SML mode. Sets can, however, create a new challenge, especially for very individualistic managers who need to learn to support others in their learning.

In Asian countries there can be the opposite situation. In many cultures, which could be labelled more collectivist, the supportive environment of the set comes as second nature. What suprises some managers is the opportunity to develop their own curriculum, and this can feel strange initially. However, SML has drawn on Eastern thinking, so that the basic ideas can make sense in Asian countries. An Indian professor, who is keen to develop SML in India, wrote to me saying: 'India is the land of Buddha, Upanishads and Krishnamurthi—SML will have its followers!' He recognized the links with Indian philosophy and saw the possibilities for an Indian style of programme. One of his colleagues also commented that 'traditional Indian teaching modes have something to contribute'. I agree.

I could go on at length referring to different cultures and their response to strategic learning and SML, but that would be tedious. As a generalization I have found that SML challenges different cultures in different ways, in terms of its *processes*. (In terms of *content* there is no issue, as the content of SML programmes is driven by managers themselves, hence immediately overcoming one of the problems in transferring standardized training courses across cultures.) An example of a process challenge is between high-context and low-context cultures.[5] High-context cultures are those where verbal communication is more implicit as the context provides the basis for understanding messages. To quote Hall:

> high context communication is one in which most of the information is either in the physical context or internalized in the person, with very little in the coded, explicit, transmitted part

of the message. In low context communication 'the mass of information is vested in the explicit code'.

(Hall,[5] p. 91).

Yamaguchi used Hall's ideas in her research on Japanese and American managers. She comments:

> In a High Context (HC) society, people tend to rely on the context in communication. They are expected to understand what one intends to mean although very few words have been said. On the other hand, the people from Low Context (LC) society try to look for every word related to the content to read the speaker's intention. Thus, in conversation with people from an HC communication society, people from a Low Context society will struggle with ambiguity while the people from an HC society may be sick of verboseness.

> The differences in American and Japanese rhetorical styles are derived from context differences as follows: In a 'low-context' culture ... like ... the United States, the lack of shared assumptions requires the American speaker to verbalize his or her message to make his or her discrete intent clear and explicit ... By contrast, Japanese is a typical 'high-context' culture ... the Japanese speaker tends to minimize extra- and paraverbal aspects of communication.

(Yamaguchi,[6] pp. 25/26)

It is clear from Yamaguchi's research (and many others) that Japanese–American communication can be a problem, and that if Japanese and American managers are in a learning context together there can be problems. However, Yamaguchi shows that these problems are soluble through managing 'context' (in Hall's use of the term). She suggests that context should at the start be low or zero and then be built up through shared language, tasks, rules and working principles. This is how good learning communities and sets work, and it again shows how important the learning assistant is in handling these issues.

Summary

In this chapter I have explored strategic learning from the perspective of the self managing learner and from the point of view of individual, cultural and other differences. I have not made an exhaustive survey of the issues, but rather shown how SML approaches can work to address some thorny issues.

Notes

1. Eco, U. (1985) *Reflections on 'The Name of the Rose'*, London: Secker and Warburg Also: Eco, U. (1983) *The Name of the Rose*, London: Secker & Warburg.
2. Ratiu, I. (1983) 'Thinking internationally: a comparison of how international executives learn', *International Studies of Management and Organization*, XIII (1/2) 139–150.
3. Harrison, R. and Hopkins, R. (1987) 'The design of cross-cultural training: an alternative to the university model', *Journal of Applied Behavioural Science*, III (4) 421–460.
4. It is difficult to be more exact than 'less than 4 per cent' as the statistics are open to interpretation. For instance, the boundary between disabled and not is open to differing perspectives. Also the statistics on the percentage of the population who are gay are controversial. However, I have erred on the cautious side in my figure of 4 per cent.
5. Hall, E.T. (1976) *Beyond Culture*, Garden City, NY: Anchor Press/Doubleday.
6. Yamaguchi, I. (1988) *Communication Skills Between Japanese and American Managers and Subordinates in a Japan–USA Cross-Cultural Corporation*, University of Hawaii: MA Thesis.

11   Conclusions and directions

Introduction

This chapter rounds off some issues. One way of being clear about an idea is to define it by what it is not. In Chapter 2 I suggested that strategic learning can be understood in part by recognizing that it is not an approach characterized by apathetic/antagonistic, reactive or bureaucratic styles of working. Here I want to say something about approaches to learning that are not SML—but which attempt to masquerade as SML. I shall also indicate some myths about SML (which are myths in the pejorative sense) as well as some real problems with the approach. Finally, I shall suggest some directions in terms of desirable actions for the future.

Not self managed learning

I want to outline here approaches that I see as outside the boundaries of SML. In some ways this is the easiest way to define SML. It will, I hope, provide a clearing of the ground and put in perspective earlier comments on SML. I shall move rapidly through a series of headings which exemplify some issues, but this is not meant to be encyclopaedic or comprehensive.

'Participative' pseudo learner centred courses

Reynolds[1] has commented on this phenomenon. 'Participative' is regarded as an 'OK term' to attach to a course, but participation in what is rarely specified. The 'participation' is almost always only in highly tutor-controlled case studies and simulation exercises: the course members do not participate in decisions about content, timing, location, learning objectives, etc.

A number of people feel they have moved beyond this by asking learners as a group to say what topics they want to cover (within boundaries preset by tutors). However, the tutors are still in charge of the class, as, of course, they control final assessment. Even this extended participation seems too limited to me.

Lee was honest enough about his experiments in learner-centredness to say:

> Evaluation mechanisms are crucial to 'learner centredness'. At the end of the day I awarded the grades, and I suppose it was awareness of the power this gave me which allowed me to delegate other aspects of the course and not worry too much about potential anarchy, absenteeism, apathy or other problems.
> (Lee, [2] p. 38)

Curriculum separate from learner

This is a major problem with independent study programmes where learners write out a plan of study and then have it approved by the institution. I have been Degree Committee Chairperson for an individualized MA student of Antioch University. They used this approach. The problem is that the 'degree plan', as it is called, was expected to be judged separately from the person. Antioch's requirement was that the degree plan should be written as a curriculum such that another person could come along, carry out the plan and get an MA.

This seems to be too tied in with an 'objective knowledge' model as it assumes that a curriculum can exist separately from its designer. It attaches a false concreteness to a process, for which we use the metaphor 'plan'.[3] In SML we do not swing to the other extreme and assume that what we call a 'contract' is a totally personal document. We expect that it should be understandable to others, but we do not expect it to exist as a disembodied entity. The contract comes out of the subjective experiences of the person and is meaningful only in the light of that person's experience. And as we are all to some extent unique, even if another person tried to carry out the 'degree plan', that individual would not do it in the same way as the person who designed it.

Oxbridge tutorial system

Sometimes when I have tried to describe what we do to someone with an acquaintance with the English higher education world, they have said: 'Ah! What you mean is something like the Oxbridge tutorial system' or, more patronizingly, 'Well, of course, Oxbridge have been doing this for centuries with their tutorial system'. It's nonsense, of course. The Oxbridge tutorial system is linked to a tightly controlled process where, despite some openness of relationships, the learner is still controlled through an imposed assessment process.

Impotent Rogerianism

Carl Rogers was not actually 'Rogerian' in the way the mythology has grown up. (That is, solely supportive and non-directive.) There is evidence of his behaving in quite 'un-Rogerian' ways; for instance, he could be quite structured and confronting. Be that as it may, there certainly is a view around about non-directiveness, and from my own research I have a nice quote which sums up one person's changing perspective[4]:

> I created uncertainty and turbulence through Rogerian non-directiveness. I refused to respond to direct requests for assistance, e.g. if they actually asked you what your solution was you'd say 'Well, I think I'd like to think that through', hence increasing turbulence and uncertainty.
>
> Previously people asked for help and I copped out—I assumed it as a sign of dependence and therefore refused to help.
>
> I now disagree:
>
> I don't see it as dependency (to ask for help)—I am prepared to share my experience/expertise.

Darwinian élitism

This term was used by someone in my research to define approaches which glorified tough individualism. This could be a problem with some organizations' approaches to action learning where they see it as a way of sifting out potential top managers (by choosing those who cope best with certain kinds of 'hairy' project). As action learning can veer towards overly-individualistic programmes, this seems a genuine concern (especially when the set is played down and the project exaggerated).

Open learning/distance learning/computer-based learning/ independent study/project-based learning

I have deliberately put together here a conglomerate of currently fashionable labels. Predefined packages (which underpin much open learning/distance learning/computer-based learning) cannot be adequately responsive to learner needs; they cannot be holistic; they can rarely be action based. Hence, on their own they are limited. That does not preclude learners on an SML programme choosing, as part of the programme, to use packaged material. My concern is only with courses which are built around such packages (even if they add on a residential weekend here and there as the Open University does). Project-based approaches also do not guarantee an SML approach.

Intrusive desire to apply one's own skills/knowledge

In one programme for which I was a 'hired in' outsider, one of the internal set advisers created many problems in the set to which he was attached, because he saw his role as a 'counsellor' and insisted on counselling people whether they liked it or not. Others have pet theories or ideas which they insinuate into set meetings inappropriately. They usually get found out. Genuine SML accepts the group's right to refuse such intrusions.

Predefined model of ideal process

Some set advisers have an idea of how a set should 'ideally' progress and try to bend the set in that way. They may have a view, for instance, that the set 'has to work through dependency/counter-dependency issues' (a common view of some T group trainers). My experience (and that of others) is that sets do not *have* to work through any phases: it is a trite truism I know, but each set really is different and one can presuppose no necessary similarities with any other set.

'Guess my list' games

In an effort to be 'learner centred' the trainer may refuse to teach, but instead sit and ask questions of 'his or her group', carefully writing up on the board or flip chart, answers that conform to what he or she wants to hear. The trainer only accepts what is part of his or her own 'map', ignoring the views of learners that do not fit.

Cutting off

Richard Bandler, one of the developers of neurolinguistic programming, was once asked in a workshop if he worked with blind people and he replied: 'All the time.' Some trainers do not seem to want to *see* (or *hear*) what is going on around them. It is not that they are unable to see or hear, but they do not know how to respond, or they feel anxious about their ability to deal with problems being raised. The easy answer is to 'cut-off', perhaps through mental or emotional withdrawal. Effective practitioners seem to 'hang on in there' even if they do not always know what to do.

Not pre-negotiated

Sometimes trainers try to change a course in mid stream. I have encountered many who have complained that they started with a standard, trainer-controlled course that was not working too well. Then they read an article or talked to someone and had a 'Road to Damascus' experience. They saw the light. In mid-course they stopped standing at the front of a classroom teaching and instead handed over the course to the participants. The trainer would explain that they were not going to teach any more, but instead let participants do as they liked.

The general result of this was mayhem, and anger from participants. The trainer would see this as a necessary counter-dependence and struggle on until they had to admit defeat.

One of the problems with this approach is that it was not the basis on which the course was set up. It is important in SML to tell people about what they are coming on. Being up-front is crucial. Participants on a programme still will not understand it fully from a pre-programme briefing, but at least they will know it is not like a traditional type of course, and hence recognize that it is something different.

Messy, unplanned programmes

Another fault with the situation described above is that the trainer may not provide sufficient help in structuring the programme. One of the ways that SML can easily degenerate is if staff do not take seriously (a) structures and (b) their own roles. The following consequences can occur:

1. Assessment is not taken seriously—people are allowed to assert that they have learned something without providing evidence of learning.
2. Contracts become loose statements of intent, which are allowed to become mere background documents.
3. Support for learners is reduced—sets meet less often and are sloppy, easy-going affairs.
4. If there is a learning community it degenerates into endless discussions of internal procedures and loses sight of its role in assisting learning.
5. Staff, for example set advisers, turn up late for meetings, demonstrate their ignorance of learning issues, refuse to take on responsibilities and refuse to learn to be better.

Degeneration into control

This, in some respects, is the opposite of the above. An example was a programme a colleague and I developed for a large international manufacturing company that had restructured its organization and dispensed with the role of supervisor, replacing it with the enlarged role of 'team leader'. The team leaders had increased responsibility and reported directly to shift managers. The company wanted a course to train the new team leaders (mostly promoted supervisors). We first had a one-day event where we explored the concerns of team leaders and ascertained what they wanted to learn. We brought in their shift managers in the afternoon and shared with the latter the views of their new team leaders. We obtained the shift managers' general support for the issues. Then we had each shift manager meet with the team leaders who reported to him and who were coming on the course (one or two per shift manager). They negotiated in detail learning objectives for the team leaders. These were set down in mini learning contracts, and my colleague and I then designed a one-week course on the basis of these precise learning objectives.

The team leaders largely managed their own learning in the course. Near the end of the week the shift managers attended the course to discuss its progress with team leaders and to plan further development for each individual team leader. The training manager was present throughout the course, and in post-course evaluation proclaimed that he was delighted with the results. He therefore decided that the content of this course would now be the content of all future courses for team leaders. He also dispensed with the one-day planning event. As far as we were concerned he had missed the point of why the first course was a success. Participants and shift managers 'owned' it, and it integrated with ongoing needs. The design we had produced allowed participants to drive the learning, and to feel a real sense of control over it. This was lost in the new trainer-controlled course.

In general, some of the problems that can occur when SML is tightened up and becomes trainer controlled include:

- mapping becomes fixed as a curriculum for all to be taught
- staff control events and learners become more apathetic
- staff deal with personal anxieties and with course problems by blaming learners
- contracting becomes perfunctory or non-existent
- the organization says it wants more structure: in reality it wants more control.

Bandwidth

SML operates within a band of possibilities. This is indicated in Figure 11.1, which shows three options.

To the left are the messy, unplanned programmes I have referred to, and to the right the controlled, curriculum-led programmes. SML can operate across a band between these, but there is a definite 'flip' in crossing either boundary. This is especially recognizable in the role and behaviour of staff on programmes. (This factor was discussed in Chapter 9.)

Figure 11.1   SML Bandwidth: spectrum of possibilities

Myths about SML

These myths[5] are based on typical questions and concerns raised by organizations or academic critics as to why they should not develop SML programmes. Some are genuine and reasonable concerns which need serious attention from SML practitioners. Others are excuses based on spurious arguments.

SML is an alternative to mainstream management education and training

It seems evident that long ago in history, even before the concept of 'management' was systematized, effective managers took charge of their own learning. The people who succeeded as managers had no courses to go on, no business school professors at whose feet they could sit, no prestigious institutions of management education to attend, no management books to read. Only in recent times has the idea emerged that 'management' is a subject to study in isolation from the work of managing. (Revans[6] has chronicled historical perspectives in many of his writings on managerial learning.)

What I find interesting is how the educational and training worlds have succeeded in developing an aberrant alternative to traditional management development. A charitable explanation would be that there has been an attempt to improve the way managers learn by teaching them in the classroom, and in the process hoping to accelerate what can be learned at work. There are various uncharitable explanations, including allegations of status seeking and job creation on the part of academics, trainers and consultants. (Revans[7] is, again, an important commentator on such matters.)

There is a danger in polarizing our perspectives on management development. In some circles there has been a debate between proponents of traditional mainstream work-based approaches (such as action learning) and defenders of the modern alternative mode of taught courses. It is clear that most managerial learning is in the traditional mode (see, for example, Livingstone[8]). Experienced senior managers typically report that the main things they have learned (that are useful to them) have come from their experiences at work (this includes observing and learning from others with whom they work). A major problem occurs because most people who write about or talk about management development are professors, lecturers, trainers and consultants (managers actually *do* it). Those who are course providers tend to believe that what they do is the mainstream and that activities where managers take charge of their own learning are the alternatives.

When I was involved in developing self managed learning programmes in a college—*because* these programmes had no predefined curriculum, *because* they were designed to respond to the precise needs of managers, and *because* staff did not impose a rigid timetable on learners—the programmes were labelled as 'an experimental alternative' to 'proper management education'. It speaks volumes for the power of articulate but misguided management educators that they are able to get away with such a stance.

At one level, however, management educators do not control what managers learn on courses, even though they try to. As Postman and Weingartner[9] point out (in quoting Earl Kelley)

> Now it comes about that whatever we tell the learner, he will make something that is all his own out of it, and it will be different from what we held so dear and attempted to 'transmit'. He will build it into his own scheme of things, and relate it uniquely to what he already uniquely holds as experience. Thus he builds a world all his own, and what is really important is what he makes of what we tell him, not what we intended. (pp.94/95)

These authors go on to say:

> In other words, you end up with a student-centred curriculum, not because it is good for motivation but because you don't, in fact, have any other choice. (p.95)

So we find that in terms of the individual manager and their learning, there can be little need to polarize the two kinds of 'learning situation' (work or course). Managers learn what they choose to learn in both contexts. The trouble is that both work and taught courses can be extraordinarily inefficient. Many managers learn little from work experience if they are just left to it without any assistance (for example, if they get poor feedback). Also we know that managers are dissatisfied when they are instructed to attend course sessions that they regard as irrelevant to their requirements.

One of our motives in developing self managed learning as a formalized approach to management development, was our desire to address these issues. It does seem that off-the-job learning can have something to offer: managers do not necessarily learn all they need to learn solely from work experience. However, the taught course mode on its own has not delivered the goods.

SML means messy, unstructured, chaotic programmes

This has already been addressed: SML has significant structuring. In the hands of poor practitioners the programmes can, of course, degenerate. In some respects the standardized training course can be an organized mess: a goulash of unconnected sessions masquerading as order by virtue of rigid timetabling.

SML is resource intensive—with standardized training it is possible to have large numbers of trainees being taught by one trainer/teacher

There are a number of responses to this.

1. The large lecture model can be low in cost but also low in effectiveness. People may learn little that is not in textbooks—and buying and reading the books could be even cheaper.
2. In SML, by dispensing with lectures, we free staff to be able to work with learners in small groups.
3. If course participants are given the budget, they can (and do) work out the most cost-effective ways of learning. They might ask for lectures (but rarely do). What we do see is learners using budgets that might have been spent on expensive glossy courses in a much more practical and focused way.
4. SML taps untapped resources, especially of existing expertise in organizations. In one company, a junior manager needed to learn about some legal issues. He asked to go on a law course. It was pointed out to him by his mentor that there was a legal department in head office, and he learned all he needed by asking them. He saved a great deal of money, not just in course fees but also in productive time that would have been lost had he gone on a course. (He learned all he needed *and* stayed in his job.)
5. Senior line managers can act as learning assistants. We have trained hundreds of managers to act as set advisers and mentors. They say that they also get a great deal out of taking on these roles. They improve as managers by

learning more about how to develop their own staff, and they contribute to wider strategic learning initiatives.

People do not know what they do not know and cannot, therefore, draw up meaningful learning contracts

Responses to this include:

1. Thousands of people have been through SML programmes, and *all* of them have drawn up learning contracts. They vary in rigour and planning, but that is to be expected. But they can *all* say something about themselves and what they want to learn.
2. Mapping processes help choice.
3. Sets provide support and challenge to help people develop meaningful learning contracts. Mentors and learning communities also help.
4. Some trainers and educators put this up as a spurious item because they feel threatened by their loss of control over learners.

Learners will set easy goals in SML programmes so it will be just a soft option

This rarely happens, and if it does, sets challenge people. Indeed the peer group is usually more challenging than bosses are in appraisals. The most common problem is that people set objectives that are too demanding, and they have to be helped to develop realism around what can be achieved in specific timescales.

Individuals may want to learn things that are not in the organization's interests

This always strikes me as a strange objection. If someone is being employed by an organization, the organization has to trust that individual to talk to customers in the right way, not to steal from the organization, and so on. If people breach such trust, they presumably are disciplined for it, but we know that people cannot be policed every second of every day. Senior managers cannot listen in to every phone conversation to check if the person is letting the organization down or not.

As Postman and Weingartner commented, people make their own choices anyway, no matter what teachers or trainers do. If someone is sent on a course, they could be asleep at the back all the time as far as the organization is aware. There is the bizarre myth that what is taught equals what is learned, so fixed curricula are assumed to control learning. This is just not true.

In SML, on the other hand, learning contracts can make explicit what the person plans to *learn*. These can be discussed and negotiated, so that there is integration between individual learning and organizational requirements. Deviations can of course occur, but they are *less* likely than with traditional training courses.

Individuals cannot assess themselves

1. People assess themselves constantly—for example, when they apply for a job they have to assess whether or not they meet the requirements. The fact that people often do this badly shows that they need assistance to develop this ability. SML does this.
2. People do it in SML programmes and in appraisal schemes based on self-assessment. It is not always easy but it happens. On SML programmes for qualifications—for example, the post-graduate diploma, an SML Masters programme, etc.—there are external examiners who check the process of assessment. They all comment favourably on the rigour and the quality of assessments carried out— and these are professors in business schools who can compare the assessments with traditional academic controlled methods.

SML is too radical for conservative organizations

I have worked in classic government bureaucracies as well as fast moving market-led organizations. Issues that arise are different and SML designs need to respond to these differences. However, in terms of acceptability, I have been pleasantly surprised by seemingly old-fashioned conservative organizations. There is a recognition now that they have to change: there is a genuine move away from the tightly controlled bureaucracy and a realization that members of the public have to be treated differently. SML fits where organizations want to move to TQM, empowerment and customer care.

Real problems   Despite my comments above, I can recognize that there can be real problems in moving towards strategic learning and learning businesses and the implementation of SML programmes. These include:

1. It does require high-quality people to implement the ideas. This quality is expressed not just in terms of capability but also in the personal security that people in senior positions need to feel. There are many disturbed people who get into powerful positions—the Robert Maxwells of this world—and they are not likely to find these ideas congenial.
2. Distortion and back-sliding can occur. Many people feel comfortable with existing ways: change is unpleasant to them and they would rather do the wrong thing that they know than something new that they do not fully understand. Lecturers get used to lecturing, and giving it up is not easy.

Directions   There is an urgent, desperate need for change towards more strategic approaches to learning. The world grows in complexity. The naive optimism of those who thought that the demise of Communism and of the USSR would produce an easier, safer world has been shown to be unreal. Wars and suffering continue because people have not *learned* to live in peace. It is a learning issue. The exhortations of politicians will not help. The kind of learning needed has to be bone-deep, second-order learning; the kind that develops unshakable commitment to ideals, and the capability to deliver on them.

These learning issues move, then, beyond the needs of companies. In many societies there are crises in health care and in education. Organizations that deliver these services are in need of strategic learning.

Research in England[10] has shown that at least one-third of 16-year-olds have truanted at some time or other in the last half term. At least one in ten is playing truant more than once a week. This situation has been known for a long time. Reports on truancy a decade ago gave the same picture—a massive rejection by young people of the way schools are organized and the way they are treated. However, teachers' union officials are reported as dismissing this evidence. They do not recognize the massive professional failure that teachers are presiding over. Their need to learn is enormous, but largely unrecognized.

Those who see the problems, and care, have opportunities to act. We have to avoid Utopian dreaming on the one hand and pessimistic depression on the other. Marien[11] calls for 'pragmatic maturity' and argues for a Taoist integration of some paired approaches, such as

* *Inspiration and Perspiration*: We need to be creative and inspiring *and* we need to work hard at the issues.
* *Realism and Idealism*: We need to keep our feet on the ground *and* leap into the air.
* *Intellect and Spirit*: We need a new rationality that recognizes the non-rational. A kind of meta-rationality that is able to reason about reason and acknowledge its limitations.

Marien closes his proposals by suggesting that if you aim high you will not shoot yourself in the foot. I would go with that.

Notes

1. Reynolds, M. (1980) 'Participation in work and education', in Beck, J. and Cox, C. (eds) *Advances in Management Education*, Chichester: Wiley.
2. Lee, B. (1985) 'Learner centred courses: a personal experience,' *Management Education and Development*, 16, 1 (Spring), 31–40.
3. This issue of the nature of plans is discussed in Cunningham, I. (1984) 'Planning to develop managers', *Management Education and Development*, 15, 2 (Summer), 83–104.
4. Cunningham, I. (1984) *Teaching Styles in Learner Centred Management Development Programmes*, PhD Thesis, University of Lancaster.
5. Many of the myths here come from discussions with Deborah Booth and Stephanie Elkin, with whom I worked on the SML programme in British Airways. I would like to acknowledge their contribution to these ideas. Also, they were clear, as British Airways HR staff, that the myths could be rebutted in the way that I have done here.
6. Revans, R.W. (1977) 'Action learning and the nature of knowledge', *Education and Training*, (Nov./Dec.), 318–322.
7. Revans, R.W. (1980) *Action Learning: New Techniques for Management*, London: Blond & Briggs.
8. Livingstone, J.S. (1971) 'The myth of the well-educated manager', *Harvard Business Review*, 49 (Jan./Feb.), 79–89.
9. Postman, N. and Weingartner, C. (1969) *Teaching as a Subversive Activity*, London: Penguin.

10. O'Keeffe, D. and Stoll, P. (1993) *'Truancy in English Secondary Schools'*. Report, quoted in *'The Guardian'*, 26 June, p.3.
11. Marien, M. (1983) 'The "Transformation as Sandbox" syndrome', *Journal of Humanistic Psychology*, 23, 1 (Winter), 7–15.

Index